EMPOWERING UNDERACHIEVERS

EMPOWERING UNDERACHIEVERS

NEW STRATEGIES TO GUIDE KIDS (8-18) TO PERSONAL EXCELLENCE

(REVISED AND EXPANDED EDITION)

PETER A. SPEVAK, PH.D.
AND
MARYANN KARINCH

New Horizon Press
Far Hills, New Jersey

Requests for permission should be addressed to:
New Horizon Press
P.O. Box 669
Far Hills, NJ 07931

Spevak, Peter A. and Karinch, Maryann
    Empowering Underachievers: New Strategies to Guide Kids (8-18) to Personal Excellence
    (Revised and Expanded)

Cover Design: Robert Aulicino
Interior Design: Eileen Turano

Library of Congress Control Number: 2005937783

ISBN-10 (paperback): 0-88282-282-9
ISBN-13 (paperback): 978-0-88282-282-2
ISBN-13 (eBook): 978-0-88282-358-4

New Horizon Press books may be purchased in bulk quantities for educational, business or sales promotional use. For information please write to New Horizon Press, Special Sales Department, PO Box 669, Far Hills, NJ 07931 or call 800-533-7978.

E-mail us at: nhp@newhorizonpressbooks.com
Visit our website at: www.newhorizonpressbooks.com

Manufactured in the U.S.A.

18   17   16   15   14   5   6   7   8   9   10

To Trish

TABLE OF CONTENTS

Illustrations and Tables

Author's Note

This book is based on both first-person research and extensive interviews with clients of the Center for Applied Motivation and their parents. In order to protect privacy, fictitious names and identities have been given to all individuals in this book and otherwise identifying characteristics have been altered. For the purposes of simplifying usage, the pronouns his and her are often used interchangeably.

The information contained herein is not meant to be a substitute for professional evaluation and therapy.

PREFACE

As a teenager, Peter was a defiant underachiever. Even though he qualified for advanced math, he remained in the lower two-thirds of his high school class. Primarily, he took vocational-technical classes and learned to weld, repair cars and do woodworking. As a student, he frustrated his teachers and parents. He thought high school was an irrelevancy imposed upon him. Even though he read avidly, He just wouldn't read what he was supposed to when he was supposed to. No one could tell him what to do. He was confused and headed nowhere fast.

After high school, he slipped into Purdue University on high SAT scores. He thought college would help him avoid having to work a blue-collar job (in factories and mills) like many of his relatives. At Purdue, he excelled—socially. Academically, he failed miserably. He arrived at Purdue in 1965 and left in 1966 during the Vietnam War.

Rather than be drafted, he enlisted in the Marine Corps. It was during his early days in the service that he had his "Aha!" experience, the moment when life hit him hard and he thought, Aha! That's what everyone's been trying to tell me! *He gained insights and made attitude shifts that turned his life around.*

After four years in the Marines, he went back to school, to Indiana University in Bloomington, and excelled—academically, this time. Then he tackled graduate school at the University of Missouri in Columbia on a fellowship. He even earned a master's degree and a Ph.D. in clinical psychology.

The underachieving kid *was* me. The man who discovered how to strive for personal excellence *is* me. I finally learned to take charge, which shaped my philosophy that "life is what you make it."

When I realized what it took to propel myself forward, an intense interest in helping other underachievers took hold. I wanted to reach them at an early age so they could effectively meet the challenges of high school, college, career and relationships—and enjoy these things much more. I wanted to help others experience the joy of fulfillment that comes with hard work. My research and the whole focus of my professional life have resulted from that intense interest. While still wandering the halls of the Indiana University Medical Center where I served as an assistant professor, I studied why people change and why people remain unchanged after they've gone through therapy. Even more importantly, I focused on the factors that would make the therapy stick.

Eventually, my philosophies on motivation and achievement crystallized, and I started putting them to work for students who were having struggles very much like my own. Fortunately, one of the results of more than two decades of work has been the transformation of many young people—students who broke through emotional walls to achieve at, or close to, their full potentials—at the Center for Applied Motivation, which I founded.

Adults have also directly benefited in some cases. I've seen parents take their new knowledge about motivation into many areas of their lives including the workplace to help the adult underachievers they manage. Also, individual adults plagued by underachievement have changed dramatically through their studies at the Center for Applied Motivation.

Parents, teachers, executives and others who care about changing those whose lives they impact so that they can reach personal excellence, we are on the same team! This book will help you gain perspectives on motivation, prevent future problems and increase your effectiveness in moving others and yourself toward self-motivation and achievement. In these pages, I'll tell you what can help you make a difference for—and *with*—your underachiever. I will help you guide your child toward greater personal responsibility and personal excellence.

In this second edition, I want to express my appreciation to the growing number of parents, educators and students who are reaching out for more information about a philosophy against the scourge of underachievement. Our experience continues to enable us to refine our methods and supplement them with new insights to aid you.

Peter A. Spevak, Ph.D.

Acknowledgements

First of all, we jointly thank our loving and supportive partners.

Peter: I recognize and thank Patricia Spevak, friend, wife and ongoing inspiration, for her support, love, sense of humor, insights, criticisms and suggestions. Her efforts have been primary in developing, applying and evolving the Center for Applied Motivation and its philosophy.

Maryann: Thank you to Jim McCormick, whose caring and intelligence bring so much to my life and my work. I also want to thank Patricia, who was *our* creative partner throughout the development of this book.

We both want to thank other members of our immediate families: Michael and Mary Spevak and Karl (who lives on in my heart) and Ann Karinch, whose solid basic values helped us form as individuals. Brother Karl also has been a great teacher of values and priorities.

Thanks also to Patrick Avon, founder of the Sergeant's Program, which was once headquartered near the Center. He brought us together.

For his graphic talents and skills, we thank Michael Gravino. We also appreciate Laura Belt of Adler and Robin Books, who brought our ideas to the attention of New Horizon Press. And thank you to our editor, Joan Dunphy, whose insight and experience added to the final product. Thank you also to JoAnne Thomas, Christina Mucciolo and Chris Nielsen at New Horizon for helping us succeed in this effort.

We also thank parents, students (especially you!) and others who, over the past twenty plus years, allowed Peter to enter your lives. Thanks also to the former client parents and students who shared their insights and personal experiences through interviews for this book.

Thanks to everyone engaged in the continuing journey of trying to make the world a better place for the children who are our future.

PART ONE

UNDERSTANDING THE PROBLEM

- Who are Underachievers?
- Types of Underachievers
- Attention Deficit and Other Disorders
- What Influences Motivation?
- Why it is Important to Motivate Underachievers
- The Motivational Circle
- Good and Bad Emotions
- Intellectual Versus Emotional Development

The Three IVEs refer to levels of human existence.

The basic level is "Surv<u>ive</u>": Will I be safe?

The intermediate level is "<u>Live</u>": Are things okay?

The advanced level is "Thr<u>ive</u>": I'm excited! What's next?

Underachievers tend to function well below their potential. Their disengagement does not usually bring their survival into question, unless they cope through substances such as drugs or alcohol. When those underachievers find themselves in desperation, they may not survive.

Usually, underachievers manage to live through a combination of personality, intelligence, judgment and serendipity. They attain a level of mediocrity—"good enough" —without much discipline, persistence or effort. They ooze along in their lives, without commitment or consistent engagement. Instead of seeking and appreciating fulfillment from work well done, they pursue "fun." They can't wait until they can stop working; the anticipation preoccupies them. Life is ultimately superficial and unfulfilling. Many become cynical and embittered, proving the truth of the saying "be better or be bitter."

What is at risk for underachievers is the state of thriving. Thriving involves being excited about life and the challenges it presents (e.g., loving your career, appreciating the world around you, looking forward to connecting with people). Individuals who thrive always find reasons to embrace life and live with passion. They realize their time on earth is limited, so they treat is as a valuable commodity, while underachievers pass time as if it were a nuisance. Thriving individuals invest energy in thriving and gain energy from thriving.

Most parents of underachievers have as their primary, long-term concern whether or not their child will advance to the level of thriving. Will they be productive citizens who are positive, engaged and productive? Will they push to their limits and achieve good things? They fear that if the underachievement continues, their child may become detached, cynical, unfulfilled, conflicted and unhappy.

When a parent deals with a child who is lagging behind, there is much self-recrimination, pain and anxiety. After all, there is nothing you want more than for your child to do well, to flourish both as a student and person. You want him or her to be productive, engaged, fulfilled and happy. Because that is not occurring, you may have the impulse to race ahead to Part II for guidance on what to do and what not to do, but don't cheat yourself—or your child. Before you start initiating changes so that your child can become unstuck and reach personal excellence, you need to read the fundamental how-to information in Part I about instilling values and nurturing positive emotions and attitudes in your child. In addition, the action items you'll find in Part II will be easier to initiate after you absorb some theoretical information about your underachiever and about your own motivation.

Once you understand the problem, you will know why your intuitive solutions probably won't work at all or won't have a lasting effect. And when you do plunge into the action items, you will be able to relate them to the theory. You'll say, "Aha! I know why this is worth doing."

Approaches that do *not* work

Power

Logic/reasoning

Skills approaches/tutoring

Together, the theories and practical to-dos in this book will give you the insight, knowledge and tools to reduce—and hopefully, even eliminate—the concern and the frustration that you are feeling about your child's unhappiness and lack of achievement in school.

We chose the word "empowering" for the title of the book because that's what you will learn to do, rather than only guide, counsel, teach or help.

People who don't feel empowered often feel as if they are being forced, coerced or controlled by others. They often do not develop a good sense of self. Things happen to them; they don't make things happen. This leaves them victims of a heartless, often unjust world in which they are not "given" good outcomes. They feel they do not have good luck. Their focus is on determining "why me?" and on whom to blame for their predicaments.

Empowering someone means transferring control so that the other person can function independently. The individual gains an appreciation that it is by his desire that he decides what he wants to do and how to do it. He gains insight.

Guiding, counseling, teaching and helping are not bad, but when they occur without the underachiever's investment in the process and without an acceptance of personal responsibility, they are ineffective. It is like pushing the proverbial wet noodle. When an underachiever is confronted with these external-controlling approaches he misinterprets others' intent. Rather than seeing these approaches as attempts to help him, he reacts as if he's being hassled. This leads to displays of frustration and irritation, either in passive-aggressive behavior, just not doing anything, or actively complaining ("Do I have to?").

With underachievers, their sense is often that they are mostly powerless. Some exceptions lie in their manipulating others and situations to transfer blame for their ineffective decisions and bad outcomes. They are the opposite of empowered. They feel helpless and develop a negative, even a cynical, perspective. This leads to resistance and continuing mediocrity, or worse.

By empowering, you place the responsibility for outcomes on your underachiever. That not only removes external blame for outcomes, but it also enables independence. The empowered individual grows toward the "no excuses" lifestyle.

CHAPTER ONE

WHO ARE UNDERACHIEVERS?

An underachiever is a child who is stuck developmentally. You may see bursts of his intelligence or take comfort in her sound values, but feel frustrated day after day as your bright, basically good child shows few signs of motivation and works far below potential. You've tried to help in every way you know how: You've tutored, you've reasoned, you've begged, you've bribed, you've punished, you've left him or her alone. Nothing you've tried has had lasting results.

"Maybe it's just a phase," you muse. "Maybe it'll pass." Teachers have said, "He will grow out of it."

The truth is, it is only infrequently that time and serendipity change underachievers. The theories in these pages will help you understand how underachievement is an emotion-based problem and the techniques will help you rouse the positive emotions, especially a strong sense of personal responsibility, that will help your underachiever get "unstuck."

The beginning of your journey to help the child is understanding what all underachievers have in common as well as the characteristics of the four distinctly different types of underachievers.

First, "underachievement" is a relative term and it applies to patterns of behavior that occur both inside and outside of school. Think in terms of envelopes of possibilities. If a genius with high standards performs up to those standards, even if he could do better, he's not an underachiever. He may lack high ambitions, but he's performing nor-

5

mally. If the child is a genius with average or low standards and routinely shirks personal responsibility to meet those low standards, then he's an underachiever. An average child who aims to do the best he can and repeatedly hits the mark is not an underachiever if he consistently turns in an average performance. In fact, if his motivation to succeed is so strong that he tries to stretch his envelope of possibility, he can be considered a high achiever. The checklist in Appendix A at the back of the book will help you determine whether or not your child fits the profile of an underachiever.

Statistics about the population of underachievers served by my Center for Applied Motivation, which has focused solely on helping unmotivated young people since 1984, illustrate key points about underachieving behavior:

- About 85 percent of the students are between the ages of eight and eighteen, with the motivational problem becoming most apparent in the early teens. The rest are over eighteen; in the latter group their parents and teachers finally realized that persistent lack of motivation was more than "just a phase." Underachievement can be a long—lifelong, in fact—experience if ignored or addressed ineffectively.

- Eighty percent of the Center's clients are male. The most likely reason for this is that girls tend to deal with their emotions more readily than boys do and utilize those emotions in the decisions they make. For many young males, this is not the case.

- The average IQ (intelligence quotient) of kids at the Center is 126—in terms of percentages, that puts them very high on the chart. Ironically, many of them get mediocre or failing grades and even did poorly on school-administered IQ tests, because they are so out of synch with the school system's and society's expectations. Many of these young people don't even know or won't accept the possibility that they're smart. Their self-perception may be that they're average because their friends are also smart; in the context of their social group, they are average. (If you live in the suburbs with a lawn, you might think everyone has a lawn.) Other reasons they don't know or don't accept that they're smart is that no one has told them they are or when someone has told them, they don't believe it; they've succeeded in convincing themselves that their productivity is low, because they don't have the brains to do better. Finally, some of them don't want to get proof that they are intelligent—they don't want to test high—because it will give their parents and teachers a factual basis for high expectations.

Jeff scored 104 on his school-administered IQ test. Indifferent to the process, he had no interest in focusing on the test and didn't trust the counselor who administered it. When he came to the Center, where he was not pre-judged to be average but rather presumed to be smart, he scored 127—two standard deviations above his previous test. That information *alone* gave Jeff the boost he needed to do much better in school consistently.

Some or all of the facts I just reiterated about the thousands of underachievers who've come to the Center probably don't surprise you. All you have to do is look in the next room and see the living proof.

The Floating Canoe

The underachiever floats in a canoe on a river and thinks: I have a paddle. I know what it does. I've watched others paddle. I see the raging river with rocks and roots. But I can't put the paddle in the river. The river takes me where it wants to go . . .

At first, underachievers have high hopes that the river will take them where they want to go—they know it will. They feel that others who tell them to use their paddle don't know what they're talking about. The voyage becomes treacherous as the canoe glides toward hazards. Either they don't notice, or they do notice and wonder, "Should I put the paddle in?" And then, anxiety sets in:

1. I don't really know exactly how to paddle. What if I do it wrong?
2. The paddle isn't the kind of paddle I want.
3. The canoe is already headed toward the rocks, so what's

> the point?
> 4. I didn't want to take this trip anyway.
> 5. If I paddle and avoid the rocks, more will show up,
>   so why try?
> 6. Why is the river doing this to me?
> 7. Where are the Park Rangers?
>
> The challenge with underachievers is to get them to internalize
> that (a) a paddle is a good thing to have, (b) they have a pad-
> dle, (c) it's to their advantage to learn how to use it, (d) it's help-
> ful to use it, and (e) not using the paddle mainly has undesirable
> consequences for them.

✳

ATTITUDE, NOT ABILITY

Students with good ability who frequently fall far short of their potential are underachievers. They are generally inconsistent in their efforts
and have a pattern of underachieving *over time*, not just periodically or
for a couple months. Even those underachievers with exceptional IQ
scores show lame performances in school and mediocre or even failing
grades. They intellectually understand what they need to do, but their
attitude is "so what?" After all, it (whatever shortcoming "it" is at the
time) isn't their fault. They blame lousy teachers, overbearing dads,
nagging mothers, crowded classrooms, bullies at school and irrelevant
homework. Does any of this sound familiar: "What assignment?"
"Don't worry, I'll take care of it." "I don't know why." "I'm bored." "I
forgot." "The teacher doesn't like me." "Don't bug me." "That grade
was weeks ago, I'm doing better now." "The class is irrelevant, I'll never
use this." For the most part, these comments represent detachments
that allow students to shirk personal responsibility for what are uncomfortable circumstances for them. They are detachments that result from
flights from their emotions.

In a forgiving society, where accountability is often seen as harsh
and mean-spirited, it is even harder for parents to take action. From
various sources, parents hear, "Shouldn't they be given another
chance?" With enough chances, there is no sense of accountability.
Personal concern of underachievers wanes as society reinforces their

assumption that everything will be forgiven…if I wait long enough. Continual moving of the line of accountability leads to manipulative individuals who do as little as possible. They take offense when someone questions their losing strategy of just getting by. They miss out on the joy of accomplishment, the excitement of engaging challenge.

While underachievement is usually pervasive, teachers are often the first to articulate the problem. They offer parents comments like, "Nice kid. Great personality. But he just doesn't do the work." Or "should be doing better." Or "not working to potential." That's the problem with underachievers. They work far below their potential and waste opportunities. Ultimately, they drag their own spirits down as well as generate unhappiness for their whole families. Parents notice the emergence of underachievement, but parental hope springs eternal—at first, they hope it will go away over time.

Most people have periods when they feel unmotivated. It's human to have transient motivational difficulties. For underachievers, lack of motivation is a lifestyle. Unfortunately, parents and teachers usually observe this unproductive coping style and think, "skills." *Maybe the kid doesn't know how to study. Maybe I should buy him a new organizer, an electronic one. Maybe he just needs more structure in his life. maybe we should monitor his assignments on the school homework listing on the internet. Maybe we should engage an "executive functioning" tutor. Maybe he needs math drills after school.* However, the problem is not ability. It is attitude. Actually, it's BAD—bad attitude disorder.

Even though the symptoms that surface are often parallel to other disorders, most underachievers have a "bad attitude" at the root of their problem. Theirs is a decision (either conscious or unconscious) to avoid, minimize, forget, be inattentive, be disorganized or be unaware. It is difficult to differentiate between neurologically-based attention problems—ADHD, for example—and a bad (unproductive/unconstructive) attitude that results in attention problems. Here's a clue: Often the underachiever is situation-specific in his symptoms. He can attend to a complex video game, but not a homework assignment, or he can remember the phone numbers of every friend, but not that he's expected to take out the trash every

Friday.

For some parents, the idea of personal responsibility for these failings seems offensive and naïve. They deem it insensitive, wrongly blaming the child for his attitude, behavior and attendant consequences. Seeing these symptoms as a *choice*, however, can help parents and kids to make a change. Even a child with a diagnosed neurological problem still has the responsibility to work toward personal effectiveness, in spite of the affliction. He must be willing to engage his reality with all of its burdens—engage so that he can learn to either overcome the disability or learn to compensate.

If you test a child enough, you will find discrepancies or variances from average. The question remains whether these discrepancies or variances cause the symptoms, or correlate to them.

Some parents spend a lot of time and money evaluating and testing. Commonly, they get a frustrating result: A lengthy, very specific report that does not help them resolve the issues. Often the reports have no integration; instead, they reflect bits of data with little relationship to each other or to the problem. There are endless scales and endless numbers on a page, like the boilerplate in legal documents. How many parents actually absorb the detailed, arcane recommendations?

Consider how your child behaves—does BAD come to mind? If so, you can take decisive action to minimize or eliminate it with the guidance in this book.

In a child of nine or ten with this problem, you may still see sparks of wanting to do well and genuine effort to change. By the time that child is a teenager, though, you may see that same underachiever resigned to mediocrity, detached and projecting the sentiment, "I don't care." It's an issue of deterioration for these individuals; at some point, they no longer feel the excitement of living. Fast forward to when the underachiever is an adult. By that time, the unproductive coping style is a habit pattern. If the adult then wants to change, it is much harder, because the habit trail is so long. As he tries to make new habits and stress recurs, he jumps right back to the old habits. This is the individual who spends hour after hour at the office working on a spreadsheet that details his retirement program instead of the spreadsheet he is supposed to do for a new project. That's surviving, not thriving.

Jason went to college after high school, but quickly dropped out and wanted nothing to do with the whole school scene. He was so detached that his only social life—in fact, his life in general for the next eight years—centered on playing fantasy games like Dungeons and Dragons. D&D players assume personas of medieval characters; some go beyond the board game and actually enact the plot with full costumes and battles. Jason's D&D friends were similarly underdeveloped adults in their twenties and thirties. None were married; none even had a long-term relationship. None had promising careers. School made Jason feel inadequate, so he turned to the one situation that made him feel confident. He tricked himself into perceiving that D&D was an important, productive and fulfilling part of his life.

Motivated students differ from unmotivated students not only in their output and grades, but also in their approaches to life—and the

Development *Toward* Maturity

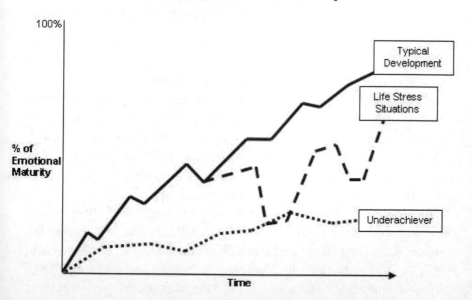

differences are mainly ones of attitude, as I indicated in the discussing of BAD. For the most part, motivated students have positive attitudes. They work close to their potential and seek out new experiences. They consistently and periodically adjust their efforts to fit the varying challenges. The phases that they go through, that might even include periods of lower productivity, don't follow predictable patterns as they do for underachievers. Motivated students may have ups and downs in a semester, but they tend to end strong. Underachievers usually start strong, but their performances soon go south and stay there for the duration. There may be a burst of activity at the end—too little, too late. If it keeps occurring, that's not a phase, it's a coping style.

It is important to note here that underachievement is not an all-or-nothing condition. It's a matter of the degree to which a person has the problems associated with a lack of motivation. At the extreme, the person becomes detached and cynical, never feeling like she fits in. On the other end, she may just be a little more bummed out than she needs to be.

✳

ATTRIBUTES OF UNDERACHIEVERS

Motivated students have three basic attributes that unmotivated students lack:

The first is an ability to **persist to completion.** Motivated students will start projects and work on these projects until they finish them, generally within a reasonable time frame. Such students will begin a semester with good effort and carry it through to final exams. When good students start their homework, they plow through their assignments until what needs to be done is completed.

In contrast, unmotivated students lack the ability to persist to completion. Usually, at the start of every grading period they promise to do better, but their efforts waiver. They just don't keep focused to the end. So the bad grades "appear" at the end of the semester—and the lectures at home begin. First you ask "why," then after a few dozen "I don't knows," you increase the pressure. Doing that may yield some effect for two or three weeks, but then the effort fades again.

The second basic attribute of motivated students that unmotivated students lack is the ability to **work within time limits**. If a project is due Tuesday, motivated students will have it done by Tuesday. Motivated students like time and appreciate the value of having an awareness of it. They use time to modulate their efforts, to organize and to keep themselves in tune with priorities.

Underachievers, however, do not consistently work within time limits. If an assignment is due Tuesday, on Tuesday when the teacher asks if the assignment is ready, the child might respond with "What? *This* Tuesday?" The same is usually true for home chores. You say, "Did you take the trash out today?" The answer is generally, "I forgot" or "I'll get it later." If yours is like most households, the trash gets taken out the same day of the week, every week. But your kid just forgets to do it or has all sorts of excuses. Time limits don't seem to matter. (Note: Most unmotivated people do not have a neurologically-based memory deficiency. Instead, they display a selective memory. A selective memory is convenient in avoiding responsibility).

Most individuals who are unmotivated have difficulty with time. If they have a watch, they may break it, lose it or refuse to wear it. (You see this with adult underachievers, too.) They are uncomfortable having a watch; it imposes responsibility. There aren't many good excuses for being late if you have a watch. Unmotivated students often arrive late to classes. Their assignments are delayed, forgotten or completed but not turned in.

The third basic attribute that achieving, motivated students have, but that unmotivated students generally lack, is the ability to **function independently**. It is important to understand that functioning independently here refers to age-appropriate independent functioning. You cannot expect an eight-year-old or a fifteen-year-old to be totally independent. And there will be a difference in what you expect from an eight-year-old versus a fifteen-year-old. Motivated students act age-appropriately responsible without being prodded.

An unmotivated student waits for others to come to her rescue. Her lack of independent functioning makes everyone else anxious.

These concerned others then try to help the underachiever. Did you ever have teachers impose weekly or daily worksheets for your child? You check the homework, you get involved, but in the long run, there is no lasting effect. Your child undermines these actions. She loses or forgets the sheet, forges signatures or makes excuses why she doesn't have it. You and the teachers escalate your attempts to organize and take control, because your child just isn't doing it. This may go on for some time, but eventually you realize that all your efforts are not having the desired effect.

If this goes on long enough for underachievers, they may fail a semester. They may fail the school year. If they do, then they have another year of living at home with their parents, which they say they don't want and at least another year at school, which they say they hate. Likewise, if they have part-time jobs, because of their irresponsi-

---

Three Attributes of Motivated Students That Unmotivated Students Lack:

- Persistance to Completion
- Working Within Time Limits
- Functioning Independently

---

bility they may get fired or at least not get promoted into something more challenging. Young people who have no sense of responsibility suddenly find themselves in their twenties doing the same thing as when they were teenagers—going nowhere. A very dependent lifestyle results. The "twenty somethings" deny themselves the very independence that they insisted throughout their lives they wanted. Their lives become a series of lost opportunities.

Underachievers ask for independence, often whine when they don't get it and get angry with those they feel are oppressing them. Because they are immature, what they want is immature independence, that is, without responsibility or accountability.

The lack of these three attributes leads to a variety of other behaviors. For example, has your child ever spent more time trying to get out of something than the time it would take just to do it? An unmotivated child might argue for twenty or thirty minutes over a task that takes five minutes to complete. It's inefficient. It's counterproductive. But it's also indicative of the child's unmotivated lifestyle and the problem has a lot to do with detachment and shirking personal responsibility.

Again, underachievement is an attitude problem, not an ability or knowledge problem. As you read the descriptions of this problem, you may identify some of the traits and patterns within yourself when you were younger or with others you know. Keep in mind that not everyone who shows some of the characteristics discussed here is an underachiever. Underachievement is not a one day or one week phenomenon. It is a pattern over time. While underachievement can occur with other diagnoses and can influence and be influenced by other concerns, the presence of underachievement needs to be objectively assessed. There are a variety of ways of doing this, one of which is to have a mental health professional conduct formal psychological testing and

Assessing Underachievement: Differential Diagnosis

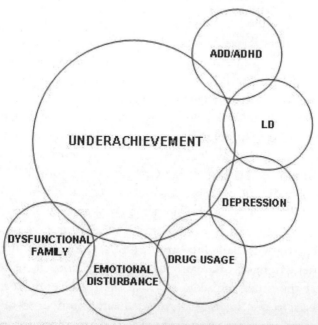

There can be an interplay between underachievement and various outside factors. Any of these problems may influence underachievement either by themselves or in combination with one or more other factors. Underachievement can also influence these conditions.

combine the results with interviews of the parents and student and a review of school and medical records.

A systematic look at symptoms is called for. Begin by watching for the specific patterns that determine who is an underachiever. Before you do, though, it is important not to confuse emotion-based underachievement with other difficulties that may have similar symptoms, such as learning disabilities, attention deficit disorder (ADD), vision problems and any number of physical ailments. Underachievement may appear as an emotional component of these other problems; it's the potential for this interrelationship that can make diagnosis of underachievement difficult. As these other diagnoses are ruled out, then the focus on motivation should begin. Here's a caution: Be wary of anyone who pins the ADD label on your child without thorough observation and assessment testing. A school counselor alone, for example, cannot make such a diagnosis.

❋

Patterns of Underachievers

Here are the key patterns of underachievers:

- They have very **selective memories.** Sometimes, it is truly amazing. When these kids want to phone their friends, they rarely need to look up the numbers. Many times these phone numbers are for acquaintances they don't even call frequently. These youngsters have no problem remembering sports scores, when certain television shows are on and upcoming social events. But, if underachievers have to remember to do homework tonight, if they have to remember to bring their books home or take out the trash, that's a totally different story.

  Underachievers have intact memories that denial has transformed into selective memories. Denial can be a useful tool in coping with daily life. At appropriate times, mature people do deny things that are unpleasant or they don't feel like handling at the time. You see a truck in the rearview mirror and rush-hour traffic in front of you is nearly bumper-to-bumper and going at high speed. What if someone in that line hits the brakes? It takes a certain amount of denial to get out there and convince yourself that won't happen. We all operate with some level of denial—we need it to function; otherwise we'd turn into hermits. Denial allows us to distance ourselves from our initial emotional reactions brought on by reality.

For underachievers, it is too difficult and frightening to face the reality that they could do better if they put as much effort into "doing" as they do "avoiding doing." Denial surfaces to "save" them from such unpleasantness and selective memory is part of the result. When they say, "I forgot" over and over again about their assignments and chores, they aren't trying to be duplicitous nor are they pathological liars. Their immature denial has created and honed very selective memories.

- Additionally, unmotivated underachieving students have **selective attention**. They don't have a neurological-based loss of attention or have an inability to pay attention. Their attention, and inattention, is selective. Either consciously or subconsciously they select to pay attention or to not pay attention. Their inattention might be selective to math, so they won't pay attention in their math classes. Or it might be selective to homework, so they won't pay attention to their homework and become easily distracted. But when they play video games or sports they love, hear CDs that engage them, or watch movies of the moment, they maintain attention very well.

  Selective attention may be mistaken for, or intertwined with, the symptoms of attention deficit disorder, but the two are different entities. You need to be aware of the differing variables before a diagnosis of attention deficit disorder is made of your child. ADD receives more detailed attention in Chapter 3.

- Another major characteristic of unmotivated students is that they **lack self-confidence**. They are not self-starters. They wait for others to guide them, focus them, push them, organize and structure them. You have probably heard your underachiever say, "I'll take care of it," but she doesn't. So what happens? First, your anxiety rises. You feel the need to help. You start organizing and taking charge. You may even go over her assignments to be sure they are done and done reasonably well. Is your child thankful for your help? Of course not. What does she do? She loses assignments, or perhaps more frustrating, completes the assignments, but never turns them in. Of course you don't know this until the grades come out and there is a big fat zero for the project. You can't believe it. The work was done, but she just didn't turn it in!

- If your child is like most, when motivational problems and underachievement occur, they usually **involve many areas of responsibility,** not just academics. Such areas include doing chores and communicating and relating well to you and other authority figures on a more mature level. This is another characteristic of an underachiever. Remember that we are talking about a basically good kid, so while your child may be driving you up a wall, the neighbors may tell you how helpful he is or how much fun she is. That's very possible, because the problems tend to show up in areas of expected responsibility with authority figures. When the pressure is off, an unmotivated child can be quite charming.

- Underachievers **intend to do well** and frequently promise themselves and others that they will. Because underachievers quickly lose their intention and put their energies into avoidance, however, parents begin to feel that underachievers do not care. This exacerbates the cycle. Parents have stronger responses and often engage in recriminations. They feel that the underachiever is numb to reality. In turn, underachievers feel bothered, irritated, defensive. Tensions rise within the family. In actuality, both parents and underachievers want the underachievers to do well.

- As is typical of immature individuals, underachievers **focus on fun and resist the developmental transition to fulfillment.** They see work as an imposition, something to be avoided. Fun appeals to basic stimulation. Impulse is fun, and usually allows them to avoid discomfort. The result of play is usually temporary satiation and relief, and it is good to a transient point. As people mature, external demands limit opportunities for fun, however. Further, a transition to fulfillment is needed. Developmental growth demands that individuals find fulfillment to be a primary source of happiness. An immature person finds it difficult to limit fun because of its basic avoidant nature. When the fun stops, reality and its demands take over.

There are secondary effects of fun. It can present a passive/aggressive message to others ("Take a leap, I'm not going to do work. I'm playing."). This is effective in aggravating mature people who expect others to work responsibly, rather than just play all the time. Another effect of playing too much of the time is that the person does not learn how to tolerate discomfort or develop skills of effective engagement. Not only is that individual then unfulfilled, but also less effective. For mature people, fun is okay, but it is usually very secondary to fulfillment. Fun must be placed in perspective. Most responsible mature adults focus on fulfillment as the source of their overall happiness.

Underachievers frustrate themselves, not just people around them, when they display these negative characteristics. These kids really want to do well, but they choose to go in the opposite direction. The choice may be subconscious—but their actions are a choice. Most teenagers struggle with their senses of identity and independence and try to separate themselves from the authority figures in their lives so that they have their own identities. The thought that they have parallel interests with these authority figures, especially their parents, makes them uncomfortable and they quickly reject such realizations, often without much thought. Adolescents may even squelch their desires so they don't appear agreeable. However, as most of us mature, we come to realize that our basic values and concerns are similar to the values and concerns of our parents and other important adults in our life. We see that working with, not against, others is more productive.

For most people, the bulk of our value core is internalized by the time we are ten to twelve years old. Of that internal value core, most

Parallel Interests — Parallel Values

```
                                    ┌─────────────────────┐
                                    │     Student's       │
                                    │  Interests & Values │
                                    └─────────────────────┘

   ┌─────────────────────┐
   │      Parent's       │         Underachieving
   │  Interests & Values │         Student's View
   └─────────────────────┘
──────────────────────────────────────────────────────────────

                              Reality

                                 ┌─────────────────────┐
                                 │     Student's       │
                                 │  Interests & Values │
                                 └─────────────────────┘
                    ┌─────────────────────┐
                    │      Parent's       │
                    │  Interests & Values │
                    └─────────────────────┘
```

are parallel to our parents' values. If parents do a reasonable job of parenting, they instill values into us through modeling, telling self-anecdotal stories, correcting, role-playing, guiding, discussing, storytelling and guided reading. Even though each person is unique—coloring, filtering and creating characteristics in a unique way—we are to some degree the product of our parents and other influential figures. Teenagers find this unsettling. In attempting to shape their own unique identities, they have a measure of discomfort with their parents. If young people go to a movie with their mothers and/or fathers, they might sit ten seats away or might even go to see a different film in the same complex just to be physically separate from their parents. If they sat with their parents, they would have to accept the reality that much of the basis for their own personal identities—their values—is closely parallel to that of their parents.

Ultimately, as these young people become more emotionally mature they will come to understand parallel interests and will accept and integrate these facts. Simply remembering this when you think about your child can help moderate your tension.

CHAPTER TWO

THE FOUR TYPES OF UNDERACHIEVERS

Even though underachievers struggle with most of the same patterns and characteristics, all children with motivation problems don't behave—or feel—the same way. Underachievers fall into four types. Each of these requires a particular kind of intervention and specific sensitivities by those attempting to help them toward personal change.

Four Types	What percent are primarily this type?
Distant	5
Passive	20
Dependent	60
Defiant	15

These types of underachievers are not mutually exclusive. An underachieving student may, at any one time, show some aspects of more than one type. Because these are developmental categories, a child may pass from one type to another on his way to increasing maturity. Patterns of a distant or passive underachiever tend to emerge early in life, dependency a little later and defiant under-achieving usually begins in the mid-to-late teens. Keep in mind that at any one point in time, though they may exhibit behaviors that fit several categories, underachievers will show characteristics that are predominately one type. This delineation is important for understanding and influencing your child. See Appendix B, "Development Level Indicators," for guidance in determining what type of underachiever your child may be.

As the four types are discussed in this chapter, it is helpful to think of your own life. We all go *through* these steps in the course of normal development. In the case of an underachiever, however, the child gets stuck in one of these developmental steps or regresses from a later stage and the characteristics become heightened and intensified. Parents frequently begin their conversation with us at the Center by saying, "He was fine up until—" Then they give an age that gives us a clue as to what type of underachiever he most likely is. "He was fine up until high school," for example, is a hint that the underachiever is dependent, defiant, or perhaps a combination.

Realizing that the motivational problem has caused them to feel as though they are growing apart from their child, the next thing par-

Levels Of
Emotional Development

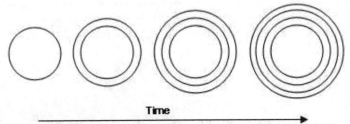

Time

Each ring represents an achieved development stage

Focus	Trust/ Bonding	Approval/ Acceptance	Dependence/ Guidance	Independence/ Differentiation	To Maturity
Significant Others	Mother Father	Parents Teachers	Peers	Self	Self & Others
Chronological Age Normally Seen*	0 – 2 yrs.	3 – 7 yrs.	8 – 12 yrs.	13 – 21 yrs.	22+ yrs.

*Approximate age range when this level normally emerges. Most children move through all these stages on their way to maturity. An underachiever becomes "stuck" at a particular stage, or regresses to an earlier one.

ents often say is, "Can you help me get my child back?" The real question is, "Can anything be done to move the child forward on the developmental track—to help him grow up emotionally?"

✳

THE DISTANT UNDERACHIEVER

Distant underachievers are detached from other people. They choose to be distant because the key issue with Distants is **broken trust**. For most of them, trusts were broken when they were very young, early in their development. Perhaps the provoking event was something as traumatic as a parent dying or parents divorcing or a parent abandoning the family. Other inciting incidents could be having someone close to them die, losing a pet, having a friend leave, frequent moves or adoption. Almost anything that creates strong emotional distress can contribute to a person being stuck at the Distant level.

Adoption deserves a special note, although putting it in this category doesn't mean that adopted children who become underachievers are more likely to be Distants than other types. A disproportionately high percentage of the Center's clients are adopted—an average of 13 percent or about four times higher than the percentage of adopted children in the United States. This fact suggests that parents need to take special steps to keep their adopted child moving along the developmental path. Even though the child usually comes into a loving family, a family that desperately wanted her, when she is growing up she often still has heightened concerns and emotions regarding her situation. The adopted child needs periodic reinforcement. Having the conversation once at an early age about "how much we wanted you" fails to meet completely and forever the child's needs. This issue has to be revisited as the child progresses through other developmental levels.

Because their feelings were hurt in the past, Distants carry the belief that trusting another person to be there for them is risky, so they choose to retreat emotionally. At their immature level of development, children with this problem feel that not getting close to other people will prevent them from being hurt again. This leads Distants to disengage from investing in their lives and from actively initiating social contacts. At school they don't easily become involved with others or with class activities—these are kids who don't look forward to recess—although they may do very well with activities that do not require much direct interaction. For example, they may be very good with computers, chess or mathematics. Often they have advanced vocabularies and technical knowledge, as well as an ability for philosophical and analytical discussions. This is how they validate their worth. This masks their insecurities and lack of close relationships.

Distant children's focus on solitary activities defines consistent boundaries for them within which they establish their identities. They perceive any changes in their closely controlled environments as threats. Close relationships would challenge their senses of identity, because Distants' identity boundaries are easily blurred. As they get older, they have few friends, if any. Emotional intimacy is avoided.

This distancing usually occurs in all aspects of their lives. Any commitment carries risks. Frequently, they will not care about anything and find reasons to remain disengaged.

Because distant underachievers are so emotionally immature, their interactions often focus heavily on their own needs rather than mutual needs. They usually have low frustration tolerance, often striking out in antisocial ways. If provoked, they may react with hostility and with no regard for consequences. They struggle to express themselves productively. They seek immediate gratification and don't understand the concept of sacrificing now to obtain future goals.

Other people easily influence Distants as they get older, because they do not want to disagree and then have to work through that disagreement. Even though they are easily influenced, however, they tend to be outside their peer groups. Distants are fragile, solitary individuals, looking and wanting to be inside.

Keeping relationships secondary or tertiary behind their individual pursuits protects Distants from the uncertainties of human interactions and the possibilities of rejection and brings instead the consistencies of predictability, which these children require to meet their emotional needs. Inconsistencies profoundly disturb them.

Their lack of positive interpersonal relationships makes it difficult for Distants to change their circumstances. It is especially important to be sensitive to distant underachievers' states of anxiety and distrust. Distant underachievers must be carefully approached in a consistent manner. Even small inconsistencies, such as being five minutes late when picking them up from school, can undermine any fragile trust established and cause them to distance themselves even more. Distants fantasize catastrophic outcomes: "Mom's not coming to pick me up! She forgot about me!"

Among the four types of underachievers, Distants are the least mature and the least developed emotionally. They are often frightened by trust and certainty while at the same time they yearn for these attributes. Repeated episodes of anxiety mark the life of distant underachievers; they follow up by distancing themselves from those things and people that brought on their anxiety. This may lead to social isolation, school expulsion, premature job transitions and short-term relationships. Substance abuse, as an attempt at self-medication, may eventually be a distant underachiever's response to inner turmoil.

When Joey was four, his father went out for cigarettes one day and disappeared. By the time he was twelve, Joey showed the full spectrum of traits associated with a distant underachiever. On his first day at the Center, he sat in a chair with the hood of his jacket covering his head. After months of sessions, he finally responded to the invitation to draw—anything—on sheets of paper. I sat across the card table and drew at the same time on a separate sheet of paper, saying very little. Joey began by drawing exploding bombs and rockets: He started to feel comfortable enough to show he had feelings about the abandonment. Then he turned the paper toward me, symbolically aiming his anger at me. I was a man and the most important man in his life had walked out on him. Therefore, I should be punished. Gradually, as he realized I could be trusted not to go away—when he saw I was consistently present and non-threatening—he started talking. Soon, Joey began extending that trust to other people and school.

❋

THE PASSIVE UNDERACHIEVER

Passives are stuck at higher developmental levels than Distants. They are passive in their own interests. The key issue for Passives is that they find their self-worths and identities externally through the approval of others. Activities and tasks center on the desire of the passive underachiever to gain approval of authority figures, especially parents and teachers, without consideration for his or her own needs. Passives feel that their adequacy as individuals is singularly based on meeting the expectations of others rather than on who they are as individuals. This creates intense anxiety—unproductive anxiety.

Generally, children between the ages of three and seven go through a normal developmental period in which they try to please authority figures, usually parents and teachers, in order to gain approval. As they acquire a better sense of self, most children quickly move through that period in which the approval of others is more important than anything else. Passives, however, are stuck at this level or they may have dropped back from a higher developmental level.

In trying to please others, Passives get so apprehensive about the possibility that they may not please the significant people in their lives and their self-certainty is so low, that their anxieties rise, overwhelming them. They freeze. They blank, responding oddly or in completely wrong ways. They end up falling short of everyone's expectations, including their own. Guilty, rejected and unhappy, they experience more anxieties, which cause even more failures. It's a circular "Catch-22" situation.

Whereas a certain amount of anxiety serves as performance cues to motivated kids, for Passives any anxiety becomes too much to bear. These children tend to collapse under it rather than use it productively. They avoid, are ambivalent or fail to respond. Because Passives are trying desperately to maintain the approval of others, especially parents and teachers, any kind of evaluation by these authority figures sparks intense anxieties. It's common for Passives to not only freeze on tests, but also confuse directions and do erratic work.

Because Passives try to achieve for others and not for themselves, they do not experience the personal fulfillment that is necessary to develop and maintain self-motivation. Their striving for others' approval is superficial to their own interests and externally driven.

These underachievers just don't have senses of independent selves. Their own needs are submerged. They are passive in pursuit of *their* own needs. Since they do not have their own needs in focus, they are constantly pressured by what they believe others may want. Things become more difficult for them when conflicting expectations or multiple-demand situations force them to make choices. Avoidance is their most common response. To the Passive, not trying means avoiding the responsibility for possible failure and resultant disapproval. Avoidance, though, leads to inadequate performance, which elevates anxiety even more.

Passives are usually so likable and try so hard to please that parents actually get anxious when their children move beyond this pattern of underachievement and progress normally to and through a dependent or defiant stage. At this point parents go from having an overly nice kid to an assertive one. The transition is jolting.

Passives can be among the most responsive children, frequently volunteering to help even if not confident that they can produce. They just want you to know that they're trying. When it comes to schoolwork or chores, they may even try to complete their work in minute detail after much discussion about exactly what they should do, but they show few elements of original thought. When asked for personal views, they are most likely to reflect the views of others rather than divulge their own thinking.

Passives smile frequently, but they seem sad. Since their self-esteem is externally based, they don't really feel good on the inside. Passives develop vague feelings of dissatisfaction with themselves and they feel trapped.

Bert: A Passive Underachiever Emerges
And Poor Teachers Engender the Problem
When Bert entered kindergarten he already knew how to read a little. He was the oldest child in what would eventually become a

group of four siblings, so he got a lot of attention from mom in the early days. A well-behaved, curious kid, he thought kindergarten was going to be great. Unfortunately, Bert's kindergarten teacher didn't teach reading and she was surly—very unlike his gentle, vivacious mother. After Bert's second day, the teacher pronounced him "uncontrollable." His mother said, "Meek, mild Bert who tries to please all the time?" "He won't do art work," the teacher said. And when Bert didn't want to do something, without making a fuss he would get up and go to the back of the room. The entire year, the teacher bored Bert and forced him to do activities he abhorred, like playing with shaving cream and singing songs he didn't like. His parents were appalled: They were called in for "crisis" parent-teacher conferences over the fact that their five-year-old wouldn't make pictures out of shaving cream!

First grade involved a nicer teacher who taught reading, but not the verbal skills that go with reading. This made the second grade teacher angry with her students who didn't have the skills they should have had by then. By second grade, Bert had a serious motivation problem. He continued his habit of getting up and going to the back of the room instead of participating in certain activities. Bert became a loner at school.

In desperation, his teacher instituted both a punishment and a reward system. Bert would have to stay in the classroom and work during recess if he didn't do an assignment during class. He would get a small gold star on his hand if he did well. This served as a cue to Bert's mother that he was "good" that day and should be somehow rewarded. None of this had a lasting effect.

By the third grade, the teacher deemed him "slow" and had him put in remedial groups, even though he tested high and read beyond his years. Bert's underachieving patterns became well entrenched. He allowed his intelligence to burst through in the form of pranks. One that the teacher found particularly annoying was his transformation of a blackboard drawing of a woman into a more anatomically correct version.

Even his parents deemed third grade "a total waste." They tried to place him somewhere else, but Bert begged them not to move him.

He had gotten used to the remedial classes; they were easy. On some level, he thought he was accomplishing something, so he could once again please his parents. The remedial reading teacher, another gem of the school system, assured Bert's parents that since he finished his work so handily, she gave him extra things to do—like wipe the boards clean.

Bert's mother was furious: "All you're teaching my son is that if he doesn't want to work, he doesn't have to work."

In order to get some schoolwork completed, by the fourth grade she and Bert's dad "became the students." They joked about it with other parents with similar difficulties—"We've already been through fourth grade"—but none of them were amused. They hired a tutor, who promptly went to the fourth grade, too. Then the jokes really flew. Bert's mother said, "I paid this woman seventy dollars to help my son with his term paper and she ended up doing it. I could have bought a term paper for less than that!"

The transition from underachiever to motivated student that began in the fifth grade meant, first of all, that Bert's mom and dad had to resign from elementary school. That included not reminding him about assignments, as well as not helping him.

The hardest part of the prescribed intervention, according to Bert's mom, has been literally keeping him at arm's length. In order to spark more of a sense of independence in Bert, who would spend an inordinate amount of time hugging and cuddling with his mother, she had to refuse some of his affection. By clinging to her he showed how much his identity was blended with hers—a common condition for a passive underachiever. The behavior was inappropriate for his age and he had to break the pattern to move forward in his emotional development.

Passive underachievers tend to fall within four subcategories: obsessive, compulsive, somatic and hysterical.

1. **Compulsive Passive** underachievers' concerns center on the necessity of order and neatness. Order and neatness seem to lessen their runaway, interfering anxieties. This compulsion for

order shows up in their attention to detail that precedes most activities. Room temperature, lighting and even the arrangement of items on the desk are vital prerequisites for beginning work. But they miss the big picture.

2. **Obsessive passive** underachievers cannot make commitments to tasks or goals. Instead, they put so much effort into checking what to do and how to do it that the tasks themselves do not get done. With that effort, they try to lessen their interfering anxieties. These obsessive passive underachievers may fall victim to stress-related physical disorders due to their excessive internalization of emotions. When asked to draw a picture, they may spend inordinate time "correcting" and delay completing. Things never seem to be good enough. They experience a lot of doubts, further heightening their anxieties.

3. **Somatic Passives**, on the other hand, are most likely to use physical distress as a way to cope with their interfering anxieties. Physical ailments become excuses to escape from rejection or disapproval. These tendencies will often become apparent when children with this problem are faced with situations such as major exams, job interviews or even intramural basketball games. The illness lets them escape a situation by eliciting sympathy from people around them; they avoid the possibility of failure through manipulation. Students like this spend inordinate time in the school nurse's office or home from school. They have headaches or stomach aches, they feel faint or uncomfortable—they have all sorts of vague physical complaints. The physical symptoms and accompanying discomfort of underachievers manifesting these signs are real, but the symptoms are caused by the stress of anxiety, tension and anticipation.

4. **Hysterical passive** underachievers have more direct approaches. They focus on acceptance and approval of their external self. They try to impress others by their exaggerated interests, their exaggerated efforts and their exaggerated disappointments when they fail. A typical move would be raising a

hand in class when the teacher asks a question, but not having an answer to the question. These students are controlled by what they perceive as the current trends and they may go to extreme lengths to try to fit that trend. These students are followers, easily influenced by others, but because importance is attached to physical characteristics, they have difficulty establishing close and meaningful interpersonal relationships. To them, the potential for such relationships is limited by their narcissistic perceptions.

Passives are very uncomfortable with their senses of self. They are more mature than Distants, but still are not sufficiently developed emotionally to face how they feel: trapped, anxious and unhappy.

When he sat down for his first session with me, twelve-year-old Kipp shyly lowered his head. He looked tonsured, like a monk. In actuality, Kipp had responded to his intense anxiety by literally pulling his hair out. As the prior school year went on, the bald circle on his scalp had grown larger.

❋

THE DEPENDENT UNDERACHIEVER

The Dependent is the most common type of underachiever.

Picture this: It's dinnertime. Walking into the kitchen, you find your fourteen-year-old working on a science project that has overtaken the entire kitchen. In order to have dinner that night, you need to "help" with the project, which is due the next morning. You become upset when you realize the project was assigned two weeks ago and now your evening is going to be spent doing homework. Your adolescent is calm and secure now that help has arrived.

While usually complaining that they want to be left alone, Dependents really want others to experience their emotions, solve their conflicts and take their responsibilities. You might say the Dependent's philosophy is "It is better to give discomfort than receive it." Dependents see emotions as something to avoid.

Dependents display selective memory and selective attention. They commonly fail to set priorities effectively, often focusing on activities that have little long-term value, while ignoring those that will impact on their futures. The Dependents' goals change frequently, are not well thought out or simply disappear. In junior high or high school, dependent underachievers often focus on subjects such as physical education, art or music while showing little interest in core subjects. And while they might channel their abundant energies into playing the guitar or in-line skating, it is common that they won't practice with the discipline and focus that could give them a competitive edge in these activities.

Much of the time Dependents say they feel bored. These kids place little importance on school and, sometimes, will even make statements about not wanting to grow up and not wanting to leave home. Missing or unprepared assignments become increasingly frequent occurrences as more responsibilities are expected of them. Dependents frequently externalize blame when things don't work out well for them. It's always someone else's fault; there were circumstances beyond their control. Their explanations serve to deny them control over their situations. This reduces their anxieties from their continual inadequacies or failures. What they really are attempting to do is avoid responsibilities—and the future—by staying dependent. However, Dependents say they want others to leave them alone. While they complain about others stepping in, dependent underachievers have created their dependency by their inactions.

Dependents feign indifference, which is a very effective way to get parents to feel the emotions that the dependent should be feeling. For example, if a dependent is failing school and his parents point out to the child that failing school probably means ending up in an unrewarding job and having a tough time financially in life, what does the Dependent do? He shrugs his shoulders and acts as if it doesn't matter. Dependents often respond with "Whatever." It almost guarantees an emotional response from the parents.

This indifference is very effective at shifting emotions such as anxiety and concern over to parents. Frequently then, when parents attempt to institute actions based on their own values—essentially taking control—dependent underachievers will usually be passively resistant to such guidance. They may not verbalize this resistance, but they will either not do what their parents ask them to or they will do it half-heartedly.

Let's say you have a dependent underachiever who has a test tomorrow, but he chooses to watch television all evening or talk on the phone with friends. At about nine in the evening, you find out about the test from another parent. You tell your child to turn off the television or put down the phone and go to his room to study. Chances are he will go to his room, sit with his books in front of him and act like he is studying. However, he will only look at his work when you walk by the room and then, only grudgingly. Mainly, he will sit there thinking about how strict you are, how unfair his teacher is for having this test and how irrelevant the class material is to his life.

With Dependents, you should think of emotions as "hot potatoes." "I feel bad. I don't want to feel bad. Here—you take it. It's too hot for me—*you* feel bad."

Usually, Dependents are quite effective at transferring emotions to concerned and caring adults. Unfortunately, if you jump in and begin taking control, trying to force compliance and personal responsibility, this can contribute to dependency. If these students get through high school because others are always guiding, controlling and prodding, they usually fail college or their employers. They aren't able to function independently, away from the support of others. It is best not to react in a take-charge manner in response to a dependent underachiever.

Socially, dependent underachievers are usually personable and active. Their attitudes toward authority are often ambivalent, though. Superficially, they respond with indifference, generally withdrawing from adults and other authority figures. They develop a degree of cynicism. Ironically, Dependents harbor resentment and anger toward individuals who attempt to control them while *wanting* that control as a way of relinquishing their personal responsibilities to others. In some cases, they may feel overwhelmed by parents or may see only the negative reinforcement aspect of their parental relationships. In either case, conflict avoidance through active or passive means takes precedence. Dependents often express anger through passive-aggressive behavior, that is, they may agree with the parent, but they won't follow through. This allows them to feel control over their parents. Additionally, they often use clever excuses to justify their underachievement in the hope this will focus attention away from them. This is a manipulative game which parents must recognize.

A significant fear for dependent underachievers is that of abandonment. These kids feel that through inconsistent and marginal performances they will become the focus of attention. Unfortunately, they usually are correct about this. In a Dependent's mind, consistent success would destroy the dependent relationship between the underachiever and the parents. Although this is true, Dependents take this to the extreme and fear appropriate independence. On a deep level, they don't grasp that if they assume appropriate independence, they can still interact, only now it will be at a more mature level. They are just too fearful of the uncertainty of change and what taking responsibility for themselves will bring. This then creates a world in which success becomes a negative and failure a positive when relating to parents. In this way, dependent underachievers stay dependent on parents for limits and especially problem solving and decision-making.

A dependent underachiever may have been a good student at one time. But just about the time when students are required to complete heavier workloads outside the school environment—a major step in personal responsibility—the dependent underachiever starts to show the signs of indifference. Soon, lost or unprepared assignments become a commonplace problem.

If parents insist on punishments and restrictions, especially if appropriate consequences are inconsistent, this further entrenches a Dependent's inverted view as he acts out the role of victim. A dependent underachiever's reliance on this rationale eventually undermines attempts by his parents to alter the underachievement patterns. Even as his dependent underachieving leads him to mediocrity or failures, the Dependent persists, all the while feigning indifference.

Parental guilt may reinforce the underachiever's reliance on displacing or shirking his personal responsibilities. By projecting such guilt on others, the Dependent continues avoiding responsibility for his own failures to achieve. One boy I treated, Buddy, had this problem.

Buddy walked out of my office with a red crease across his forehead.

"What's that?" his father asked me.

I told him that after I had asked Buddy where his journal entries were and he produced nothing, Buddy spent the rest of the session crying with his head resting on the edge of my desk—hence the crease. Buddy tried to pass on his pain to me—like a hot potato. He wanted me to accept responsibility for his journal entries and the strategy hadn't worked.

Buddy's parents said that he commonly would enlist them to supervise him for three or four hours in a homework assignment that should have taken thirty minutes.

✳

THE DEFIANT UNDERACHIEVER

Defiant underachieving usually begins in the mid-to-late teens and these young adults tend to be very insecure in their emerging independence and maturity. Of all the types of underachievers, they are the farthest along developmentally—the closest to being mature—but this weakness in their independence holds them back.

Many Defiants are openly rebellious. If you say "up," they say "down." If you agree and change to "down," they will say "up." They have difficulty accepting that their teachers, counselors and especially parents are generally correct about life's connections and the need to fit themselves within a social context. They are conflicted. External authority stirs that conflict—as do limits, expectations and any other boundaries.

This creates turmoil and confusion for them. They tend to act-out by arranging confrontations and by only rarely using either negotiation or compromise. If you go past almost any high school in the morning before classes start, you'll see the kids who have odd hair-styles and strange clothing loitering off school property. Maybe they're smoking. Generally, they look rebellious. These tend to be Defiants. They'll sneer at anyone over thirty. They spend much energy trying to be confrontational in ways that they think are clever. Favorite pastimes include "catching" parents doing things that are forbidden and pointing out illogic, irrelevancy or inadequacy in adults. Depending on the intensity of their defiance, this can range from mildly irritating to outrageous. Defiant underachievers will pro-voke "oppressive" behavior by authority figures in order to ensure the continuance of their rationalizations of underachievement. Defiants truly have "attitudes."

Adults sometimes have a hard time *not* agreeing with Defiants or getting a kick out of what they say. Woven into their refusals to study could be some persuasive and entertaining arguments about the irrel-evance of the subject matter, for example. "Who really needs Emily Dickinson's poetry?" can sound like a legitimate question to a parent who owns a shoe store. The underachievers don't understand the value of acquiring discipline through a range of schoolwork, of men-tal exercises to stimulate their brain, of expanding interests and being well-rounded individuals, and they shut these messages out when parents and teachers express them.

Tim: A Defiant Underachiever
Responds with Rapid Changes

Tim had a rocky beginning in school because of an undiagnosed ear problem. Until the second grade, neither his teachers nor his par-ents realized that he couldn't hear some of what was said in class. His second grade teacher actually thought he was "slow" or might have attention deficit hyperactivity disorder (ADHD). He went through standardized tests that revealed he had learned to read by memory. Despite that, the tests showed he had the verbal skills of a seventh grader. His hyperactivity, the therapist concluded, was just a cover-up for not being in tune with the rest of the class.

Over the next few years, Tim struggled to catch up. His mother helped him with homework regularly and he showed an enormous capacity for learning. Then he'd go to school and blow it on the test. He would get nervous. Finally, he lost interest in trying and became demonstrably more defiant. If his parents said, "Up," he'd say, "Down." They said, "Black," and he'd kick back with "White." Compromise was not in his vocabulary; he was right and he knew it. Finally, he turned to sports where he could enjoy and excel in purely kinesthetic experiences. School took a far back seat to soccer, rollerblading and snowboarding, in which he easily channeled his high adrenaline into high performance. He convinced himself that he didn't need school at all. He would be a professional in-line skater.

When his parents told him that wasn't realistic, he fought with them. "They don't get it," he complained. "They don't know how good I am."

Tim's parents did, in fact, realize that their son had a lot of talent, but they began an intervention program, because they wanted him to have options besides skating.

At the time that Tim and his parents began the program early in his sophomore year of high school, he had a 1.8 grade point average. Progress came quickly for Tim; his grades went up each semester for the next two years. By the time he was completing his senior year, Tim had taken his GPA to 3.5.

Tim's steady and relatively rapid progress from defiant underachiever to excellent student is not unusual—it just can't be expected with every underachiever. It does highlight the fact that Defiants are closest to maturity than other types of underachievers.

The intervention that kicked Tim off to a fast start involved exercises in negotiation and compromise. He learned to make deals with his parents about when and where he could skate; his compromise to study harder had the effect of ratcheting up his grades. For that, he quickly got the satisfaction of having accomplished something. His parents acknowledged his success and began displaying more trust in his judgment. He lost interest in his rollerblading friends, who were younger, and gravitated toward more activities with his classmates. By the time he entered college and began a pro-

gram in economics, he had so much trust in his own judgment and intellectual skills that he took over management of a small investment pool with the same zeal he had earlier put into sports. Tim graduated from Shippensburg University of Pennsylvania with a degree in finance.

Defiants, like Tim during his high school years, are just beginning to see themselves as responsible individuals, but they haven't solidified their senses of self. While striving to find what roles they play in life, it becomes critical for them to have unencumbered success as individuals. Any criticisms or other suggestions of inadequacy result in distance, defensiveness and arrogant behaviors from them.

Defiant underachievers develop difficulties when they are unable to easily achieve personal goals. They then hesitate to implement personal choices when they begin to realize that the potential for failure is real. Instead of accepting that they're still developing, they flaunt

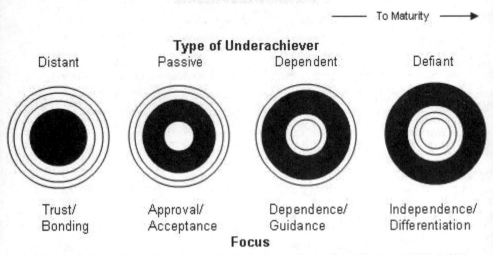

Levels of Emotional Development In Underachievers

———— To Maturity ————▶

Type of Underachiever

Distant	Passive	Dependent	Defiant

Trust/ Bonding	Approval/ Acceptance	Dependence/ Guidance	Independence/ Differentiation

Focus

The Focus is overly enlarged and dominant. An individual perceives and interprets the same situation in different ways depending on his or her particular level. Motivation approaches must be specifically tailored for each level.

their *false* independence by being contrary. This serves to protect their sense of individuality while they avoid truly being independent with the incumbent responsibilities. Through their defiance, they reduce the anxieties of potential failures by gaining transitory senses of control and minimizing their needs to deal with reality in more productive and responsible ways.

Kristie, one defiant girl at the Center, asked, "How much you makin' on this Coke machine?" When she was told the Center made nothing on the machine, that it was there strictly for the convenience of clients, she snapped, "I don't believe you. You must be makin' tons of money on this thing!"

David, another child I treated, wanted me to convince his parents to allow him to have a Mohawk haircut. I said I was willing to go along with that as long as he would have it cut ear-to-ear instead of back to front. He backed off when he realized that I wasn't willing to engage him in an obviously arranged argument about his hair.

How might each type of underachiever react to having a test tomorrow?

Distant:	Go into denial about it. If pressed about it, get depressed, refuse to discuss it.
Passive:	Go through the motions of studying hard. Maybe try to figure out the exact test questions and spend a lot of time talking about the test, but prepare only superficially. Be extremely anxious, even making a point of saying how ready he is. In the morning, he may feign sickness and ask to stay home.
Dependent:	Feign indifference and wait until the last minute to study, thereby forcing parents to crack down and/or coach the child through a study session.
Defiant:	Refuse to study. Perhaps launch into a diatribe about how unfair the testing process is or how irrelevant the subject matter is.

The four types of underachievers—Distant, Passive, Dependent and Defiant—are the four stages of development in which under-achievers may get stuck. As you will see in Part II, the interventions that can help them move forward have some significant differences so that understanding the pattern your child has developed is important if you are to help him or her.

CHAPTER THREE

ATTENTION DEFICIT AND OTHER DISORDERS

How common are attention deficit disorder (ADD) and attention deficit hyperactivity disorder (ADHD)? What about dyslexia and other learning disabilities, which some research affirms are physiological problems—how often are they at the root of underachievement?

Most motivational problems of children who come to the Center are emotional problems; some involve interplay of physiological and emotional factors. Sorting one from the other can be tough. Overactivity, impulsiveness, aggressive behavior and forgetfulness can all be signs of a purely emotional problem as well as symptoms of ADHD, for example.

A passive underachiever, Ricky never told his parents or his first or second grade teachers that he couldn't read what was on the blackboard. He memorized many lessons after simply hearing them, so his vision problem went undetected in those early school years. The learning difficulties his myopia caused very likely reinforced his negative self-perception. Until he got glasses, the simple fix for his physical problem, addressing his developmental problems through counseling would have been premature. Even after he got glasses, he had to play catch-up in school, because those years of memorizing damaged his ability to read, so the interplay between his learning difficulties and emotional issues continued.

*

LEARNING DISABILITIES

Learning disabilities include a broad range of learning difficulties, but for our purposes of discussion, the term will apply only to children with disorders of basic processes involved in understanding or in using language. That includes speaking and writing problems associated with apraxia, reading problems such as dyslexia and difficulties with listening, spelling and doing mathematical calculations.

A motivational problem can make it look like a child has a learning disability and vice versa. Unlike drug abuse or family dysfunction, however, which can both cause and be caused by a motivational problem, the motivational problem cannot *cause* a learning disability. On its own, the learning disability makes it harder for the affected child to learn.

Professionals look at three aspects of a child in order to refine a learning disability diagnosis and figure out how best to manage the problem:

1. General intelligence. It's important to determine whether or not the child has the natural ability for higher performance than she's achieved in the past.
2. Areas of impaired functioning. Tests for perceptual (reading), math and cognitive difficulties help define what kind of neurological-based learning problems the child has.
3. Areas of strength. What does the child do well? Under what circumstances does he learn easily? The answers to questions like these prove very useful in designing remedial programs.

It seems like a reasonable assumption that tests related to these three areas would yield clear-cut guidance about helping learning disabled kids. They don't. States and school districts may have different criteria that establish a disability. A child's test results in one region might qualify him for assistance from the school system, whereas in another region, they might not. The fact that divergent criteria exist does not necessarily mean that people in one school district are heartless and cheap and in another district they're the opposite. Diagnosing the severity of something like a learning disability means assessing a lot of variables. It isn't as if "normal" is precisely one set of attributes and everything else is a disability. It's arguable that everyone has at least a hint of disability. Keep in mind that some experts argue that more people receive learning disability diagnoses now than in previous years, because the tests are more comprehensive. These new tests can, at times, indicate subtle cases and lead to specific skills training, which can profoundly affect a child's scholastic progress, self-esteem and his emotional state in general. In short, diagnosing a learning disability isn't accounting. It involves interpretation that covers emotions as well as abilities. And emotions are slippery! Parents often find it frustrating that so many variables surround their child's learning challenges.

While struggling with the physical aspects of the problem, parents and their LD kids need to accept that the diagnosis of a learning disability is not an excuse for not achieving. It is an indication of a physical problem that needs to be addressed so achievement can occur.

The motivation to achieve is uniquely important for a learning disabled child. In a way, the child's challenge is like yours when you have a blinding headache and still need to participate in an important meeting. Aspirin helps a little, coffee helps a little, but after that it's your pure desire to perform well that helps you the most. Unfortunately—and this is something parents need to remember— the "headache" doesn't go away the next day even though therapies are in place. The desire to achieve has to remain strong to carry the child through the tangle of psychological and neurological factors making his life difficult.

This is a lot for a child to manage. It's easy to see how a learning disabled child might have trouble staying motivated.

Some parents want simplistic actions to solve their learning disabled child's underachievement problem. However, this is rarely the case. After an LD diagnosis, parents and teachers have an obligation to react and interact in different ways that will help the child and that means addressing both physiological and emotional issues. The child has an obligation to do something about his or her problem, too. First, he has to be brought toward an understanding of the problem so he can make changes in his life and speak up about his special needs. Otherwise, he can feel as distanced from the teacher and other students as a physically disabled child who can't get his wheelchair through the classroom door. Second, he needs the positive attitude toward change that comes with motivation. The ability to change will help him become a resilient human being who can land on his feet despite his physical challenges.

❋

ATTENTION DEFICITS

The debate over the defining characteristics, biological involvement and treatment of chemo-neurological-based conditions referred to as attention deficit disorder or, when heightened activity is also present, attention deficit hyperactivity disorder, is inflamed but quite legitimate. Such debate is a good thing, hopefully leading to further clarity and definition about the disorders. Parents should be very cautious, however, about anyone instantly diagnosing their child as having an attention deficit disorder.

There are those who feel that ADD and ADHD do not exist and others who feel that they are relatively common. Most professionals stay away from those extremes, yet they have their own battles about symptoms and treatments. According to a 1998 National Institutes of Health Consensus Statement on ADHD, "Although an independent diagnostic test for ADHD does not exist, there is evidence supporting the validity of the disorder." At the same time, NIH notes that research suggests that the disorder affects only three to five percent of school age kids and within that range, there are varying degrees of severity. Even so, in some school systems a much higher percentage of students are being *treated* for attention deficit disorders, often with some kind of psychostimulant. The Office of Drug Enforcement has identified areas with almost no use of methylphenidate (Ritalin®, Methylin®, Concerta®) or amphetamine prescriptions (primarily Adderall®), but has also documented that, in an alarming number of communities, 10 to 20 percent *or more* of the student population receives stimulants for ADHD treatment. And in a percentage that mirrors the latest figures we have at the Center, 80 percent of the prescriptions that pediatricians write are for boys.

DEA points to a spillover problem affecting undiagnosed children, as well. Along with the rise in prescriptions of stimulants for school kids—there are about 11 million methylphenidate prescriptions per year and six million amphetamine prescriptions—illegal sales have jumped. Methylphenidate produces many of the same effects as cocaine and other "recreational" stimulants, and their availability in school means that children with the means and desire to buy drugs can easily make a deal at recess. DEA warns parents that adolescent abusers commonly crush methylphenidate tablets and snort the powder to get high.

The question is, when is the taking of the drug justified and in the interests of the particular child? Without a clear consensus on standards that should be used for diagnosis of ADD and ADHD, firm diagnosis can be tricky. There is a broad range and degree of symptomology. Assessments are sometimes too brief, too limited or just plain inadequate. As the NIH report indicates, there is actually *no definitive test* for attention deficits, that is, nothing like a blood test or a brain scan that yields a "yes-or-no" diagnosis. There is some emerging data from neurologists, but it is not established, consistent or definitive. One of the problems is that some doctors, educators and parents misunderstand or disregard the limitations of this research, jumping to blind acceptance and making exaggerated claims.

The principal method of diagnosing ADD now consists of either systematic or informal observations by parents, teachers and other professionals. So, in the absence of a definitive test, accepted standards and diagnostic criteria, over-diagnoses and misdiagnoses are common occurrences. To make matters worse, many who are rendering these diagnoses are not fully qualified or educated on the disorder.

Some of the current behavior checklists used by parents and teachers are useful, however some are just not reliable. Among the most frequently used checklists are the Connors and the Achenbach Scale. Even though they are the most popular, they are still not completely accurate in diagnosing ADHD and should only be used in conjunction with other assessment tools. In other words, even if a child does come up "positive" on a checklist, that does not necessarily mean the child has an attention deficit disorder.

Some professionals rely entirely on checklists of behaviors and don't include a range of factors such as family history and functioning, which could have a profound effect on their diagnoses. They also bypass useful and reliable tests for learning disabilities, personality disorders and intelligence. Even though a student may display some of the symptoms, that doesn't necessarily mean that the student has an attention deficit disorder. Emotional difficulties, learning disabilities, developmental delays and family dynamics need to be ruled out. The diagnosis of attention deficit is often made before these other areas are explored for a number of reasons.

One of the most common reasons is that it takes time to assess areas other than behavior and some people don't want to make that expenditure of effort and money. A second reason is that many people feel there is a quick and easy answer for attention deficit treatment: "Give the kid a pill." Treatments for other, more complex causes of an underachievement problem can be much more involved and may take more time. Third, some prefer to have a biological explanation for a problem, thus minimizing the personal responsibility of all concerned. Finally, a relatively large attention deficit industry has formed. Some individuals and companies make their living off the ADD diagnosis, so caution regarding that diagnosis and treatment is wise.

Key Factors and Assessments
In Making an ADD Diagnosis

- Genetic background
- Developmental history
- Family history and functioning
- Social history
- Observations through a behavioral checklist by parents, teachers and significant others

- Overall behavior
- Neurological assessment
- Computerized performance testing
- Personality evaluation
- Intelligence evaluation
- Achievement testing
- Learning disability testing
- Psychological diagnostic interview

One thing professionals do agree on is that when attention deficit disorder is accurately diagnosed, medication can be effective. However, when it is misdiagnosed and the child instead has emotional or developmental difficulties, **these difficulties may be increased with the medications given for attention deficits**. Additionally, these medications may cause side effects such as mild insomnia, appetite reduction, palpitations, abdominal pain, lethargy and other symptoms that can have a negative impact on the child. Will they have an effect in later life? The NIH Consensus Statement notes that there is a paucity of data providing information on long-term treatment beyond fourteen months.

A simplistic, give-'em-a-pill view of the underachievement problem ignores the fact that, even when a biological component is present, there are usually emotional outgrowths of the problem that should be addressed. Also, while the affected individual bears the ultimate responsibility for achievement, parents, peers, teachers, friends and family are all influential toward positive change. Even when there is a significant biological component, it would be an error not to assess and treat the emotional components that generally are found with attention deficit disorders.

Keep in mind that underachievers frequently exhibit attention difficulties and, while it is possible to have *both* an attention deficit disorder and underachievement, in most cases underachievers will show a selective attention, attending when they want to and when it serves their purposes.

If your child is able to pay attention to things she likes and generally ignores the things she doesn't like, then it's more likely she has a motivation problem than attention deficit disorder. She has selective attention. (Although there are some professionals who claim that the inability to focus on a single subject such as math is a form of ADD.)

Again, for some families a diagnosis of ADD takes the focus away from personal responsibility—away from the need to change and change their life through their own efforts. There are entire families who have secured a diagnosis of ADD. What are the chances of that statistically? There is no definitive proof one way or the other. The way of life in a household like that becomes one of "Did you take your medication?" Learning the skills and strategy to get past the motivation problem becomes a minor, if any, part of the therapy. Some parents will persist in visiting professional after professional until they find someone who will give them a diagnosis of ADD or some other biological problem as the causal factor in their child's underachievement.

It's ironic that in schools that declare themselves a drug-free zone, medication to "calm kids down" now has widespread use. Some kids actually turn it into part of the drug problem, because they don't really take their medication—they sell it to other kids on campus.

Casual evaluations and misdiagnoses do a disservice to the school system, to the student and to the student's future.

CHAPTER FOUR

WHAT INFLUENCES MOTIVATION?

Now that we have looked at the type of underachiever your child might be and how this impacts his particular behavior, we can turn to the major problem for all underachievers: motivation—the force that compels us to act. Throughout life, motivation presents one of the greatest challenges: keeping it high enough to manage consistency of effort, utilization of our potential and dogged direction toward goals. Adding to the difficulty, all of these efforts must continue in the face of changing circumstances.

Motivating factors may be as basic as a glass of cold water on a hot day or a paycheck at the end of the week. They can also be complex, such as the need for fulfillment, friendship, love, prestige, power and financial independence. Different motivational factors are more or less important to us at different points in our lives. One of the keys to becoming a motivated and motivating person is to develop the sensitivity to identify those various factors and to react to them appropriately. It is important to "know yourself": to understand how you feel and what you want to do about your situation.

Motivating factors fall into two major categories: external and internal. External motivational factors include rewards like money, gifts and praise that come to a person from other people. Internal motivators include the desire to work to the best of our ability, the feeling of accomplishment a person receives when work is done and a sense of fulfillment. External attempts to motivate should be seen as

49

an adjunct to the more lasting internal motivators. Used alone, external motivators are often superficial and usually don't produce lasting results (How many times have you said, "If you get good grades, we'll get you xyz?" How few of you have found your underachiever's behavior change, in response to that prize, to last over time?). But don't reject them out of hand. Attempts at external motivation need to be keyed into internal development. This can be enhanced through the use of personal relationship factors. Do occasionally give rewards and incentives, but deliver them personally and with caring for the individual. Don't just leave your daughter's allowance on the dresser or slip the bonus or incentive into an envelope. Personal enhancement will pay many long-term benefits.

Internal motivation is the key to resilient, long-term motivation. It yields fulfillment and, ultimately, real happiness. High achievers and very motivated people tend to develop their internal sources of motivation. They achieve because it makes them feel good. That

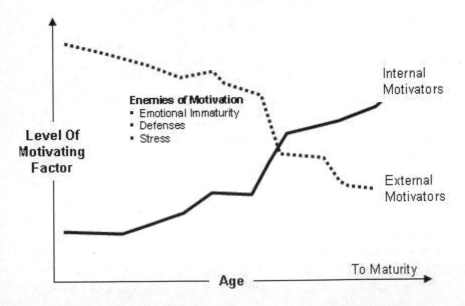

Internal vs. External Motivation
Effective Motivating Factors

Level Of Motivating Factor

Enemies of Motivation
- Emotional Immaturity
- Defenses
- Stress

Internal Motivators

External Motivators

Age — To Maturity

sense of self-accomplishment is primary. A person who takes pride in himself and sees himself as a productive member of society will prevail. Even when surrounded by others who aren't highly motivated, the achiever will persist in his efforts.

So what influences that all-important internal motivation? There are two factors, **innate personality** and **environment**, between which there is constant interplay.

Many parents ask, "What exactly did we do to create this problem?" They think of a sibling who is an unhappy adult, smart, but still dependent on his now elderly parents (or a responsible, successful sibling) to bail him out of one bad situation after another. This leads to the question, "Is our family genetically cursed?" They compound their guilt by second-guessing their parenting decisions. When junior was three and wanted that candy bar at the grocery store, should we have said, "No?" Those nights when he was restless, should we have let him cry himself to sleep instead of rocking him for an hour?

Motivation problems emerge for several reasons. It is extremely difficult, if not impossible, to clearly determine the exact root of the behaviors. Underachievement has diverse causes: genetics, modeling, enabling others, over-reliance on defenses for escape, delayed personality (i.e., emotional development) and more. To that list, you might even add serendipity.

Recent genetic research has yielded a new crop of theories on the possible biological basis of various emotional characteristics. These theories have rekindled the old "nature versus nurture" debates when discussing mental and emotional concerns. While these studies have shed light on the presence of a biological ingredient in certain human behaviors, it is important to remember that an individual's personality and behavior are very complex and simple answers don't suffice. The biological components of a behavior problem can vary from being minor in their effects on the situation, to being significant factors, to being the causal factor. (Knowing more about possible genetic causes would surely benefit clinical psychologists as well as scientists who work with laboratory rats.) Formal testing, observation and history are key to assessing the impact of personality factors on the

Narrow The Focus To The Cause(s)

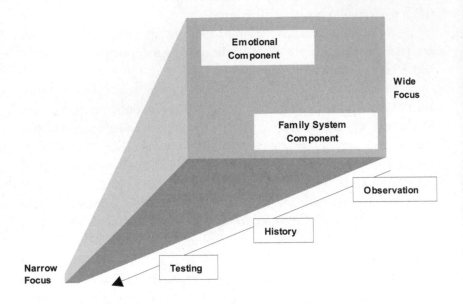

presenting symptoms and the degree of any possible biological/neurological involvement.

Depending upon one's innate personality, an individual may be *at risk* for becoming unmotivated and being an underachiever. This is not to suggest that no matter what a parent does and no matter what the circumstances are, certain individuals will be motivated or unmotivated. Actually, it is harder to sort out than that. However, there is a matter of degree for being at risk that is part of innate personality in the way an individual responds to various circumstances.

We have often seen a family history that contains individuals who mirror the underachievers' way of coping. Given that problems with motivation are somewhat common, that it exists in family history does not, it itself, show causality. There is the possibility, however, of a genetic component that influences the wiring of the brain such that the unmotivated individual is more likely to have a low tolerance for discomfort. Such a low tolerance may lead to detachment when uncomfortable. Coping mechanisms that contribute to insulating the underachiever from the discomfort of a challenging reality may over time become entrenched. Such entrenchment then further cements the coping style. In the longer term, the individual becomes "unable" to face things—and becomes ineffective. The negative spiral toward cynicism, detachment and sadness begins.

Are models of underachievement—in the extended family, neighborhood, media, or parental history—a causal factor? At a minimum, those models probably contribute to reinforcing unmotivated behavior. The majority of parents are usually well intended, but even so parents' negative emotions can leak into behaviors, and as a result, produce unintended models.

In an underachieving student for whom a biological factor such as attention deficit hyperactivity disorder (ADHD) is significant, pharmacological intervention may help in addition to learning compensation skills. Nevertheless, the student's sense of his or her emotions, self-esteem and ability to function independently and responsibly within the context of both work and play is still key. The child's sense of these factors has to be addressed, as do other emotional areas. In those underachievers for whom there are no significant biological impairments—and that's roughly 95 percent of those who come to the Center—the influence of systems and relationships is primary. Just as the cause of the problem takes many shapes, so do the resolutions of underachievement, including appropriate defenses, modeling, empowering, prompting, personality development (which may include therapy) and consequential experience (through living). Parents shouldn't lose sight of the fact that they are an integral part of the solution no matter what the causal factors of the child's problem are. They should not harbor an illusion that a magic pill or a tweak to the hypothalamus will suddenly turn their child into a highly motivated student. Parents must see themselves as an influential aspect of the student's potential change. Many times parents need to modify their concerns and their responses so as to shift emotions, appropriate responsibility and control to the student.

Despite the importance of parental influence, parents shouldn't jump to blame themselves solely for their children's "faulty wiring." Kids develop reaction patterns as a result of many different influences inside and outside the home. For example, it isn't uncommon for families with more than one child to have just one underachiever. The home environment may be the same for all of the kids, but each one's school experiences, social interactions and perceptions could be quite different. Nevertheless, parents can look to themselves for some insights into how they *may* have influenced their child's level of motivation and emotional development.

In order to do this it is useful to divide the environmental influences on motivation into two types:

- Home influences.
- Societal influences.

※

HOME INFLUENCES

One of the frustrating and perhaps guilt provoking aspects of parenting is the feeling that comes from the thought "I should have—" or "If I had only—." Many parents of underachievers feel that something they either have or have not done has caused their children's underachievement. However, it is important to realize that when your child was six and whined for a popular toy in a crowded department store or demanded a candy bar in the checkout lane of the grocery store, you did not trigger the process of underachievement by saying, "No!" You did not trigger it by offering a swat on the bottom once when your five-year-old threw his Halloween candy at his little sister. Any one specific act on your part did not create a problem, but a pattern of acts over time can have an effect—positive or negative.

In some instances, reviewing the past helps parents think through and unburden themselves of unproductive guilt, learn from their experiences and correct unproductive parenting habits. However, despite poor patterns in the past, it is most important that parents of underachievers look to the future and to potential changes in both the underachievers' patterns and in their own reactions to the underachievers. A focus on the past is mainly an exercise in intellectualization and guilt. What has occurred has occurred and cannot be changed. In tennis, the advice is, "Don't play the last shot!"

There is *potential* for instability from the factors such as being adopted, moving, parental unemployment, parental deployment, parental separation or divorce, parental remarrying, parental illness, death of a loved one, sibling leaving for college, friends leaving, family financial uncertainty and other instabilities. These factors should be confronted and attendant emotions expressed.

Resilient individuals can experience many of these situations, yet remain well-balanced, understanding their emotions and accepting the situation without any corrosive effect on themselves. These individuals do not avoid or minimize their emotions, but rather use them as cues to engage the circumstances and get a grip on feelings.

However, most motivationally challenged individuals want their world to have predictability minimal risk. When these factors occur they create a world that is less certain. The underachiever's emotions are swirled, weakening their ability to work through the matter clearly. Instead of taking on the situation, they expend considerable energy denying their emotions and avoiding working through their loss or uncertainty.

If parents have these factors within the family, the most productive response is to discuss the situation openly—and periodically—so each family member's emotions about the situation can come out. Everyone needs to know what can be done, what cannot, what is being done, what will be done and any "unpredictables." The family needs to aim for and try to achieve certainty.

What should be your personal expectations as you try to raise your child? First and foremost is the attempt to **instill good values** such as honesty, doing one's best, productivity, consideration of others, politeness, respect of other's views and so on. Through modeling your consistent behavior and sharing your feelings and opinions, values are usually instilled in children by the time they reach adolescence. If you think you haven't had success in developing values in your child, merely lecturing her will not do the job. Show her by example.

A mistake that many parents make in an effort to help their children learn values is to give them too much information too soon, before the children are either emotionally or intellectually ready to handle that information. Instead of helping children internalize values, they may overwhelm them. Children come away from such encounters feeling that life is too complicated or that they are somehow responsible for all of society's ills.

Do not treat children like little adults. Their personalities, as well as their coping mechanisms, are not fully formed. Overwhelming children can cause them to lose optimism and joy for life. Demonstrate values and give information relating to values to

---

Role of Values

- Help us understand our emotions and sort through feelings
- Enable us to use our emotions productively
- Give us time to sort our motives, perspectives, priorities and responsibilities
- Allow us to act with a level of consistency, predictability and understanding
- Serve as a compass for action

Results of Using Values

Access values + Use them as guides = More rational response to events

Immediate results:
- Control over impulses
- Ability to interact on a higher relationship level that reflects respect

Long-term result:
- Basing our actions on our values ultimately makes us happy

children when they are able to use that knowledge, both intellectually and emotionally. For example, most parents teach their children
that it is wrong to kill another person. For a very young child that is
enough information: Killing is wrong. As a child matures, parents
can add views on killing in self-defense. Later, issues related to war,
mercy killings and so on, can be introduced and discussed. To fling
opinions about these issues at a child in an attempt to engage his
mind before he is ready to handle such concepts confuses and overwhelms the child and, in fact, stifles positive development.

Some parents who have come to the Center have seen good
results in reinforcing and clarifying values through a lightly structured exercise such as this one:

- Write out your core values. List the ones you feel are most
  important, then branch to secondary values. Discuss them with
  your spouse or other important individuals in your life and
  refine your list. Give yourself a few days to think about these
  values, then make additions or changes as necessary.
- Provide a copy of your values to your child. Let your child
  know you've been thinking about values and that it is important to discuss them occasionally. Briefly—very briefly—tell
  your child why these values have meaning for you. You don't
  have to talk specifically about each one.
- Ask your child to make a list of values that he or she feels is
  important.
- Set a time for a family meeting where everyone involved will
  talk about values.
- At the meeting, have everyone bring his or her list. Discuss similarities and differences. Get into specifics. Discuss examples of
  good values and poor values. Discuss how values sometimes conflict and why they may differ from person to person. Talk about
  how people can change. This should be a lively dialogue. Try to
  keep the atmosphere light so that none of the exchange takes
  the tone of lecture. Check sarcasm and cynicism at the door.
- Make a conscious effort to show your values by the way you
  lead your life. Let your kids see that your actions link to your

values.

Regardless of the approaches you use to transfer good values to your child, how can you be reassured that you've succeeded? You can only be reassured by the overall pattern that your child displays in living his or her life. Is he generally behaving with the appropriate values? When he makes mistakes, does he learn from them? Don't overreact to misjudgments. React dispassionately and influence your child to rethink and explore the basis for his decision. He has to explore his *emotional* reaction to his circumstance. Assist your child by helping him express his emotions through **words**. Model this by **telling** him how you feel (not showing him). Do this a few days after the incident so that emotions are no longer strong and swirling.

Children will try unacceptable behaviors—this is normal. Actually, it's normal for them to venture beyond the completely acceptable as they come into adolescence, but an early warning sign that parental guidance may be deficient is if they go wild as young children. Consider this as you review the illustration of the Behavior Orbit:

- In early years, children stay in the clear area, generally not doing wrong. There may be slight incursions into the gray area, but they are unintentional. Parents simply need to respond promptly and bring their children back into the center.
- In adolescence, children may "try their wings" and go into the gray area frequently to test limits. Even though it is disconcerting for parents, in many ways it is preferable that children stray when they have parents to control and limit the unacceptable behaviors and to give guidance and knowledge.
- If children want to try unacceptable behaviors, but wait until out of the control of parents, the results are often more severe than if they had done so earlier. In addition to instilling values, parents can **instill effort** to some degree. These might be considered preventative measures in developing motivation:
- Serving as good role models. When mom and dad extend themselves, displaying effort as part of their natural style, the children learn by imitation. Enjoy effort, don't habitually complain about "having to do" things.

- Encouraging children to make extra efforts and letting them see, feel and understand the benefits that come from making those efforts. This is a gradual process of acknowledging small incidents that allows children to understand that you and other people appreciate their efforts in a variety of forms and that such efforts can make them feel good. To focus only on circumstances requiring large efforts and those with large results makes the goals appear unattainable or gives the impression that if the tasks are not "big deals," then they aren't worth the effort. In reality, just as learning to run begins with many baby steps, motivation is developed from experiencing many small efforts and resultant satisfactions. This becomes an *attitude* and a way of life. Children then see challenges as possibilities. Efforts yield satisfactions. Over time they become resilient, effective and focused on the efforts.

Behavior Orbit

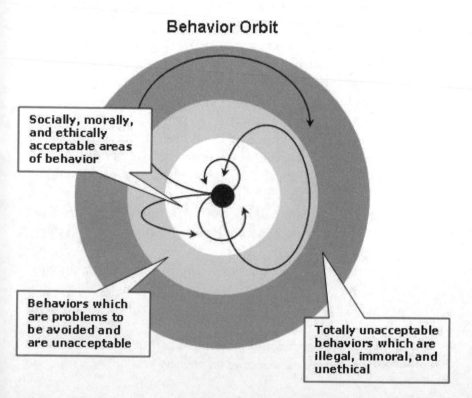

Socially, morally, and ethically acceptable areas of behavior

Behaviors which are problems to be avoided and are unacceptable

Totally unacceptable behaviors which are illegal, immoral, and unethical

Over time they also learn the proverbial work ethic, a belief in work as a moral good. Anyone knows that work can be dirty, difficult and monotonous, but people with a work ethic are more likely than people who lack it to find excitement and fun in work. They link work with productivity. For people to be happy in life, two factors are crucial: One is good interpersonal relationships and the second is a feeling of productivity. That feeling feeds motivation.

Actions like these instill in a child a desire to exert effort and develop a work ethic:

- Point out to a child when she does something that pleases. You don't have to make a fuss over your child cleaning her room, but you can say, "I noticed you cleaned your room. Thanks! It looks nice." As the child matures, acknowledging an action some time after it has happened is very powerful: "I wanted to let you know I was very proud of the way you helped clean up after the party last week." The fact that you not only noticed, but also appreciated and *remembered*, is a great source of motivation for a child. These micro-recognitions do a lot to boost a child's self-esteem and provide guidance toward the value of effort. (It works with adults, too, as any good manager knows.)

- Show sensitivity to the positive efforts of others. How often have you gone into a store for an item, couldn't find it and asked a clerk if the store had any more? The answer is usually, "Everything we have is on the shelves." In contrast, isn't it refreshing when the clerk offers to check the stockroom and does so with a cheerful attitude? Direct your child's attention to such efforts. Mention the positive attitude of the clerk. Let your child know that putting forth extra effort is a good thing, perhaps by letting him know that you've written a complimentary note to the clerk's manager. By doing this, your child will learn not only what is good for her, but also that others notice and appreciate effort. It will sensitize her to the various values of effort.

- In a positive way, remark about insufficient effort. When the clerk in the store gives the "on the shelves" answer, mention it to your child: "That person seemed so unhelpful and unhappy. Not like the clerk who helped us last week." You have to be careful, though, not to belittle true effort or demean the results of your child's, or anyone else's, genuine effort that is inadequate. A statement interpreted as putting down the child will do more harm than good. Talk about insufficient effort in a dispassionate manner: "Jack is a talented natural athlete. I wonder if he could break the school record if he really focused his training?" The focus should always be on the *effort*, not the individual or the result.

Your success in actively attempting to instill values and effort in your child hinges to a great degree on the amount of certainty in the child's life. "Certainty" implies a high level of stability, durability, assurance and truth in behavior. Certainty may include relative predictability in family, friends, school, chores, jobs, residence, lifestyle and guidance from interested, trusted adults. Developing children want and need certainty.

Consistency and certainty are especially important if an individual is insecure or not yet mature. As children develop emotionally and intellectually, their need for certainty lessens, but it never totally disappears.

Stability, through predictable aspects in their experiences, allows children both the energy and the time to think and to make decisions. With this predictability, they are less distracted and less preoccupied with their basic needs. They are more likely to expend their energies in emotional and intellectual growth. This enables them to develop their senses of values and personality. It allows them to have secure bases from which to compare their thoughts, feelings, reactions and decisions as they go through life. It cultivates perspective. It gives them confidence as they struggle with personal development and grow into their views of the world. A child with a reasonable world of certainty is apt to be engaged, self-motivated, clear on values and future-focused. What then occurs is a cat-and-mouse game

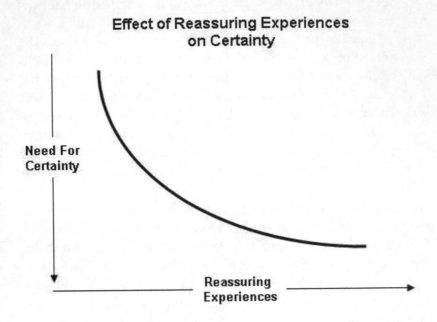

Effect of Reassuring Experiences on Certainty

in which he begins to step gently into risk, learns to gauge it, make appropriate assessments and consciously chooses a course of action.

Certainty:
Children need all aspects of it for normal emotional development
Stability
Durability
Assurance
Predictability
Reliability
Clarity
Truth in Behavior
Consistency

In most cases, a child who does not have enough certainties will find it difficult to relate to others, to develop a sense of self-confidence, belonging and self-motivation. When much of a child's experience is unpredictable, that child will spend a considerable portion of her emotional and intellectual energy in trying to anticipate and in trying to predict what will happen next. The absence of core certainties leads to *personal* uncertainty (indecision, detachment, interfering anxiety, self-doubt and so on). Children experiencing uncertainty will often divest themselves of active views, replacing them with reactive and defensive postures. They try to protect themselves. This often results in underachieving behaviors and low motivation, which then undermine their experiences and possibilities.

With underachievers, feelings of personal inadequacy are triggered. For them, inconsistency equals unpredictability equals confusion and doubt. These kids spend considerable time and energy *seeking* certainty. Many of the children who do not find it in their families and homes seek it through peer groups—sometimes with disturbing results. Often they will seek certainty in mediocrity, a downward adjustment of their expectations. Mediocrity may not be what they want, but it is predictable for them and thus accepted by them because it is certain. Indifference and nonchalance then become primary modes of reacting.

Cliff: A Genius Chooses Mediocrity
To Restore Certainty in His Life

Cliff hated school even though he was a genius. In fact, it was his love of math and solitary activities that made him the brunt of jokes at school—by teachers as well as fellow students. Teachers would chide him mercilessly for not living up to his potential: They told him he'd never go to college, no matter how smart he was. His parents told him to talk to his teachers, but he had grown afraid of them.

Cliff was in a high school program for gifted and talented students so virtually everyone around him qualified as a "superachiever." In order to increase his comfort level about even showing up for school, Cliff gravitated toward the other low performers in the program. He said these friends made him feel "less isolated," but maintained the real reason he hung out with them was that they had so much in common, like a love of computer science. Primarily what this small band of unmotivated kids had in common were patterns of underachievement that they inadvertently reinforced in each other.

As Cliff's parents actively tried to guide him away from those patterns, Cliff lost interest in those friends. He found he didn't have much in common with them after all.

After pulling himself together during his junior and senior years in high school—and nearly tripling the 1.3 grade point average he had earned at the end of his sophomore year—Cliff went off to one of the top universities in the country. As for his "best friends," one took on menial work after dropping out of high school and one tried to get into college, but was rejected even by schools with low admission standards. He, too, took a job with little future.

Cliff visited them after his freshman year of college and it made him sad. They had "slipped into a hole" and showed no signs of trying to climb out.

❋

SOCIETAL INFLUENCES

Society and culture can create an environment that engenders achieving and underachieving behavior, too. Depending on where they grow up and what they observe, children can develop either disproportionate senses of entitlement or resentments for high achievement.

For example, kids who realize that entire television channels are devoted to their interests and that designers create clothing specifically for them may grow up with the impression that they are the center of the universe. If you're the center of the universe, why work hard? Parents (and grandparents) can unintentionally contribute to the development of a sense of entitlement by omitting an important word: *No.* Do not give your children everything they want. Pandering to them only leads to later internal confusions and struggles. Be selective with "yes" and "no." Your children need to understand they co-exist in a context. Children who grow up with such senses of entitlement can honestly believe that things they want will come to them and that the world, or at least the United States, is a veritable cornucopia. Families will often unwittingly reinforce this perception in subtle, ostensibly harmless ways. A common one is the Christmas or birthday gift list. There is no sense of wonder to receiving gifts that are responsive to a list. The child has little or no perception that there was effort involved in finding something he liked and that the giver enjoyed hunting for something special. Searching for a gift is an element of stretching an interpersonal relationship. It reflects reasonable risk-taking in the relationship, which strengthens the resilience of it.

It is important that your child feel loved, wanted and special, but you must balance that with placing age-appropriate demands upon him to respect others' sensitivities and needs. You do not want your child to be self-centered, oblivious to others and to his impact upon others.

Many students who come to the Center share an extra challenge with the children of high energy, high achieving parents in places like Silicon Valley, Manhattan and other supercharged cities. These young people are growing up in areas like the suburbs of Washington, D.C., where the philosophy of "motivation breeds success" has devout followers in all political parties and from many nations. Even if parents try to establish a balance in a child's life at home, the fact that they may both work in demanding jobs in the context of an achievement-focused community can affect that child's perspective. As children observe the stress and hectic pace of their parents' lives, they may come to see personal responsibilities as overwhelming burdens.

In terms of a child wanting to achieve, the impact of the particular school a student attends is limited, although we see a preoccupation with it, especially in supercharged urban areas. We could focus on many different angles of the school experience: **class size** (large and impersonal vs. small and individualized), **teacher type** (caring and supportive vs. demanding and unforgiving), **mode** (private vs. religious-based vs. public vs. home-schooling), **location** (community vs. residential boarding) or **geographic setting** (urban vs. suburban vs. rural). We all agree that it is important to give the child the "best" setting, but it is not especially important or useful to be concerned about these different angles to the exclusion of internal factors such as personal responsibility, ability to defer to authority, personal engagement and emotional maturity. Many high-achieving parents have educational consultants who "help" them expend considerable energy and funds on finding the "best" setting. While this effort is not fully misguided, there needs to be proportionality. For the investment in time, funds and effort, is there a reasonable return? In comparison to the child's attitude taken into the setting, setting factors pale. It is more difficult, yet more productive, to overlook inadequacy of the setting and expend energy on **being adequate.** In trying to be adequate, an individual accepts personal responsibility for his situation.

The way society reacts to young people's choices about everything from premarital sex to underage drinking can also impact on their emotional developments. I saw the societal wink and nod about marijuana use—the substance was accepted, at least at one time, by many Baby Boomers as a harmless party drug—have deleterious effects on one of my clients. He was caught selling pot at school. Distressed as they were, his parents thought, "Finally, he will have to face the consequences of his behavior. Maybe this will be the kick in the pants he needs."

The school, a self-designated "drug-free zone," only suspended him for two weeks. He was allowed to turn in his homework the entire time and make up any tests he missed when he returned. The system reinforced his conviction that he could slide though life getting away with all kinds of things. "Right" and "wrong" had no meaning or influence.

Too often, our flexible and tolerant society focuses on being nonjudgmental. It is as if we have a floating ethic, with no right and wrong, only "maybe," "sort of," or "in this instance." Children need adult guidance—guidance as to what is right or wrong—to help them sort through the myriad choices they face daily. When they are adults, they can soon enough consider the gray areas and seemingly endless possibilities that confront them.

Media Influences: The Good, The Bad and The Ugly

Media can affect motivation in good or bad ways, depending on the level of constructive access, self-discipline, and critical thinking involved. Here are key - and + factors related to media:

Television Shows (sitcoms, reality shows, docudramas. . .)
Negatives
   Mindlessness
   Superficiality
   Distortion, such as fictionalized history, altered to reflect cultural or political bias; corrupt values portrayed as normal/acceptable
   Draw on available time

Positives
   Diversion to relieve stress
   Information
   Socialization, so a child can discuss shared experiences with other children; proper behavior portrayed

Television News Programs
Negatives
   Single-mindedness, or the absence of competing ideas
   Brevity, regardless of the complexity of issues
   Designed for adults, so children can be overwhelmed by the pessimism, horrors, challenges
Positive
   Information

Video Games
Negatives
   Replay button, therefore able to ignore consequences
   Detachment from reality
   Draw on available time

Positives
   Development of thinking
   Stress reduction/entertainment
   Coordination development

Opportunities to bond. Playing a game with your child
is like "tossing the ball."

Internet

Negatives
Inappropriate information (incorrect information, porn,
subversive information)
Draw on available time

Positives
Information access
Potential for growth through exposure to other ideas,
thoughts, systems, etc.
Opportunity to develop critical thinking in sorting
through volume of information
Entertainment

IM'ing/E-Mail

Negatives
Draw on available time
Inappropriate reinforcement of negative ideas, con-
cepts
from friends
Positives
Social interaction
Information sharing

As the chart indicates, media are part of that "system" that has
specific ways of undermining a child's perception of what is appropriate and responsible. The problem is that most children do not
have *models* of appropriate and responsible use of media, especially
computers. The main guidance they get is time limits on use.
Parents can help children use media to develop critical thinking, to
improve their ability to sort information. Parents can also model self-
discipline and discuss their self-imposed limits (How many adults
limit their own time with media?).

One of the main problems of media is their attractiveness
through entertainment value. The underachiever wants to avoid dis-

comfort. What better way to avoid discomfort than immersing one's self into mindless sitcoms, fun video games or IM'ing for hours about superficialities? In the 1950s television appeared and children disappeared. They stared at the tube for hours, restrained only by their parents ordering, "Shut that thing off and go outside and play!" Now there are many more avenues for detachment-and they are more stimulating, enticing and distracting.

Parents should set reasonable limits related to age or maturity, and gradually modify them with the goal of having a child who can self-discipline. The child needs to be able to modulate his impulse to lose himself in distraction.

Home and society are the context within which one lives one's life so it makes sense that, between innate personality and environment, the more influential of the two factors on motivation is the environment. The variety of personalities of the people around us as well as more general environmental factors creates and affects every one of us. An incredibly complex mix, these factors contribute eventually to how we handle our lives and whether we become motivated or unmotivated. These factors are not permanently fixed, though. They are in flux. They can be influenced and individuals *can change*, although as you may already know, inducing an unmotivated individual to change is not easy.

Good intentions get you started, but they are not enough. Delving into motivation means taking a look at a range and blend of factors that influence behavior. For individuals who are trying to overcome a lack of motivation, it means they must get to know and understand *why* they do things and what their emotions, values, motives and priorities are. This may mean changing the way they see themselves and others and changing the way they do things. Change can be scary for anyone. We have to be willing to face the unknowns that change produces. Many times underachievers prefer the "known" of underachievement to the "unknown" of trying to achieve.

For an underachiever, fear of these states can be grossly exaggerated:

failure	pain	rejection
embarrassment	being hurt	hurting others
seeming stupid	being different	loneliness
being misunderstood	dependence	the unknown
losing what you have	not measuring up	success

In general, underachievers have many fears. These anxieties are part of why they are stuck emotionally. Fear of failure. Fear of success and of what success entails. Fear of taking reasonable risks. These fears prevent unmotivated students from achieving. This can all be overwhelming for underachievers. From these children's perspectives, we are expecting them to do the impossible, even though at some level they really want to change. Actually, the change the under-achiever needs to accomplish isn't large—he just feels that it is.

Among the other external components of underachieving behavior is self-doubt caused by repeated instances of failure, for whatever reason. Perhaps a big brother or sister always beats the younger child at games. Another problem may be the absence of appropriate pressure from parents to meet reasonable performance standards. Either ignoring a child or allowing him to "get away with it" time after time is a lack of appropriate pressure. (Some parents will actually do their kids' chores rather than go through the hassle of fighting over them.) Finally, a corrosive relationship with parents—mixed messages and other inconsistencies—is often a big factor. A child who has been embroiled in a contentious divorce and whose parents are at war for both control and attention, for example, may well fall victim to this.

On the flip side, a reasonable childhood—an appropriate level of stress and the knowledge of how to use stress as a cue, reasonable and consistent expectations, healthy affirmations of self-worth, enough emphasis on trying your best, basic consistency in treatment and messages—all contribute to normal motivational patterns.

CHAPTER FIVE

WHY IT IS IMPORTANT TO MOTIVATE UNDERACHIEVERS

In the *short* term, while underachievement is discomforting to those who are motivated and to those concerned people, especially parents, around underachievers, it may have only a moderate, negative impact on the child. Underachievers might get ever deteriorating grades or repeat a year of school. They may have tense relationships with their parents and other adults. They may be socially and emotionally immature. But these short-term motivational problems, once corrected, do not necessarily leave long-term consequences. It is *chronic*, long-term underachievement that produces unhappy individuals and stressful, problematic relationships.

Chronic underachievers have a set of common challenges. First, they must decide to change, that is, cut off all possibility of not changing, so that they will have a more reasonable and productive life. In the immediate, however, underachievement reinforces itself. Their behavior patterns allow underachievers to avoid unwanted stress, to deny what is really happening in their lives and to create unrealistic dreams about their future. Because they can often defend these fantasies with skewed logic, they have no pressure to change how they behave. Additionally, because the underachieving behavior is self-reinforcing, underachievers have persistent tendencies to underachieve **even after they transform into achievers.** This means that they must remain vigilant, anticipating their tendencies and behaving in such a way as to not act on their underachieving tendencies. For example, a former underachiever, now a productive adult, may have to stave off tendencies to daydream when working on a spreadsheet.

Underachievers are
Fearful
Uncertain
Uncomfortable
Distressed
Angry
Unhappy

Underachievers miss the worthwhile challenges and true joys of life. They're so uncomfortable with their emotions in general that they inadvertently deny themselves pleasure (they don't have fun at the same level

Possible End Results of a Lack of Motivation

- Ineffectiveness
- Defensiveness
- Over-reliance on others
- Denial of reality
- Disillusionment
- Disaffection
- Superficiality
- Cynicism/sarcasm/criticism
- Rationalization
- Anger
- Detachment
- Low self-esteem
- Remorsefulness
- Confusion
- Absence of fulfillment
- Pessimism
- Loss of opportunity
- Unhappiness

as other kids) as well as cause themselves emotional—and sometimes physical—pain. They duck when they see reality coming at them.

In a sense, underachievers—adults and children—have a peek-a-boo lifestyle.

One of the interesting and fun things about very young children is that they like to play peek-a-boo. You look at them, run behind the door, then pop out and say, "Peek-a-boo!" They squeal with surprise and delight. You can repeat this over and over and get the same reaction every time. Why is the child so enthralled and excited by this seemingly inane act? The very young do not have a sense of constancy—that things exist even when they're out of view. It is an "out of sight, out of mind" viewpoint taken to the extreme.

If this behavior continues into adolescence and beyond, however, it ceases to be even slightly amusing. Many underachievers, even when they're fully aware of the existence of responsibilities like homework, manage to act as if those responsibilities do not exist. When authority figures bring those responsibilities to light by reminding them, they have only slightly different reactions than the little child who is playing peek-a-boo—they now cringe rather than giggle. The authority figures also have serious reactions rather than playful ones because the underachievers are expected to be beyond this "game."

One day, Jeremy, a teen I counseled, tried to play this childish game. When his mom came to pick him up at the Center, she asked me, "Where is he?"

"I left him in the waiting room," I said.

"I looked there already. I didn't see him."

So we both returned to the waiting room and looked for Jeremy. There he was, curled up under a chair. Some part of him thought he could literally make himself disappear by hiding. This time his behavior was not treated as "cute." Our discovery was the rude end of his peek-a-boo strategy.

The cause of a peek-a-boo lifestyle is the refusal and inability of underachievers to face their situations maturely and with any consistency. Their emotional development in this regard has not advanced beyond that of a younger child. Rather than have the strength of personal conviction to face the challenges of reality, even though it's sometimes unpleasant, they choose to deny, ignore and selectively attend to reality. The lifestyle becomes so ingrained that they are not aware that the peek-a-boo effect occurs. Such children may be continually surprised when confronted time and again with reality. This often results in a response like "I didn't know" or "I don't know" from the underachiever and in further frustration for the parents and teachers.

Later in life, more often than not, this lifestyle also results in a mediocre existence and maybe even self-medication through drug, alcohol or food abuse. Unmotivated persons are not necessarily total failures, they just aren't successes on any meaningful level. They survive, but don't thrive. They are unhappy, lose opportunities, feel they have few choices—the edge to their lives is gone. They develop a growing and evolving cynicism and become detached from life and other people. They are reactive rather than active. Unsatisfied with their situation and themselves, they still do nothing to change.

Change of Focus (Perspective)
Half Empty vs. Half Full

Negative focus
Unproductive/inappropriate action
1. disengaging
2. denying
3. minimizing
4. rationalizing/intellectualizing

A negative focus tends to yield minimal productive results. The tendency is for increased use of inappropriate defenses. The child believes the outcome will be bad, and his actions then ensure it-the self-fulfilling prophecy.

Positive focus
Constructive/productive action
1. engagement
2. clarity of goal
3. effort
4. accomplishment

Positive thinking has value. The child focuses energy and effort on engaging the process and enhancing outcome. Optimism, coupled with realism, helps to clarify the goal and focus effort. The end result of the positive focus is personal growth through accomplishment: I tried. I overcame. I succeeded.

Bart, one young man I treated, possessed soaring ambitions to have his own car, do "what I want to do," and "do my own thing." Planning and making certain levels of commitment, however, were out of the question. The future was irrelevant.

We all know adult underachievers like Bart. These unmotivated adults are not fun to be with. They feign indifference, but they are always complaining about something. Yet, as much as they complain, they do nothing to change their circumstances. Problems always seem to plague them, but do they change their patterns of behavior to improve their lot? No. They are given opportunities, but they don't benefit from them. They feel everything is a hassle. They either don't even try or repeatedly undermine themselves.

In contrast, motivated persons have the capacity to experience real happiness, recognize that they have choices and feel engaged by life. They seek fully satisfying experiences and savor them when they occur. Everything is an opportunity and, even if difficult, this opportunity is viewed as a challenge to be used for the betterment of themselves or others.

Adults seen at the Center who are in their twenties, thirties and forties and who have a problem of low motivation frequently are chronically depressed. While they have been avoiding and denying their feelings for years, they are finally so uncomfortable that they decide to seek help to try to change these long-term patterns. Because the patterns are so ingrained, however, change is very difficult. Many give up. Most adult underachievers don't even try to change or push themselves to find out what they can do. They intermittently feel, *If only I had—* . The end result is unhappiness and mediocrity—possibly until the day their lives end.

Parents who look down the road and see this vision of their child's future face a spectrum of choices from "letting them fail" through seeking professional help. There are risks in all approaches, but it is important that you make a resolution to do something constructive to stop the spiral of failure.

Underachieving behavior can simmer for years with "good enough" even enabling the student to attend a respectable college. In Ernie's case, he went to college for three years and, by his own admission, "didn't accomplish anything. I wasn't getting anything done in my life." Diagnosed with depression, nothing the MDs prescribed or said helped him. He began to self medicate with drugs and alcohol.

At best, he had a rocky relationship with his parents: "I was on edge all the time. Hypersensitive to anything they would say. They were scared to say things to me, even the most mild of criticisms or comment. They were worried about how I'd react. So I avoided my family."

His mother remembers that, when Ernie was spiraling downward, his choices "shocked his father and me, as well as him. We tried to help him through school counselors and teachers, but his heart wasn't in it. We tried to get help at home—nothing made an impact."

When Ernie came to the Center at the age of 22 (through his parents concern and pressure), he worked at a daycare center for 20-25 hours a week and mostly slept during his downtime. He desperately needed a plan of action, measurable achievements, and a sense of accountability. He needed a way out—a productive way out.

After establishing a trusting, working relationship with him, I strongly recommended some changes in his life. "Go out and get another job," I told him. Immediately, to support that goal, we developed a systematic plan to seek employment and arranged for his parents to change some of their expectations and responses. I introduced Ernie to the "No Excuse Lifestyle." In the area of accountability, I helped him understand: You have choices. If something good happens, it's your doing. If something bad happens, it's your fault. Ernie adds, "I never heard, 'You have to do this or that.' Instead, I heard challenges and questions like, 'Don't you think this would be a good deci-

sion or action?' Dr. Spevak guided me as I worked my way toward good decisions."

Ernie quickly got another part-time job in a bookstore—an environment that stimulated him. In just over a year, he went from working part time at that store to being the youngest general manager in the company. While still managing the bookstore he has also returned to school to complete his degree.

"Being brutally honest with Ernie made a difference," his mother says. "Dr. Spevak painted the picture of how inertia would defeat him."

❋

LET THE CHILD FAIL

One of the most obvious options for parents is to ignore the pattern of underachievement, leaving possibilities to fate and hoping that the child will change. The child's failure will convince her to change, say the proponents of this position. This choice as the *sole* way of dealing with the problem does a number of things, including create a tension in the family that can become very disruptive. This choice also contributes to lowered self-esteem for the underachiever. The unpredictable nature of emotional development will surely remain unpredictable in the absence of attempts to influence or guide the pace or course of development. There is the slight possibility that everything will work out well without change. More likely, though, the child will spiral downward with negative assists from lowered self-esteem and growing self-doubt.

Within the context of deliberate intervention, however, "let them fail" can be a useful tactic. Chapter 10 covers when and how to employ it.

❋

WAIT AND WATCH

This option ranks just barely above the "Let the Child Fail" option as far as action is concerned. There is a serious limitation to a laissez-faire attitude in that possible intervention opportunities may be missed and parental concern seems to be lacking. In those circumstances, however, where there is not a definable problem, only a vague feeling about the existence of a problem or the problem has been evident only a few weeks, limited "ignoring" may be the best route. This involves ongoing observation to see if things either deteriorate or continue without positive change. Usually, this option is a predecessor to one of the next two options. It is expected to be a passive process without intervention. When you observe both your child and your reactions and responses to your child, this could be viewed as fact-finding. A caveat is that underachievement tends to be easier to change when the child is younger (i.e., the younger the better). As a person grows a history of this behavior, not only does he cement unproductive habit patterns and negative coping patterns, but also the demanding reality of "life beyond parents" looms, creating ever more need for the underachiever to rely on underachieving perspectives and habits.

❁

BECOME MORE INVOLVED

This is primarily what this book is designed to help you do, in a way that's appropriate for the type of underachiever in your family.

Becoming more involved can include a number of approaches, frequently with intervention by the school. Parents and teachers often intuitively select one of these starting points, without having a sense that they're on or off track:

- Provide more structure
- Institute a monitoring program
- Study child development and actively apply the appropriate knowledge
- Make adjustments in the family system

As a precautionary note, parents who choose to become more involved may fall into the trap set by their growing concern for their child and by their own internal logic. Without intention, parents may become contributors to the underachievement problem as they begin to structure their child's behavior too much, in an attempt to force their child to change from a pattern of underachievement. Rather than becoming more independent and less underachieving, the child frequently becomes more dependent and continues with the underachievement pattern, often with renewed vigor. For example, a child might complete his or her homework diligently when supervised closely, but somehow "lose it" or "forget" to turn it in at school. Further, parental concern and periodic disappointments may cause the parents to function as "emotional thieves." They get so excited about a success that they cheer—thinking that will encourage the child. They get so bummed out about a failure, you'd think it was their own. The child sees the parents' reactions and doesn't have to experience the emotion on his own. His own emotion becomes unnecessary and redundant, because the parents have already experienced it—stolen it, in fact.

Many parents mention that educators, extended family members, and other "interested parties" often accuse them of not caring or being bad parents if they follow my philosophy of transferring the anxiety back to the student through gradual, parental distancing. Help those well-meaning individuals understand the logic behind the approach I recommend. Many of them misinterpret the intent of empowering the underachiever to make other, better choices. They see our approach as some form of abandonment. Similarly, they misinterpret both the underachiever as "crying for help" and their own resultant need to micromanage the underachiever. Remember the three approaches that don't work: Power, Logic and Skills Training. Additionally, because of the frustration encountered by the parents and the teachers, often these parties come to be at odds with one another, forgetting the real focus of the problem—the underachiever.

Brenda and Ronnie:
Siblings Falling Into the Same Trap
For both Brenda and Ronnie, siblings just four years apart, grades took nosedives in middle school. After their parents went

through the initial disappointment with Brenda, they refused to believe that a second child would repeat the pattern of underachievement. Just like his sister, Ronnie started hanging out with "airheads," as his parents described them. Ronnie's and Brenda's rooms were buried in clutter and their schoolwork showed a complete lack of organization and effort. Ronnie, who had been meticulous about his work and routinely completed school projects—he was the one who would win scholarships to the best schools, his parents thought—suddenly stopped showing any promise.

Brenda openly resisted doing her work, which earned her repeated punishments, but Ronnie took a passive-aggressive approach. He would say, "Okay," when his parents told him to study. Then he would go to his room and do something completely different. Sometimes he spent study time writing nihilistic verses about school and the world in general. Mom and Dad didn't really have proof he hadn't studied until the test results came in.

When their parents attempted to intervene, first with Brenda and then with Ronnie, both kids rebelled. They resisted any conversations or exercises meant to address their problems—problems they denied existed. Brenda assumed she would grow up and just get married and Ronnie convinced himself he'd go to California after high school and ride BMX bikes for a living.

To get them moving towards personal excellence, Brenda and Ronnie's parents had to back off from their nagging. The rules about study times did not have to be changed, but the approach the parents took to enforcing these rules did. They learned to focus squarely on their children's choices: "I wonder why you chose to fail that course?" and "You seem to choose to study certain subjects and not others."

As much as the kids resented them at first, the exercises they performed at the Center helped Brenda and Ronnie focus on what they really did choose to study—what they liked about school. When Brenda kicked into high gear after intervention—a change that took a few years to effect—she went on to college and became a psychology major. Ronnie allowed himself to enjoy and excel in Latin, history and philosophy. In contrast to his sister's slow change, Ronnie had some life experiences that turned him around more quickly.

His dad started having Ronnie work for him in his carpet installation business. He gave Ronnie the most onerous and physically exhausting jobs so his son got a good dose of what blue-collar life was like. When Ronnie complained, his dad said, "That's what the people who work for me do every day of their lives. It never changes. It never gets any better. Is that what you want?"

By the time he was a junior in high school, Ronnie woke up to the fact that he wasn't good enough to ride a bike professionally and he knew he didn't want to work for his dad his whole life because the labor was grueling. By the next grading period, he had achieved a 3.0 and he kept his grade point average high until he graduated.

❋

ENGAGE PROFESSIONAL HELP

For many parents, the choice to seek help from a counselor, psychologist or other professional depends on their tolerance level. Sometimes they act at the first signs of a problem, but often they wait until the problem corrodes daily family life. Making the decision anywhere along that spectrum is a difficult and personal one.

Before choosing this option, observe your child for a while, then attempt intervention. This conservative approach is recommended to avoid overreaction by the family. A small number of underachievers quickly demonstrate that they are amenable to change. It is helpful, though, to have the child evaluated by a psychologist if underachievement symptoms persist. The student's intellectual potential, achievement level, emotional maturity and the possible presence of learning disabilities should be determined so as to eliminate these factors as causes. The psychologist can then diagnose the problem and guide the parents in evaluating their observations. This allows for establishment of reasonable parental expectations and to see if, indeed, the child is underachieving.

Remember, to be identified as an underachiever, the child should have at least a several months pattern of underachievement. The underachievement generally surfaces both in academic areas, as well as in other, nonacademic responsibilities.

With few exceptions, up to the age of eight, parents should restrict their actions to observing and to limited parental interventions. Until about age eight, wide variations in development occur that can be considered normal. Pushing the child too hard at this time can be counterproductive. Every so often, parents will come to the Center with a very young child. They complain that their five-year-old would rather play with Legos than use flash cards to learn a *third* language. Their expectations are out of whack. I offer to treat the parents, instead of the child.

After age eight, if patterns of underachievement continue, other response options should be seriously considered. Allowing the underachievement to progress, generally means the unwanted patterns will become more firmly ingrained and, therefore, more difficult to change.

The greatest risks lie with letting children fail and ignoring their problems. The belief that if only these two approaches are used the children will change is doubtful and very limiting. When positive action is called for, parents must be ready to assume the responsibility for taking it to correct the problem of underachieving children.

CHAPTER SIX

THE MOTIVATIONAL CIRCLE

Underlying the theories and therapies in this book is the conviction that motivation is emotion-based. Essentially, events trigger emotions. Relatively mature kids and adults can identify their emotions, which become cues that help them access their values. Following those values can then lead the person to productive action. That action then leads to a new event and re-evaluation of the new event. This is the Motivational Circle™.

To illustrate how the motivational circle works, consider that Peter and Paul both have to write history papers and they both want to see an action movie that just opened. Paul is mature; Peter is an underachiever. Here are the boys' contrasting situations:

Paul:	Peter:
Whole Motivational Circle	Broken Motivational Circle
Event: History paper assigned	**Event**: History paper assigned
Emotions: Anxiety, tension, anger	**Emotions**: Anxiety, tension, anger
Internal Response: Emotions are uncomfortable, but they become a cue to values	**Internal Response**: Emotions overwhelm him, scramble his focus; he can't tap into values
Values: "Do your best." "Work hard."	**Values**: "Do your best." "Work hard."
Action: Completes history paper on time	**Action**: Bypasses values, goes to movie

Motivational Circle

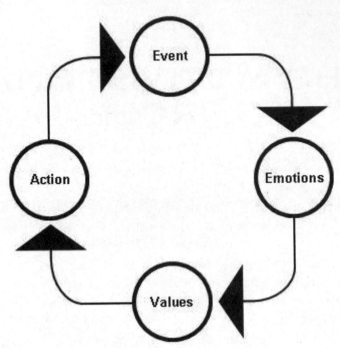

Result: Satisfaction and fulfillment at having completed the work; pleasure that he earned a grade that reflects his effort. He feels good and he anticipates feeling good the next time around the circle. Paul goes to the movie on the weekend and enjoys it.

Result: Anxiety at not having completed the work; pain that he got a grade that reflects no effort. He feels bad and he anticipates feeling bad the next time around the circle. Peter's enjoyment of the movie is muted because of guilt and anxiety.

The cycle starts all over every time some new "event" occurs or as new situations require attention. If the end emotions are pleasurable like Paul's, the person's values are reinforced, more positive productive actions follow and so it continues. The motivated individual then feels good about his actions and about himself.

The Motivational Circle occurs frequently in people's lives, maybe even dozens of times per day, in conjunction with all types of events. Many people follow the whole circle's pattern automatically. For example, you see a neighbor struggling to carry a large box (the event). You have an emotion, such as empathy or concern. You access your values: "Help a person in need." You take action: You help the neighbor carry the box. You don't have to think deeply and ponder actions like this in most instances. Perhaps in those situations that are more frenzied and complicated, with more important circumstances, you might purposefully sit and ponder how you feel and plan a course of action, but through most of the day this is done relatively automatically. You have integrated the Motivational Circle. Not only can this occur dozens of times each day, but also several events can occur simultaneously. If the Motivational Circle in a child or adult's life does not operate smoothly, life will not go smoothly for that individual.

A person like Peter has a motivational problem, so he responds differently to pressure than would a mature individual. Instead of analyzing the situation and reacting with constructive action to alleviate the pressure he feels, Peter resorts to defense mechanisms—procrastination, detachment, magical thinking, intellectualization, minimization, projection, denial and so on.

The Effect Of Pressure On Unmotivated Individuals vs. Motivated Individuals

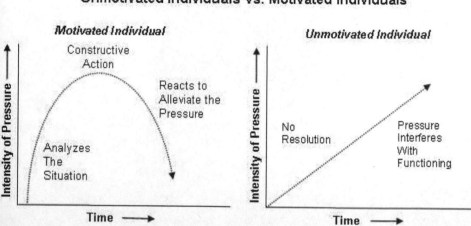

Peter gets stuck in part of the circle. He has the event—the assignment of a paper. He has emotions about that—maybe apprehension, anxiety, doubt, fear, discomfort. He might even have the same emotions as Paul, but Peter's are exaggerated, because he has a history of not following through. Emotions like pressure and tension due to assignments with deadlines are a little uncomfortable for any student, but an unmotivated student like Peter can't handle the discomfort. He is either unwilling or unable to sort through his emotions, to understand why those emotions are there and to use those emotions productively. So what happens? He dumps the emotions, that is, he uses emotional defenses to try to feel better. The underachieving student may just ignore the negative emotions, hoping they will go away. He skips values and jumps to action, impulsively going to the movie—anything except paying attention to those negative feelings. However, the emotions don't go away. They just are moved to the background. The feelings are repressed, not removed. This causes additional distress and more negative emotions.

Another emotional defense underachievers utilize may be denying the feeling: *Oh, I'll do okay in the course even if I don't turn in this stu-*

The Motivational Circle:
Controlling Our Decisions

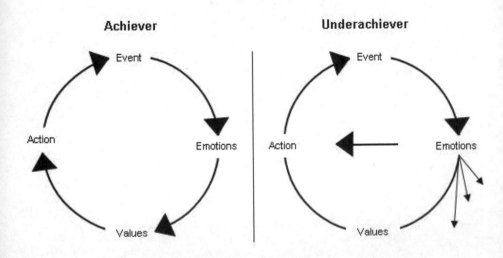

Achiever

Event

Action

Emotions

Values

Underachiever

Event

Action

Emotions

Values

pid paper. Unmotivated students frequently minimize, repress or deny their emotions. These students take a deep breath and think, *It's just not worth worrying about*. That thought may immediately help them feel better, but the unpleasant reality is still there intruding on their dream world. They just don't do anything about it, while internally, because they have good core values, they feel guilt and frustration.

Our internal defenses help us survive feelings or situations that scare us or make us feel threatened, inadequate or unable to cope. When used judiciously, they help us effectively cope with the complexities of life; however, when used too quickly, too frequently or inappropriately, they can distort reality and detach us from coping productively.

Examples of defenses underachievers use may include:

- **Avoidance** – An attempt to postpone or escape an aversive event or situation and thereby avoid the anticipated (or unknown) outcome. It involves more than just trying to get away from a situation, however. It's also an attempt to get away from the emotions associated with it.

- **Denial** – A refusal to accept something as reality. This is an unconscious, non-malicious attempt to protect oneself from something hurtful or difficult to accept. As discussed in Chapter 1, denial is not the same as lying. Lying is a deliberate attempt to deceive with an untrue statement.

- **Projection** – An externalizing of wishes that leads to a distortion of reality. It is attributing qualities, actions or characteristics to a person or object where they do not belong, so as not to confront the true nature of a situation.

- **Rationalizing** – The justification of an attitude, idea or action that is unreasonable, illogical or for which the true motive is not recognized. It is an effort to distort reality so as to cover up mistakes, misjudgment or failure in order to protect one's self-esteem.

- **Repression** – An unconscious exclusion from the conscious mind of objectionable acts, memories or ideas, so that the conscious mind is not aware that the offensive material exists.

- **Minimizing** – A lowering of the degree or a lessening of the affect or value of an act, prospect or influence in order to make it appear less important.

These and other defenses allow people to disregard uncomfortable emotions as cues to help access their values and ultimately lead to productive action. If a person is unmotivated, usually there is very little action taken. If that person acts at all, his actions tend to be based either on avoidance or on not getting caught. Other times, the actions are impulsive and without consideration of the consequences. The result is the same: No productive action occurs. The person hides from himself and others the fact that there is, as in Peter's case, a paper due tomorrow. He denies the fact that he is avoiding and tries to minimize the circumstance so that no one else notices.

Through example, anecdote and counsel, parents create and reinforce a value core in their child. The value core is made solid through consistency, caring and making the child exercise the values. Through values, we filter our desires, leading to appropriate actions.

The value core is usually intact and established fairly well by age 12. When the value core is sheathed in defenses, however, it is not readily accessible. In order to be self-driven, we must have clean access to and understanding of our value core.

An onion has a core with many thin layers enclosing its nub. In seeing defenses as layers of an onion with the value core in the center, the mechanisms can be better understood (Figure A). It is appropriate

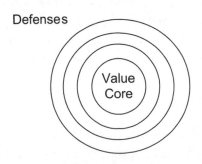

Figure A

to have some defenses. Without defenses, we would never leave our home for fear of getting mugged or being bitten by a dog, so some defenses allow us to function, to take reasonable risks.

When there are too many defenses or they are assessed too quickly and often, as in the case of an underachiever, there is a problem. In that circumstance the individual becomes reliant on defenses, automatically adding layers of defense to protect and limit vulnerability to stress and hurt. For example, if I am "defended" about my grade I get in math, if I get a bad grade, it does not really bother me. This often leads to utterances such as "so what" or "who cares." The "well-defended" individual can have a minimal reaction to events or possibilities that might make another person act to avoid them.

Defenses hinder reality from being accurately viewed and understood. Defenses "save" the underachiever from appropriate emotions. Because of this state of numbness to reality, reactions may be wrong, inappropriate or non-existent. There is little learning from experience.

Reality approaches and the underachiever either deflects or distorts it. It is deflected (Figure B) if it is not too serious or sharp, so it remains at the level of a minor irritant. The underachiever in this instance either feigns indifference or passively deflects (*e.g.,* "Don't worry. I'll do it later"). It is distorted (Figure C) if it carries a serious, harsh or unavoidable message. As it breaks through defenses, the individual struggles to avoid through distortion and misinterpretation. Eventually, many underachievers react with anger and hostility, sug-

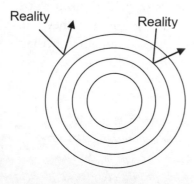

Figure B

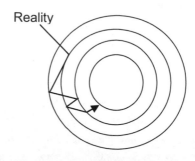

Figure C

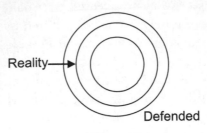

Figure D

gesting injustice or unreasonableness of reality. In either case, they react ineffectively, do not use their value core to guide them and may be defensive in whatever response they show. Those defensive responses may be passive or aggressive.

When confronted with an unpleasant reality and if their defenses are not strong enough to "defend" from it, underachievers may add another layer of defense. Layers can be transient or situation specific. They can fade after the challenge is met by productive coping. For underachievers, most layers stay, however, and become part of a continuing build-up. Reality moves further away as does the ability and likelihood that the underachievers will effectively respond. Ultimately, they have to spend more energy and time on defending, rather than on productively coping. This is a losing strategy that leaves them ineffective. They know what is "right" and what they "need to do," but either show no response or an ineffective one.

For productive change to occur the levels of defense need to be minimized or discarded. Underachievers must accept that they will be better off if they face reality and base their judgments on their clear values. They need to strip away the defensive layers.

Andy: He Wasn't the Only One Who Was Stuck

When Andy's mother looked back at the generations that preceded her son's, she saw distinct reasons why her son might emerge with emotional development problems. She felt he had been set up for them well before he was born.

Andy's great-grandmother had kicked her husband out of the house because he ran around on her. As a result, Andy's grandfather became a breadwinner at age eleven. He had no time for childhood and, when he had his own children, he had no time for their childhood. When Andy's father, Ray, would misbehave, his dad would threaten to dump him at St. Joe's orphanage—and Ray believed his father would do it. The logical outcome of having such an emotionally unavailable father was to become the same kind of emotionally unavailable father to his own son.

By the time Andy reached high school, he made below-average grades in most subjects and showed the classic defensive behavior of an underachiever: He hid his feelings by feigning indifference to his failure. That would temporarily alleviate his anxiety and keep his parents at arm's length. He didn't want his mom to get upset and figured his dad wouldn't get involved anyway.

Nevertheless, the parents did see the bad grades as a sign of a problem and they addressed it by taking Andy to a psychologist. Unfortunately, what they didn't realize was that the psychologist they chose had an expertise in criminal behavior. Andy was traumatized whenever he sat in the man's office—books on criminal tendencies lined the shelves. Andy thought his parents knew of the psychologist's speciality; he wouldn't say anything negative about the therapist because he was afraid that would convince his parents he was headed for a life of crime.

When nothing changed, Andy's parents brought him to the Center. Andy discovered that he had no clue how to deal with emotions and that a big part of the problem was that no one had taught him how. "People model what they see," he now explains, "and my parents did not know how to deal with their emotions. I saw my role as trying to fix them, but I didn't know how."

During his sessions, Andy felt invited to express his emotions and he enjoyed that. He also made practical gains in school. But the root of the problem was still there. At home, he felt that emotions were not welcome.

Finally, because of Andy's needs and his growth, the parents sought help through therapy. They began engaging in the kinds of exercises that could help them get emotionally unstuck. They practiced showing their feelings, modulating their emotions and inviting their son to open up with them.

Andy eventually married a woman whose family, he says, "in terms of emotional expression, is the opposite of what mine was." He also joined his father's small business and works side by side with him on a daily basis.

The endless loop of event-emotion-values-action can also become short-circuited when a child either does not have a solid value core or rejects her values. When the loop starts, she tries to decide how the event relates to her values. If the values are jumbled, they do not provide her with the stability of consistent guidance. She flounders and takes a shot in the dark. Eventually, she becomes less capable and effective and probably feels confused and unhappy.

As I've indicated, for most motivated individuals the Motivational Circle occurs with little conscious effort. Achieving individuals have the ability to take uncomfortable emotions, fully experience them and understand what they feel and why. They then use those feelings to access their core values. The values usually include such basic concepts as "do your best," "be honest," "do a good day's work," "care for others" and "be responsible for your actions." Accessing those values provides *guidance* for motivated people and this leads to productive action.

The Motivational Circle Applied

<u>Achiever</u>
Event step: "Please mow the lawn."
   automatically proceeds to
Emotion step: Feels desire to help even though he'd rather play ball

<u>Underachiever</u>
Event step: "Please mow the lawn."
   distorts request and motive, so
Emotion step: Feels put upon; request wrecks his free time.

Achiever	Underachiever
automatically proceeds to	*emotion not a cue to action, so*
Values step: Accesses value to be helpful and obedient	**Values step:** (Step not taken; values there, but not accessed)
automatically proceeds to	*impulsively tries to avoid, so*
Action step: Mows the lawn.	**Action step:** Says he feels sick.
Event step: Dad tells him how much he appreciates the help and what a good job he did.	**Event step:** Dad tells him he's disappointed he can't help and asks what the problem is.
automatically proceeds to	*distorts degree of criticism, so*
Emotion step: Feels pride and a sense of accomplishment.	**Emotion step:** Feels guilty and worthless; dislikes himself.
automatically proceeds to	*has inflamed reaction, so*
Values step: Accesses value, "It's good good to be productive."	**Values step:** (Step not taken; value there, but not accessed.)
automatically proceeds to	*impulsively reacts, so*
Action step: Tells Dad, "Glad to help."	**Action step:** Tells Dad: "You're just trying to punish me!"

Of course, in life things do not always occur in a simple form. The Motivational Circle can get very complicated because we may have several events occurring at the same time. Some may be more important than others, some may contain incomplete information, some may have many sub-event categories and some may unfold over long periods of time. Nonetheless, each of these events brings emotions. A person must then decide which of these is important and demanding. This is how we establish priorities for our actions. Frequently, however, we may be in various stages of action with a variety of events. Being able to clarify and understand our emotions as they relate to events and then access our values as they pertain to those emotions and events, enables us to act productively.

The unmotivated individual breaks the circle, runs from discomfort and remains ineffective, conflicted, detached and unhappy.

Chapter Seven

Good and Bad Emotions

The force of emotions pushes us toward or away from actions all the time. Inappropriately strong emotions can incite destructive, including self-destructive, actions—a common occurrence for the underachiever. Conversely, weak or retarded emotions allow an underachiever to languish through inactivity.

Part of the challenge that underachievers face is that they don't know where their emotions lie on a scale of intensity. For example, they may not perceive anger as an escalated form of discomfort, but rather as the sole expression of it. As a corollary, they commonly lack emotional vocabularies that reflect degrees of feeling. They are "pissed off" or "feel awesome," but you probably won't hear them say they are "uncomfortable" or "delighted." They may also not grasp both the positive and negative nuances in a word like "excited." These black-and-white emotional experiences are aspects of what causes them to lose the utility of emotions in sorting priorities and moving toward positive actions.

Parents of underachievers often serve as *enablers* when they see this happening. Parents are usually well intended, but it is as if parents feel their child will be too hurt by his own feelings. Sure, many feelings are uncomfortable. Discomfort, to a degree, has practical benefits. Discomfort allows us to scan our situation, anticipate, plan and productively engage. Without discomfort, we would ooze along, waiting for others to warn us, to think for us and to do for us (that sounds like underachievement to me!). Ironically, by parents "saving" children from distressing feelings, they create someone who runs from emotion, is not using emotion productively, is not resilient and is fearful. One child cries bitterly because his homework isn't done—his whole world is falling apart—so mom and dad do the assignment and the child simply records their answers. Another teenager yells at a teacher and earns detention for two weeks, so the parents dutifully make a special trip to pick him up from school instead of making him take a bus home. These parents haven't sorted through their own emotions; they soothe themselves by providing superficial aid to their "needy" child. One of the most dramatic examples of this kind of enabling behavior involved a grossly obese man whom fitness guru Richard Simmons tried unsuccessfully to help. So fat he couldn't even move to get food for himself, the man gained weight steadily because people around him brought food to him in bed—they enabled him to be over 800 pounds.

What role does enabling fulfill in parents' lives? If it's one parent, does he have a problem with his spouse? Is mom vicariously trying to live through her child? Are both parents avoiding looking at their own personal development? Do they have subconscious motives like wanting their child—perhaps their youngest—to stay home longer? Often, there's nothing "wrong" with the parents. They engage in enabling behavior because they don't know another way of dealing with the problem. Their actions may be well-intentioned efforts to avoid confronting the child and hurting his feelings. Unfortunately, the action is wrong and the result unwanted. The exercise of sorting through emotions, identifying them and figuring out where they lie on the intensity scale *before* taking action is something that will help both the underachiever and his parents to break the cycle of enabling behavior.

Emotion words are very personal; everyone has a slightly different ranking scale. Appendix C contains a list of emotional vocabulary words that may help you and your child pinpoint your emotions and describe the intensity of your feelings. (Megan, one of the teenagers who came to the Center, first condemned this list and the ranking exercise as "stupid." She later made a point of saying the list was one of the tools that helped her most in understanding her emotions.)

Degrees of Upset
Irritated/disgusted/*pissedoff*/angry/outraged/OVERWHELMED/SHOCKED

Degrees of Joy
Contented/*comfortable*/pleased/happy/delighted/THRILLED/ECSTATIC

Understanding emotions involves more than assessing their relative intensity. It is also useful in many cases to see an emotion as a fabric of different threads. For example, "discomfort" can include apprehension, displeasure and embarrassment.

❃

USEFUL URGENCY

Urgency is another complex emotion, which, because of its key role in motivation, deserves special attention. Urgency is composed of discomfort, anticipation, anxiety, uncertainty, necessity and a sense of time. Depending on the circumstance provoking urgency, that emotion might also encompass appreciation of one's responsibilities and a fear of failure.

All the emotions taken together in "urgency" provide cues to positive action in a motivated individual. How can you develop this useful urgency in your child? Those children who lack motivation are especially distant from their emotional lives. They see urgency as bad, anxiety-provoking and something to be avoided. The most effective way for you to teach this useful attribute is by modeling. You must show your child how you use urgency effectively to help you decide to act or not act. As part of this, dissect the process of deciding to act into:

1. Emotions around the sense of urgency,
2. Cues to action,
3. Cues to time constraints,
4. Resultant emotions upon completion.

Demonstrating the process of urgency and how it occurs in your life will help your children. It is through this vicarious learning that they come to appreciate the positive effects that a useful sense of urgency can impart.

Also, try to explain and demonstrate to your child the important balance between urgency and complacency. The ability to establish priorities for one's responsibilities is a critical skill. If you have several responsibilities, the best way to handle them is to place them in an order that correlates to your sense of urgency for each task (more urgent tasks are put at the top of the list). You can help a student, and especially an underachiever, by explaining how you do this, then showing him. A child needs to see that no one can do everything at once and that attempting to do so causes intense frustration. A much more successful way of solving multiple problems is prioritizing and solving them one at a time. A child will absorb this message on some level even if he rolls his eyes and feigns indifference. When a child has difficulty setting priorities, you should ask leading questions about the order assigned to completing tasks. Which task is more important and why? What would be the results if it were done this way or that? Guide, but don't be so direct that you impose *your* priorities. You need to react, of course, if he strays far from the mark in setting priorities and the result would be harmful, however minor errors are a learning experience. Let the child figure those out.

In addition to modeling, you need to react in a dispassionate way to any lowered sense of urgency in your child. This does not mean you should be unconcerned. Rather, your comments should guide them: "*I wonder why* you are choosing to ignore that project" said without judgment or regard for an answer. Or you might say, "*I wonder how* you would feel if you got that project done early?" If the proper sense of urgency results in a positive outcome, the comment might be, "*You seem* to feel good that you got the project done early," or "*I wonder how* you feel now that you finished that project?" Give the child time to reflect and respond to his or her own feelings, then you can say yours. A word of caution—and you'll see this offered many times throughout this book: **Don't steal the emotion from your child**. Even if you feel like jumping for joy, calling all your relatives or taking out a full-page advertisement to publicize the fact that your child got something done on time, remain moderate in your response. Your child should feel good about his achievements—certainly more than you (at least outwardly). React appropriately and be sure not to give "negative praise," such as, "I'm glad you finally did well since you're always screwing up."

A sense of personal urgency is one of the most productive attributes you can help your child cultivate. It allows the child to proceed without the vigilance of others.

The world is full of people with good intentions who promise to do things and have great ideas, but ultimately do very little. Frequently, there is a lack of urgency to begin, to continue or to complete a task. For those without this sense, many potential paths of accomplishment remain unexplored; a sense of efficacy is not developed and self-esteem plummets.

❄

GOOD AND POOR SELF-ESTEEM

Much has been written about self-esteem and much of it is wrong. For too many people self-esteem means "making them feel good by never hurting their feelings." That kind of warm-and-fuzzy treatment will not develop good self-esteem. It gives the entire concept of self-esteem a bad name and actually harms the individuals targeted by it. Good self-esteem grows through real accomplishments, large and small. This is the positive kind of self-esteem that failing kids need, but as parents and teachers have found out, it is precisely the kind most difficult to achieve.

Like urgency, self-esteem plays a critical role in motivation with underachieving children, who experience it in some painful ways.

Self-esteem comes in two forms: Good (high) self-esteem and poor (low or false-high) self-esteem. Unmotivated individuals have poor self-esteem, even if they project self-confidence.

Good self-esteem is positive self-regard, but it is not an inflated sense of self. It is not about putting oneself above others—wanting pleasure, position or power for purely selfish reasons. It is neither self-serving nor self-centered. With appropriate, positive self-esteem, an individual considers abilities, limits and consequences. It enables a person to interact with his or her reality productively and to experience emotions clearly. It feeds a person's desire to want to experience all of his or her emotions, both comfortable and uncomfortable ones. The connection between effort and outcome is understood and respected. Appropriate positive self-esteem does not seek undeserved positive outcomes for the sake of outward praise. It does use negative situations as learning experiences from which one can grow. **Positive self-esteem is a confidence in one's self that is earned and justifiable.**

Positive self-esteem is also positive self-regard in a context. That context is self in relationship to society, from the close society of friends and family all the way to the global society. What this means is that people who have good self-esteem have a range of powerful, success-oriented traits—confidence, resilience, character, personal responsibility, purpose, honesty, self-discipline, competence, courage, vision—and they see challenges as opportunities. They understand their abilities, feelings and motives and relate these to their values. They also have concern and respect for others and others' capabilities.

Good self-esteem has a balance. This balance is between accepting yourself and having others accept you for who you are, while maintaining your values within a social context.

In contrast, poor self-esteem is self-centered, but not in a positive manner. Poor self-esteem has two sub-categories: false high self-esteem and true low self-esteem.

1. **False high self-esteem** is focused on the self only. With false high self-esteem comes inflated expectations, excessive concern with self, grandiose acclamations and strong projections of self over others.
2. **True low self-esteem** is also self-focused, but in a negative way. Individuals with low self-esteem feel incapable, depleted, unable to control, overwhelmed, put-upon, left out and disrespected. In essence, they lack self-confidence.

Self-Esteem: Effects on Attitude

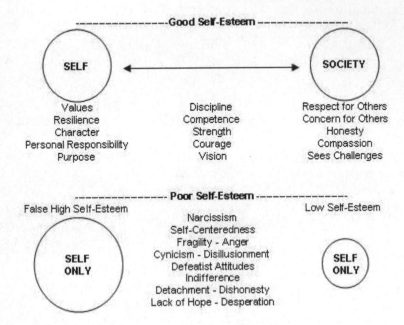

---------------Good Self-Esteem---------------

| SELF | ←————————→ | SOCIETY |

Values
Resilience
Character
Personal Responsibility
Purpose

Discipline
Competence
Strength
Courage
Vision

Respect for Others
Concern for Others
Honesty
Compassion
Sees Challenges

---------------- Poor Self-Esteem ----------------

False High Self-Esteem   Low Self-Esteem

Narcissism
Self-Centeredness
Fragility - Anger
Cynicism - Disillusionment
Defeatist Attitudes
Indifference
Detachment - Dishonesty
Lack of Hope - Desperation

SELF
ONLY

SELF
ONLY

Both of these categories of poor self-esteem have elements of narcissism, self-centeredness, fragility, anger, victimization, cynicism, disillusionment, defeatist attitudes, indifference, detachment, dishonesty, lack of hope and desperation. Rather than seeing new situations as challenges, these persons see new situations as hassles.

Think of good self-esteem as a clear, polished lens. Reality travels through it and is not distorted, rather it is focused and sharpened. This leads to workable emotions. That does not mean that the emotions are necessarily uncomfortable or comfortable, bad or good. It just means that they are not distorted. They allow the individual to see clearly what the circumstances are and make appropriate responses.

Poor self-esteem of either variety is a distorted lens. The picture of reality through the lens is unclear and vaguely defined. This leads to both limited and confused emotions. These distorted cues are not

Self-Esteem: Effects on Reality

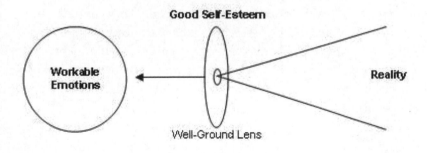

Good Self-Esteem

Workable Emotions

Reality

Well-Ground Lens

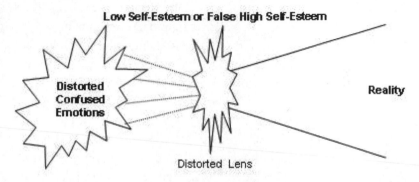

Low Self-Esteem or False High Self-Esteem

Distorted Confused Emotions

Reality

Distorted Lens

helpful in allowing people to accurately access their values and make decisions. They yield false data. Decisions based on distortions of what is really happening tend to be inappropriate and counterproductive. So, good self-esteem is necessary to avoid misinterpretations of reality as well as to provide the self-tools necessary to take positive, productive action.

In kids as well as adults, many factors and experiences can work together to cause an erosion of positive self-esteem or plant the seeds of poor self-esteem. The broadest of all the contributing factors, and one that hints at the nature of the others, is the "wimpization" of America.

To some teachers and parents, competition is a dirty word. They deal in absolutes: Every child always gets a gold star just for turning in a project. Every kid always gets to hit the ball, no matter how many swings it takes. Grades are bad; just go to school and learn.

Scores are bad; just go out there and play the game. Their philosophy is that, if the kid doesn't get the gold star or hit the ball, it hurts his self-esteem—that any "failure" hurts self-esteem. They subscribe to a simplistic view that good self-esteem can be obtained by mainly having loving, caring parents and a loving, caring environment that rewards a person's behavior affectionately and without limit. That is definitely not enough to achieve and maintain high self-esteem. These people are well-intentioned, but misguided.

In reality, pandering to a child hurts his or her self-esteem. Resiliency will suffer. If a child doesn't *earn* the prize, self-esteem will not develop. If she doesn't appreciate the value of "If at first you don't succeed, try again," a fundamental lesson of success will never take hold.

Milton Bradley and other board game manufacturers put suggested ages on the outside of the box to indicate not only what ages will be interested in the games, but who can *honestly* win at them. Candyland is a game of pure chance; a five-year-old can win it honestly. A mom who repeatedly allows her nine-year-old beat her at Monopoly, however, has not honestly accomplished her intended goal of building self-esteem in the child. Self-esteem comes with honest accomplishment.

Some schools also degrade students' academic accomplishments by lowering standards. They allow kids to offset a lack of regular effort with extra credit projects, always grade on a curve and teach with the lowest common denominator in mind. In the interest of having the kids do well in school, they create a non-competitive dream world. Any self-esteem that does result from these misguided efforts is weak, riddled with doubt, non-resilient and false. Aside from the emotional problems that the approach fosters, it also results in many college freshmen having to take remedial courses. To help avoid this, students must be held to reasonable standards throughout their early years.

✳

DEPRESSION

Does underachievement cause depression, coexist with depression or is underachievement caused by depression? Not only is there a question of, "Which came first, the chicken or the egg?" but also, "If there is a chicken, will there necessarily be an egg?"

Depression does not always result in underachievement. More likely, depression will contribute to detachment that can be seen as less personal control, less responsibility and less apparent concern. Underachievement, if it occurs in a depressed child, will coexist with the depression. It will be associated with it, but the two problems will require different, if complementary, courses of action.

Underachievement does not always result in depression, either. When it does, it is generally reactive or situational. It will go away when the child rekindles his motivation. An underachiever may act "bummed out" because he is upset about his condition and shows it through detachment, hostility or nonchalance.

If you say yes to many of the following symptoms, your underachiever might be more than "bummed out." Consult your physician to determine if a depression is present that might benefit from medication.

- Depressed for several months
- Detached from previous attachments
- Turning his emotions inward, except for unmodulated outbursts
- Having difficulty sleeping or sleeping too much
- Experiencing major changes in appetite
- Reporting hopelessness or helplessness
- Seeming sad much of the time
- Feeling discouraged

Medication as an adjunct to other interventions can help an underachiever who is clinically depressed. Do not blindly embrace a diagnosis of depression and rush out to buy pills and herbs however, without having a physician thoroughly examine your child. Otherwise, you will fall into the same pit as parents who early on seek a simplistic answer to complicated motivational problems by only considering that a medical condition such as ADHD is impairing their child.

B<small>UILDING</small> G<small>OOD</small> S<small>ELF</small>-E<small>STEEM</small>

The key to building good self-esteem in your child is for that child to experience productive accomplishments that include good interpersonal relationships. Good emotional development creates the environment for this to happen. Appropriate emotional development leads to young people having concern for others and becoming self-aware. Being self-aware allows individuals, even at early ages, to know and understand their emotions, values and abilities. This in turn allows them to understand their motives, to plan, establish priorities and set goals based on values. Because our values are our internal stability and the guide through which we obtain our character and on which we base our decisions, this planning or goal setting leads to constructive action and accomplishments. That, in turn, builds good self-esteem. These elements and actions are interdependent.

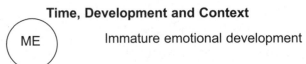

Time, Development and Context

ME   Immature emotional development

Figure 1

Underachievers have difficulty with time, anticipating outcomes and consequences, and projecting themselves into a context of others. Usually, they are self-centered and do not like to think of past or future. Now is most important to them (as in, "Am I having fun now?").

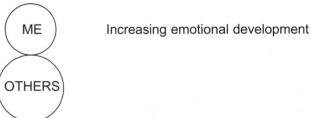

ME   Increasing emotional development

OTHERS

Figure 2

As individuals mature they begin to appreciate they are in a context with others and other things (systems). Others begin to encroach. This begins the development of anticipation related to other people: if they are pleasing others, getting along with others, and meeting their expectations. Their sense of self over time begins to develop. They learn they have lasting impact.

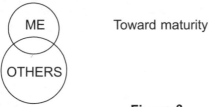   Toward maturity

Figure 3

As emotional development continues toward maturity, there is an acceptance of context—it matters. A priority is anticipation and planning as it relates to self and others. Outcomes are real and important.

In immaturity, time is attenuated. Gradually, as individuals develop, they accept the inevitability of the demands for self-development. They learn the nature of choices and accepting responsibility and outcomes for their choices. Additionally, they come to accept that in order to be effective, they must accept the context of others. They must be considerate of others and their impact on them. They learn from their past and come to understand that what they do today can carry into the future.

Good self-esteem in children and adults not only comes from having nurturing and loving people around us, but also comes from experiencing the challenges of life. It comes from experiencing struggle and disappointment and learning how to survive, to be resilient, to adjust behavior to get a better result and to prosper. Making mistakes may bring about negative consequences, but then the mature response is to adjust one's actions and try again. I know children are not born mature, yet instilling respect for effort and mistakes plus the attitude of trying again is essential if parents are to help them attain that quality. If the child makes further mistakes and there are more negative consequences, the thing to do is make further corrective adjustments based on the new knowledge and to continue to do so, until the mistakes grow smaller or disappear. This will not happen, however, without an awareness of feelings and values. There must be self-awareness.

Self-awareness enables us to understand our motives and set priorities for our needs. All of this takes a certain amount of positive self-esteem to be able to handle, but in turn it also builds self-esteem. It all works together. It kind of happens at the same time—dependent and interdependent. That is why building self-esteem is a slow process that starts small and gradually builds. You cannot teach self-esteem to a child, but you can develop it. Again, positive self-esteem stems from real accomplishments, large and small, and healthy relationships.

Often, self-esteem classes advocate having the participants visualize their unique qualities, repeatedly telling themselves how good they are and thinking about the potential results of future accomplishments. These actions do *not* develop self-esteem. Similarly, the "wimpization" approach—giving awards and certificates of achievement or excessive praise when nothing significant was accomplished—does *not* build true self-esteem. These methods can instead build cynicism, distrust and self-doubt (often camouflaged by "false high self-esteem"). Children learn eventually that there are individual differences in abilities, efforts, outcomes, attributes and attitudes. If adults are telling them that every person's abilities are equal or that their accomplishments, even if dramatically different from others' accomplishments, are worth the same praise or reward, children soon realize that they are not being told the truth. If adults do not tell the truth in these areas, can they be trusted regarding other things? This leads to confusion, distrust and feelings of self-doubt. It actually makes a child feel worse to get unjustified praise than no praise at all. Praise becomes meaningful for the child when the accomplishment has true merit. Any temporary self-esteem boost gained from distortions and false praise is merely artificial self-esteem—frail and, ultimately, meaningless.

This is not to imply that children should only be acknowledged or praised when they do something outstanding. Everyone needs a pat on the back occasionally to boost morale. Small recognition for small accomplishments is fine. This **micro-recognition** is appreciated and can be very beneficial, especially when it focuses on positive personal attributes or effort, not necessarily on outcome. Problems are created when excessive recognition or rewards are given for accomplishments that do not warrant them. Sometimes this is a judgment call and an occasional slip will not cause lasting damage.

Rather than viewing your child as a fragile individual who must be constantly protected from a reality that might assault his emotional well-being, you must provide realistic growth opportunities tailored to the child that allow for meaningful, significant recognition of real accomplishments. **Treating a child as capable of significant actions leads that child to do significant acts. This builds positive self-esteem.** Even when the child fails, if he sees the information gained from that failure as a learning experience, his self-esteem improves and growth in character occurs. Learning from mistakes can be very positive. When a child learns to improve, overcome and control negative situations so that those situations are not repeated, self-esteem builds. Becoming more effective makes a person feel good.

Positive experiences engender feelings of happiness, success, self-worth, empowerment, joy and satisfaction. Negative experiences can cause discouragement, uncertainty and anxiety. However, from negative experiences can also come persistence, flexibility and resilience that lead to using constructive criticism as an assessment of goals and the motivation for positive change. An important insight for every child to learn is: **Failing is different from being a failure.**

A lot of kids who come to see me have keen interests in extreme sports involving tricks on skateboards, in-line skates, bikes, skis and snowboards. One of their perennial heroes, even after his retirement in 1999, is Tony Hawk, a legendary skateboarder. One story that intrigues them is that Hawk attempted for ten years to do a 900-degree rotation on a skateboard. The day in 1999 when he finally accomplished it, he tried and "failed" ten times before he succeeded and made skateboarding history. As much as they admire him for trying, they don't necessarily make the connection that they can do the same kind of thing in their lives—that by learning from their supposed failures, they, too, can become successes in some areas of their lives.

Your child must learn that when the results she achieves are less than desired, if her effort was good she will be able to use her newly gained knowledge for improved results with the next try. When challenges are met with resilience, a child learns, "I feel good about myself and my efforts—no matter what happens, I'll be okay and I'll keep at it."

Developing positive self-esteem requires a continuing interaction between parents and child. This requires a certain amount of two-way openness. This openness may be slow in developing, especially on the child's part, but it is necessary for growth.

As a parent, here are a few things you can do to improve your child's positive self-esteem:

- **Have consistent and clearly defined goals, rules and limits.** Every child should know what is negotiable, what is not negotiable and where the child has self-discretion.

- **React consistently** and, if possible, as a team with other authority figures (such as: the other parent, relatives and educators). Inconsistencies and mixed messages deflate and confuse children.

- **Give continuity of concern.** No matter what the situation, listen respectfully. If the situation is negative, explain why it is and give appropriate consequences, but *always* discuss positive alternatives. Try to facilitate the child finding appropriate alternatives, rather than you lecturing him with the answers. Emphasize the failings of the circumstance, not that the child is a failure. This may seem like a subtle difference, but it is a very important one. For example, your son doesn't turn in an assignment and gets a zero for the project. Instead of saying, "You can't do anything right," say instead, "That project probably would have gotten a very good grade if it had been turned in on time." Be consistent with positive situations also. Be careful not to say something like, "You did well, but—." That *but* makes the positive into a negative.

- **Minimize your emotional reactions.** State your feelings plainly, but without showing strong emotions. Let your words convey your feelings, not the tone or volume of your voice. This is hard to do, but try. Remember to use a variety of words to describe your feelings; you want to build an emotional vocabulary.

- **Have responses stressing your values and understandings.** Remember positive as well as negative consequences should be appropriate to the circumstance. Try to enforce a natural consequence for a particular circumstance. For instance, if your daughter tears up the neighbor's flowers by running through them, don't just take money out of her savings to pay for the flowers. Instead, have your child purchase new flowers and plant them in the appropriate space, cleaning up the mess she made. It is okay to take some time to come up with an appropriate consequence to negative behavior. Just tell your child you need time to think about her actions and that you will have a response by a specific time, then be sure you do so.

- **Focus your praise on effort,** but only secondarily on results (while still giving the results their proper due). Encourage the effort. For some kids it may be beneficial to break large chores down into a series of small tasks. This enables the child to progress through small *completions* without being overwhelmed, as the work moves toward the ultimate goal. When you do this you may state the ultimate goal, but then state your smaller step. For instance, you tell your son, "We're going to clean out the basement, but first let's get the stuff we need to start." Then list the tools, boxes and such that you will need. At each new phase announce the next step or, even better, ask your son what should be next. If he gets it wrong, say something like, "Yes, but how do we get there?" or "What do you think about _?"

- **Monitor your use of "positive" and "negative" so that you are not inappropriate in either area.** Minimize your use of cynicism in front of your child. Work towards eliminating it. You may be just blowing off steam, but kids won't take it that way. Kids will misinterpret cynicism as a coping mechanism. Cynicism, when used inappropriately, is a drain on motivation.

Let your child see your positive side. Be realistic, but save any cynical or sarcastic remarks, no matter how clever, for other adults who understand that you are just venting.

■ **Be available and be "askable."** Let your child *know* and *feel* that he can come to you for anything. This means not only saying you are available, but also giving that impression and truly being there for him. Even if you don't have the answers or it's not appropriate for you to give the answers, help him find resources where he can get answers to his academic, as well as personal, questions. Share some of your experiences. Let your child know that you don't have all the answers to life's questions, but discuss scenarios, options and alternatives with him. Tell anecdotes that stress values, reasoning and problem solving. Very importantly, when your child does come to you, give him your undivided attention. Put down whatever else you are doing and focus on him. If he wants or needs a big block of time that you can't give right then, set up an appointment for a time when you can. Then be sure to keep it.

Self-esteem To-dos for Parents

■ Have consistent and clear goals, rules and limits
■ React consistently
■ Listen respectfully
■ Don't add "but" to a compliment, regardless of the situation
■ Minimize your emotional reactions
■ Have responses stressing your values
■ Focus your praise on effort
■ Monitor your use of "positive" and "negative" so that you are not inappropriate in either area
■ Be available and be "askable"
■ Be friendly, but not a friend

- **Be friendly, but not a friend.** Children want authority figures. When your child becomes a mature and independent adult, then friendship is appropriate. Kids want limits. They want reasonable expectations, even if they seem to resist. Be open and friendly, but give them factual and realistic responses. They need adults who will give them adult perspectives and adult guidance. When they trust you, they will use you as a resource and use your knowledge in their own personal growth.

Remember to let your child know that all emotions are useful, whether they make us comfortable or uncomfortable. They are cues that help us access values and move into productive action.

CHAPTER EIGHT

INTELLECTUAL VERSUS EMOTIONAL DEVELOPMENT

Underachievement is a problem based on emotional development. Lack of motivation arises when children get stuck in development or regress to earlier stages—not in terms of their thoughts, but of their feelings. Even though underachievers may intellectually understand what must be done to achieve, they don't change because of their emotional immaturity. They understand, but they can't move forward. Motivation flows from the interplay of chronological-age, intellectual-age *and* emotional-age components.

What underachievers want and need are both intellectual and emotional levels of understanding. An underachiever has to learn to clarify his or her emotions and that clarity will lead to the *application* of intellectual understanding. This state is called a *working knowledge*. Experiences that throw off the complementary relationship between intellectual and emotional activity can delay acquisition of working knowledge. For example, if you get angry at your child for a bad test score, you can cause your underachiever to shift her focus away from her emotions and on to you. She needs practice working through the problem emotionally, then applying an intellectual resolution to it.

A high school sophomore who took the SAT's early and scored at the ninety-eigth percentile may walk through the door at the Center with his parents biting their lips in frustration. Why? He is chronologically fifteen, intellectually nineteen, and acts like a twelve-year-old. His behavior is pre-adolescent, his interests are pre-adolescent, even his friends are pre-adolescents. At the same time, he's the intellectual equal of most college students. While students like this *understand* what they should do, they won't do it because of their lagging emotional maturity. Parents become especially irritated and frustrated when this occurs: "Why doesn't he just do it; it's not that hard!"

When emotional development lags, responsible behavior will lag. The person's maturity will be less than expected for someone of that chronological age. This immaturity causes confusions, uncertainties, detachment, anxiety and maybe depression. The result frequently is underachievement.

Most parents tend to interact with their unmotivated children on the kids' intellectual levels, which are usually quite high. They expect their children to do what needs to be done. This adds to the parents' frustrations when these kids underachieve. You probably take your child's underachievement personally. Don't. Generally these kids are not purposely striking out at any particular person. You just happen to be close by. It is very difficult for a motivated individual to appreciate how controlling underachievement can be, how powerful it is and how difficult it is to change.

Again, these children are reacting on emotional levels that are considerably below their chronological ages and often even further below their intellectual ages. Because of this, the actions of unmotivated students frequently run contrary to logic. You know that your child knows how to do the work, but she just will not do it, and your frustration mounts as you lecture, plead and cajole. You need to keep in mind that your child is probably as frustrated as you are, even though she usually won't say so. While the problem may appear illogical and unsolvable on the surface, there is hope. The first step in fixing the problem is understanding it.

We all pass through various developmental levels or stages on our way to maturity. Depending on the individual, some stages may be brief and some long, but we keep progressing, even if it's in fits and starts. The problem with underachievers is that they are unable to move forward developmentally in a consistent manner. They are stuck.

Unable or unwilling? Why won't the underachiever "just do it?"

This is a question that has not only plagued parents and teachers, but also creates great consternation in underachievers. Many underachievers are perplexed: They "want" to change, but don't. They are unable because of stunted emotional growth, but their will definitely comes into play. There are mechanics involved in change. These are small, somewhat insignificant, do-able, but that does not mean they are easy to accomplish. For instance, relative to school performance the steps leading to success are: Exert consistent, strong effort; pay attention; take notes; write down assignments; complete assignments; hand in assignments; study; take tests. In order to have success at home: Reassure parents and self through reasonable attitude and behavior (*i.e.,* do chores, don't complain, meet expectations, modulate emotions, apply consistent effort). Other examples of "simple" mechanics: (a) smoking → don't buy or use cigarettes; (b) weight loss → eat less and exercise; (c) drug abuse → stop ingesting the noxious substances. Problems solved! It's as easy as that, or is it?

So why don't we readily do these mechanics? Significant factors are the lack of emotional facility (maturity), the lack of emotional utility, and competing interests. We don't have access to our emotions. They may be jumbled, too uncomfortable to face, conflicted or confused. Also, we don't understand how to use our emotions appropriately. Additionally, competing interests, things that we favor in the short term, but are at odds with others goals, side-track us.

Having clarity of emotions is key. We must be willing to face our emotions, many of which may be very uncomfortable. We must be willing to be uncomfortable, which runs contrary to most people's desire even though discomfort benefits us by bringing us information. That information helps us set priorities and explore our intentions, as in, "Why am I so uneasy about this? What did I really want as an outcome?" Ambivalence often arises from doubt of our basic motives, plus a variety of fears, including fear of outcome (change), fear of failure or success, and fear of offending. Further, emotions tend to be fluid and are often conflicting and confusing. It's like trying to hit a spinning, zigzagging target that is also changing shape. It is a challenge, but a worthwhile one.

How can an individual attain "clarity?" It is a process of exploration. First, we must have clarity about seeking clarity. Doubts, hesitancies and fears must be aired (and overcome). We must develop awareness of our emotions that may be many, changing and blending. This requires quick recognition of emotions and a willingness to feel those emotions (even if uncomfortable). Sometimes emotions blend, creating a challenge to differentiate just what we feel. Dissecting and clarifying emotions is like looking at balled string of Christmas lights. Every new, hybridized emotion is like a new string of lights that's added haphazardly. Understanding it involves "re-feeling" or perhaps, feeling for the first time. We may not know how to react. We have to define the feeling and learn to modulate our responses. This sounds complex, and it is. It takes practice. There are several factors involved: willingness to experience emotions, willingness to assess emotions, willingness to possibly gain new understand-

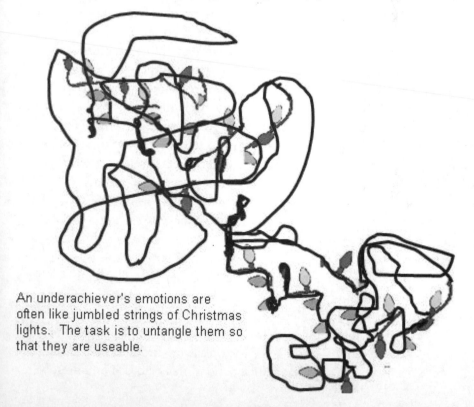

An underachiever's emotions are often like jumbled strings of Christmas lights. The task is to untangle them so that they are useable.

ings and perspectives and willingness to accept personal responsibility for priorities/change/adjustment/acceptance.

Clarity is reduction or elimination of ambivalence. With clarity we experience certainty: we know how we feel and we know what we are going to do and we know that we'll do it.

No matter how much a person says "I want to" and "I'm going to" take charge (intention), if clarity is not attained and maintained, any change will be short-lived, if it occurs at all. Emotions are key to engaging the mechanisms of success. Clarity is a process, not an event—a process that needs to be a willing habit.

Underachievers cannot make constructive, consistent choices well because they lack clarity. They are overwhelmed with ambivalence, and they make confused choices that reinforce the performance borders they can't seem to cross.

John said he couldn't tolerate being at home with his parents. He couldn't wait until he left because his parents "bugged him." But because of his mediocre performance in high school, he positioned himself to be accepted only by a local junior college. Ironically, while at junior college, he remained in his parents' home—the one place he supposedly didn't want to be—and the conflicts with his parents intensified. Logic dictates that if John really didn't want to stay with his parents, he should make choices that would get him away from them. His parents had the resources to send him away to school, but he chose (even if subconsciously) to not put himself in a position to take advantage of that.

Why do underachievers make these bad choices? Situations that challenge them to grow up are clouded. They are having a lot of discomfort with their circumstances and their emotions. They do not, however, explore their emotions in such a way as to more clearly understand how they feel. Often, they experience terrible ambivalence and several changing emotions that become blended and confusing to them: "I want to be independent and live in my own apartment, but I like having a nice home to live in with a full refrigerator and access to a car." Because they do not work their way through these emotions in systematic, effective ways, their actions may be based on unresolved ambivalence about growing up, about becoming independent, about a mature relationship with their parents and so on. They don't think through potential actions and resultant consequences.

Are underachievers aware of these action choices? Usually not. Underachievers do *not* tend to see that their world is mostly the result of their choices of how to behave. It is their perception of choice that must change if they are to productively live their lives.

The reality is that you choose to act in certain ways and there are consequences for those choices. Some are immediate, some longer term. Some are desirable, some unpleasant. Underachievers use defenses in order to avoid consequences and personal responsibility for those consequences.

From their point of view, they are being told they have to do all sorts of things that they wouldn't choose (e.g., chores, homework, thinking about the future). Their world is full of impositions and they are generally irritated. Because they are protecting themselves from their various emotions (many of which are very uncomfortable for them), they do not understand how they really feel. They tend to make choices based on impulses—uncertainty and avoidance—rather than on thoughts and values. By trying to avoid reality, they often are in states of denial, minimizing their responsibilities for circumstances and acting accordingly. This denial and the intense internal conflicts these individuals experience drains their abilities to act productively; they become unmotivated. This is what happened to one client, Carol.

Carol habitually lied about attending classes. She skipped school frequently and lied to everyone in authority, including me, about it. In a completely frustrated state, her mother told her she could not go to college. Her mother's friends supported her decision. Don't let her go, they urged. She'll fall flat on her face.

I disagreed. I felt Carol had developed enough and had enough insight and working knowledge to make the move. I told Carol's mother she must push Carol out of the house—put pressure on her to make mature choices by letting her go off to school. Then Carol's mother was furious with me as well as her daughter. I told the mother that she should be honest with herself: She wanted Carol to stay home, even though she said she wanted her out of the house. I told her she was taking action to undercut Carol's attempts to grow up.

Carol went off to school. She called during her second semester to say she was not "burning up the world with her grades," but she was getting C's or above and working part-time. With excitement in her voice, she said she made it through the first semester and would be doing better next semester. She also said a number of her college friends hadn't returned after the first term. She made her mother proud and proved that friendly advice isn't always the best.

Given that unmotivated students like Carol are usually unaware of the various choices they have when they are making decisions that affect their futures, and given the dynamics underlying the choices, how do parents go about helping them? The underachiever needs to recognize the defenses he uses to avoid reality, as well as his tendency to use them too quickly and too often. The awareness helps him (1) resist the tendency to use them, and (2) give clear consideration of the consequences of his choices. He has to ask himself: What outcomes do I desire? Pushing himself to explore what-ifs can help him determine why he needs to change his behavior.

You should discuss in an unemotional, nonjudgmental manner that there are usually many choices, and that certain choices create their own set of circumstances. Some students are so into denial and so repressed that they cannot see *any* choices, so they do nothing. In these situations, you may have to give concrete examples of choices. Often, it is helpful to diagram the available options and the potential consequences. It is also important for the child to understand that if the result of a particular decision turns out less than expected, then another choice should be made, and on and on, until his choice leads to a desired outcome. The conversation should be unemotional, although goals, consequences and values should be discussed, and the choice should be left to the child unless his choice paves the way for disaster.

It is very important that others help unmotivated kids to see that, especially as they get older and independence is being gradually expanded, most circumstances in life are products of their choices. It is not just that underachievers are "lazy." Avoid using terms like that or excusing bad choices. If you use excuses to justify your child's bad choices, he will tend to believe he has no control. You need to point out that there *is* control in the form of choices. If your child gets a bad grade on a test because he chooses not to study, the main question should be, "*I wonder why* you made that choice?"

You can help the transition from your child's view that things are "fate" to things are "personal choices and personal responsibility" by removing the heat of emotion from your responses and by putting the appropriate responsibility and emotions onto your child. Don't accept your child's emotional burden. The burden is his; he needs it. This can be very difficult because underachievers tend to be effective at manipulating parental emotional responses. Look at it as a game of "hot potato" in which the unmotivated student consciously or unconsciously aims to throw the emotions onto the parent so that the parent will take care of situations. Stay unemotional, but not unconcerned. Essentially, by refusing to take on the emotions, you are saying, "It's yours. It's too hot for me." You won't improve matters by blurting out, "Do whatever you want," or "I don't care." The most productive response is to express that choices are available.

Over time, when systematically confronted about various realities in terms of choices, feelings and values, underachievers will see when their choices are illogical. When this happens, they begin to make better decisions.

PART TWO

SOLVING THE PROBLEM

- Approaches to Motivation—What to Avoid
- General Interventions
- Summer and Holiday Interventions
- Specific Interventions—How to Motivate Each Type of Underachiever
- Maintenance and Prevention Exercises
- Staying Fit for Intervention
- Teacher/Parent Cooperation
- Intervention When You Aren't Around

In Part II we will give specific guidance on new actions to transform underachievers into performers. First of all, don't get angry at yourself for having tried the intuitive interventions that we counsel against. Simply move forward with your underachiever by implementing the approaches that we have found to be effective.

As you approach intervention, remember that not all unmotivated students act the same, nor are their circumstances the same, nor are they all at an identical developmental level. Because of this, remediation must be specific for the individual child. Within a broad framework, however, unmotivated kids have similarities according to the four types of underachievers and they all follow generally predictable patterns and respond in similar ways to influences around them.

The chapters on specific interventions for your child suggest a number of exercises to do. Commit to doing an exercise a couple of days in advance. You don't want to seem intrusive in your child's life—you want the exercise to seem natural even though you've planned it—so think about family experiences, school events and other aspects of your child's life which naturally give rise to the exercise. Use the exercise as it relates to those real circumstances.

A caution is in order as you begin: As you see developmental changes occurring in your underachiever, adjust the interventions accordingly. For example, a passive underachiever, who is much younger emotionally than a defiant underachiever, will probably pass through a defiant stage (however brief) as he or she moves toward emotional maturity. Don't stop the intervention, thinking, *I want my quiet, accommodating child back*. Instead, adjust the intervention to your new situation... and be glad for the change.

This section also includes a suggested system of actions you can take to stimulate the emotional development of your other children, as well as to keep a young *ex*-underachiever moving toward maturity.

Important Changes in an Underachiever

When the underachiever chooses to change, what changes first? Attitude changes first, and then academics. Attitudinal changes tend to be as follows:

ATTITUDE	
FROM	**TO**
Hassle	Challenge
Dread	Positive Anticipati on
Irritation	Acceptance
Anger	Acceptance
Not Communicating Directly	Talking/Discussing
Rigidity	Consideration/Negotiation, Compromise
Detachment	Engagement

CHAPTER NINE

APPROACHES TO MOTIVATION— WHAT TO AVOID

Sometimes you have to fight the natural urges of a "good parent" to be a good parent. It's the paradox of living with an underachiever.

To be a good parent, you may have tried to help your child by doing the following: instructing and guiding, inducing a little guilt occasionally and encouraging suitable behavior. Unfortunately with underachievers, the effect of these parental behaviors is often the opposite of what you intend. What may work well with a motivated child does not work predictably with an unmotivated child. This presents a special challenge for parents who are raising an unmotivated child in the same household with an achiever or two: For an underachieving child, there must be a difference in child management. You have to employ somewhat different sets of parenting behavior for the motivated and for the unmotivated siblings. Parents may figure this out, but then rely on their intuition to dictate how to coach their unmotivated child. It often gets them nowhere.

When a child is unmotivated, parents usually rely on three intuitive strategies—**power, logic and reasoning** and **skills training**—which give rise to a mix of intuitive tactics. Quite naturally, parents see themselves as armed with the power to change their child's life. They are in a position to remind, insist and, when all else fails, they figure: "We can giveth and we can taketh away!" Good parents also think about the future, considering the consequences of their actions or inaction—positive and negative, internal and external. They present their logic and reasoning to their underachiever, perhaps in the form of a lecture, with the assumption that their intelligent child will understand and respond accordingly. The third strategy is to try to make the child learn more of what she doesn't want to know with a tutor, a set of tapes or work organizers that end up in the trash.

Ineffective tactics result from parents' attempts to use power, logic and reasoning and skills training:

- **Intensifying the parenting.** This is like speaking English louder to a non-English speaking person in the hope he'll understand you. The impulse begins when the child resists suggestions about improving or changing. The resistance is usually passive rather than openly defiant. For example, the child forgets, only does the task at half speed or at half quality or completes school assignments, but doesn't turn them in. Raising the intensity of parenting to deal with the problem involves repeated directions and orders that get louder and louder, extra involvement by parents and increasingly harsh penalties. The result is a deteriorated relationship between parent and child—one marked by escalating tension. The unmotivated child merely defends against this intensity, becoming even more determined in his passive resistance.

- **Lecturing.** This is also like speaking English louder to that foreign visitor. Parents see lecturing as a potentially useful tool with the purpose of breaking through to a child on a logical level. They may repeatedly present life's connections, drawing the correlation between action and outcome: "This happens if—." If the child didn't "get it" the first time, they offer the lecture again…and again…with ever-increasing length and intensity. About the sixth time around, the child just sees his unreasonable parents moving their mouths. He rolls his eyes. Resentment builds in everyone.

- **Teaching organizational skills.** You would think that teaching a person some skill that he doesn't seem to know, but needs, would lead to learning and application of that new knowledge. The underachiever may learn, but does not apply what he may know. At the beginning of each school year, organizational systems appear in stores. Logical, handy, attractive—effective, if used. Parents frequently will invest in those systems and spend much time trying to help their child learn the system. This usually deteriorates when the unmotivated student disorganizes the organizational system or "forgets" how to use it and continues along his own path. Through their lack of application, these students remain disorganized and transfer any anxieties back to their parents. Parents are often disappointed, shocked and dismayed that the student didn't take advantage of the system. Then comes the gnawing frustration.

- **Reminding.** Most parents of unmotivated children find reminding to be one of their frequent daily parenting behaviors. If the parents themselves have to be reminded to do something, they feel bad, complete the task and integrate the bad feeling, which then minimizes the possibility of having to be reminded again. Parents see the value of being reminded through periodic prompts. Unmotivated children see being reminded as being hassled. The "reminder" reminds them of something they are trying to deny and repress—their responsibilities and how they should feel if they shirk those responsibilities. The effect of reminding is, therefore, opposite the desired one. Mainly these kids get irritated at their parents, feel nagged and retreat into greater efforts at avoidance. It is better for a parent to limit reminders, but be consistent with consequences. When it's practical, if there are natural consequences for an underachiever not remembering, make him aware of them and then let the consequences take their course. Don't expend your energy telling Janie ten times to take her bike out of the driveway. After the second reminder, let the truck run over it! Seriously, take the bike and offer to let her earn it back. If Jimmy "forgets" what you told him about wiping his feet and he dirties the house - have Jimmy clean up before he can do the things that he wants to do. If a natural consequence is not handy, make up a consequence and consistently apply it.

- **Rewarding.** If someone completes a task, she should receive a reward. Right? Well, with the underachiever this approach becomes distorted. Either the underachiever minimizes any motivating effect of the reward or the reward becomes the goal to be pursued at almost any cost. Either she acts as if "It isn't worth it" and finds no motivation in the prospect of a reward or she'll pursue the prize regardless of what it takes to attain it. Promised a new skateboard if he completes all his home and school assignments in a given week, the underachieving student may plagiarize to get a paper done or bribe a younger sibling to do his chores. He seeks the reward regardless of the quality of his work, ignores values of honesty and disregards the value of the task. Internal rewards are not part of the thought process for him.

When a motivated person receives an external reward, it is an adjunct to an internal reward system that operates regardless of the external. The achieving individual's internal rewards are good feelings. Personal fulfillment through an internal process occurs first.

For the underachiever, the internal process is not functioning. Instead, the reward becomes the goal and eventually it becomes seen as an entitlement. Underachievers seem numb to the internal rewards that come from putting in good effort. If they do work toward rewards, they do as little as possible, try to manipulate others and will probably deny the truth—all in an attempt to acquire the rewards. At the extreme, they will demand the rewards and then be angry with others when they feel the rewards are being unjustly withheld. As mentioned earlier, another possibility is that these kids will denigrate the rewards, saying they aren't worth it or they didn't want them anyway.

Because underachievers are not well aware of their emotions, their internal reward systems don't operate well. Self-pride in effort does not surface for them and they can access only minimal initiative and self-motivation. They seem lazy even in consideration of compelling external rewards. For example, a good education holds promise for many more positive opportunities, but the underachiever seems indifferent to this fact.

■ **Punishing.** Punishments are as ineffective as rewards for the underachiever. With most children, external punishments have both the effect of teaching and of deterring. They learn and then anticipate. For underachievers, however, punishments have the effect of cementing these children's projections of their dissatisfactions onto others. In their minds, they become more "right." They feel they didn't do anything wrong; their parents are simply unjust, unreasonable, too tough and insensitive.

Underachievers' internal controls, brought about by awareness of emotions and values, have been repressed and denied. Because they do not readily anticipate consequences, their behaviors are ones of neglect toward tasks and indifference toward consequences. These children minimize any potential punishments as they might effect their behaviors.

The effect of punishments and potential punishments on underachievers is to further drive their emotional focus away from their own personal responsibilities. This allows them to project responsibility for their situations onto others and onto circumstances. Punishment, for the unmotivated, does not teach. It does not deter. The intent of punishment is distorted. It creates angry underachievers who still won't do anything for themselves. The inefficacy of punishment on an underachiever can be seen in Gregory.

Gregory's parents insisted that they were consistent in punishing him for neglecting his schoolwork. It was a system of "Do better or we'll take away—." (Fill in the blank.) They took away television privileges. Gregory decided he didn't like television anyway. They took away movie privileges. Gregory decided he didn't need to see movies. They took away video games, Internet access and the CD player. Gregory became the smiling kid in the empty room who still wouldn't do what his parents wanted! Gregory simply adjusted to each punishment without changing his behavior in the least.

What's a parent to do? Don't avoid punishment completely,

but make it brief and enlightening. Make it businesslike. You can generally accomplish this by requiring thought and discussion. For instance, have your child sit in a certain chair or go to a designated area of the house to give thought for fifteen minutes to these questions: *Why did you do that? How did you feel before you did that? How do you feel now? How do you think I feel? Why have I had you think about this? Did you learn anything? What should you have done differently?* Then have your child come to you to discuss his thoughts on these questions. If the discussion is insightful and honest, that is the end. If not, have the child repeat the process and talk with you again. If the child continues to resist, continue the process the next day a couple of times (at a time convenient to you). Do this until the child has an insightful discussion with you. With some children it is better to have them write down their thoughts instead of, or in addition to, discussing them. (Some kids have a hard time with oral expression, but communicate well when they write or draw.) Save the really big consequences like a weekend grounding for the truly large infractions.

Equipped with background on what doesn't work, you may now appreciate a story that hints at the kind of intervention that we at the Center have found effective. In the next few chapters, you'll see how kids like Brad—and, more importantly, how *your* underachiever—can reverse their fortunes with the help of your systematic guidance.

Brad: An Underachiever is Turned Around
Through Systematic Interventions

At the age of fourteen, Brad would refuse to flush the toilet. Mom would do it eventually. He would refuse to do his homework. Mom would do that eventually, too. His older sister would complain, "Why can't I just have a normal brother?"

Brad had been "a very easy baby," according to his mother, a middle school teacher, but became difficult as a toddler and stayed that way. A very bright kid, he had a mature ability to conceptualize and make correlations that surfaced early. One time when he was barely four, he pointed out to his mother that if the letters "t" and "p" on a stop sign were reversed, you could make the word "spot."

During the second grade, his mother took him to Johns Hopkins University to be tested for entrance into a program for gifted and talented students. He passed the test, but never attended the school, because more school was precisely what he did not want. Incidents like this were routine: Brad's teacher would assign twenty math problems. He would do five correctly and stop. He wouldn't even look at the other fifteen. He knew how to do all of them, but he was "bored"; he didn't want to work.

A very creative kid, he would play endlessly with trains and Legos. He would pretend to be a weatherman, showing where it would be rainy or sunny on the maps behind him. At the same time, he would refuse to focus on his homework, which often drove his mother to spend hours coaching and nagging him through homework at the kitchen table. A few times, his mother recalls, he got frustrated with this homework process and completed the work in a few minutes.

During the fifth grade, he re-qualified through Johns Hopkins for a gifted and talented program, but again his mother chose not to send him because his effort in school always fell short. She had him tutored instead. He thought that was great, because he'd play stupid and the tutor would do the work for him.

Pre-adolescence brought some new ideas to Brad—he was convinced he would be a rock star. He repeatedly made a point of telling his mom that she was never getting any of his millions, because she had no faith he would be a rock star. "You're gonna be sorry when I'm rich!" he told her. He continued to stay on the fringes at school, earning mostly C's until his mother discovered at a teachers' workshop that Brad's problem had a name and a system of intervention to go with it.

Brad deeply resented being told he had a developmental problem and he resisted intervention. To his parents, he projected his belief that the psychologist who developed these interventions was a con artist.

By the time he was sixteen, after more than a year of intervention, Brad had gradually transformed into the "normal kid" of his big sister's dreams. He got good grades, earned the privilege to get a driver's license and got a part-time job. At the age of seventeen, he announced to his parents that he wanted to open a Roth IRA. He invested his own money in the stock market and began taking business classes in preparation for college. Based on his SAT scores and most recent grades, Duquesne University accepted him.

Brad's mother cites the following two interventions as the hardest but the most rewarding.

1. **Let him fail and take responsibility for the consequences.** Previously, Brad's parents would "help" him with his work. Backing off was a radical change and one that Brad's teachers even criticized. His mother cautions: "When a teacher calls and says that he hasn't done his work and you say to her, 'I know that—there's nothing I can do,' then you better be prepared for the lecture on your job as a parent." The teachers didn't understand that Brad's parents had not given up, but rather they were engaging in consistent and systematic interventions. Chapter 19 covers the process of introducing teachers to the methods described in this book.

2. **Remind him daily through processing comments that his behavior reflects his choices.** Asking, "I wonder why you chose not to do that English paper?" then walking away was a big change for a mother who was accustomed to nagging her son. Processing comments receive a great deal of attention in the upcoming chapters.

CHAPTER TEN

GENERAL INTERVENTIONS

It's now time to set down the iced tea. What does that mean? Often, the families of unmotivated kids have avoided focusing on painful or troublesome areas of their lives for years. They arrive at states of balance that might be labeled "veranda relationships."

Veranda relationships evolve over time through much "taking for granted" and through becoming familiar—patterns that frequently lead to unproductive casualness in relationships. People don't normally try to create veranda relationships. They take shape as parties indirectly acquiesce without ever honestly discussing the difficulty that won't go away. It's as if two people who irritate each other are sitting on their veranda, each with a soothing glass of iced tea. The weather is balmy, birds chirp in the distance. Looking over to the side, they see children playing and neighbors waving pleasantly. On the surface, everything is just right.

If you have adjusted to veranda relationships in an effort to avoid confrontations and difficulties, you've reacted in a normal way, trying to keep relationships intact without overreacting to each and every disagreement. Nevertheless, if you want to help your underachiever, you will have to set down the iced tea. You may take offense at this and feel a bit resistive. Many families who have veranda relationships come to the Center and say, "We've worked hard to get to this relatively calm state with our child. Why are you asking us to change?"

I tell them that change is the only way their underachiever will get on the track of personal excellence.

The interventions discussed in this chapter and the next will require some changes in the family system in order to help your underachiever get in touch with his or her emotions. That can be unsettling for everyone, but the changes will hopefully lead to communication and resolution. They lead to real stress relief at home. Veranda relationships, on the other hand, are just part of the atmosphere in a quiet, but not necessarily happy, home.

In order for you to begin an intervention program, no matter what type of underachiever you have, you have to make interrelated shifts in your attitude and communication style and—with some overlap—changes in your household rules and how you enforce them. This chapter addresses the first set of general interventions. Chapter 11 is all about rules with value.

- **Be understanding, but not accepting, of underachieving behaviors**

You may have looked at your child once or twice and yelled, "I want you to change your habits starting right now—just do it!" He's stuck. He can't "just do it." You need to understand the complex situation he faces. That's part of resolving the problem and the reason why Part I of this book is devoted primarily to the theories related to underachievement. Understanding does not mean you change your tune and say, "Oh, well. If that's the way you want to be, that's okay." You don't want to shirk responsibility to guide your child. If you merely accept her underachieving state, then you accept her failure. Your triggers of action are going to be pressed and you're going to lash out indiscriminately or in some other way give the child a hard time. Being understanding will put the problem in context and alleviate some frustration. It allows you to develop a systematic approach to addressing the problem, to deal with it constructively, the way you would deal with a problem at work. Being understanding means pulling back from taking it personally, but still doing what is most effective for your underachiever.

It takes energy to *not* accept underachieving behavior. Some parents don't have it and they ooze into an accepting stance, comforting themselves with the mantra, "He'll grow out of it." Generally, the quicker you recognize the problem, the easier it is to resolve and the less entrenched the unwanted behavior will become. Understanding puts an obligation on you to research, read and learn about the problem, to talk with other parents and meet with teachers. You can't be "too busy."

■ **Be consistent**

Keep a notebook to help yourself with this suggestion. If you have either given consequences or observed certain situations with your child that require intervention or comment, write them down so that you can go back later and refer to them. This is helpful for positive references also. Sometimes we all need help to remember exactly what happened and what was said at an earlier time. While this may seem somewhat mechanical, it is especially useful in establishing and stabilizing consistency.

While the degree and type of response might vary from child to child, consistency for each individual is important. Consistency allows a child to learn and understand what is expected. It means having a firm base on which to develop and build. Lack of consistency is frustrating and confusing for children.

To enhance consistency, if there are two parents they need to act as a team. Take the time to confer on decisions. Always support each other in front of your child. Sure, individuals have differing child management and teaching perspectives, but parents need to be consistent *together* regardless of their marital state. Don't let your child split you as a parenting team, pitting one against the other. Iron out your parenting differences in private and support each other in front of your child.

Children need certainty over time and over situations so they know that when a particular situation comes up, particular outcomes are going to happen. A bulb lights up: *When this happens, here are the limits. Here are the boundaries. This is what I should do.* Then children can begin to make useful generalizations: If they aren't allowed to stay at Bowl-by-the-Sea after 9 o'clock, they probably aren't allowed to stay at Bowl-by-the-Bay after 9 o'clock, either.

- **Become dispassionate in dealing with your child**

    Act and react without strong displays of emotion. You are not alone if your first reaction to this is either, "I can't—he goes out of his way to make me angry!" or "But I care about her—how can I not show my feelings?"

    Underachieving children, because of the frustrations they cause, often create emotionally charged confrontations, many times over the most insignificant occurrences. These blow-ups drain families, driving parents close to the edge sometimes. Have you ever been unable to go to sleep because of worry? One of the necessities is for parents to remain—or become—dispassionate.

    Being dispassionate does not mean you are uninvolved or somehow shortchanging your child by repressing the full power of your emotions. Instead, it means you express involvement in a way that can help him. You continue to provide the guidance and structure that an underachiever needs, but you do it without displays of strong emotions.

Elements of the dispassionate approach

1. A non-excited tone of voice

2. Decrease in volume of the discussion-using a quiet tone of voice

3. Avoiding arguments and excessive reasoning that can become never ending

4. Avoiding personal attack

5. Not trying to have the last word

How many times have you become upset over bad grades when it's your child who should be upset? He thinks, *I don't need to get upset. Mom and Dad are already doing it for me.* When you "steal" your child's emotions like that, you encourage him to focus on your emotions and ignore his own. He also feels that you will take the responsibility along with the emotions. The result is that he, in the heat of your outburst, acts indifferent or even offended. His appropriate emotions have been stolen. He acts as if he doesn't care.

Similarly, if your underachieving student does well, it is not helpful if you get too excited prior to your child experiencing and expressing her emotions about the success. After your child has expressed herself regarding the situation, then share your feelings about it. Even then, keep the emotional level low. Convey your emotions through dispassionate speech, not through heightened actions or intensity. If your child chooses not to express her feelings, use processing comments such as, "I wonder how you feel about—"

At this point, you may be asking, "How in the world am I going to pull this off?" Start by monitoring your reactions.

Monitor your reactions in terms of both their level of emotionality and their intensity of presence. To clarify, emotionality can be both the use of words that incite and the volume of that expression. Intensity of presence is best described as an attitude or aura you project. For instance, when your children walk into the room and your intensity is high, they *know* that you are angry, upset and so on. You don't have to say or do anything.

You can monitor your reactions by rating each one. While the rating is somewhat arbitrary, you are setting up your own baseline. It becomes an important tool in finding the patterns of *your* emotionality and intensity.

- After you've experienced a particular event, rate your emotionality and intensity on a scale from one to ten, with one being "not at all" and ten being "the most."
- Do these ratings at the very end of the day for several days to establish your baseline, then do them again periodically to establish an awareness of your patterns. Try to lower your emo-

tionality and intensity in the situations that trigger high response. Eliminating your feelings is not your goal; being dispassionate is. Start with bringing the tens down to nines at first. Then bringing the nines to eights and so on. Keep track to know the results of any efforts you are making to reduce your emotionality and intensity.

- Keep track of what circumstances and types of circumstances triggered a particular level. You may find it helpful to use the format suggested by Appendix D, the "Emotion Situation Gram."

- Over time, try to bring the levels down. Don't burden yourself with unrealistic expectations of what you will accomplish. If the intensity of your emotions hits ten when your child tells you late Sunday night he didn't do his weekend homework, be happy if you bring it down to a nine by Tuesday, when he tells you he didn't do Monday's homework. And when he tells you the same thing the following Tuesday, consider you've made great progress if you only hit a six.

Re-engage this rating periodically to keep an awareness of the tendency of underachievers to transfer their emotions to their parents. It is difficult for both underachievers and those around them to change these ingrained patterns of transferring emotions. This is especially true if these patterns have been present for a while. The idea is not to become unconcerned—continue to "parent." Set rules, expectations and consequences, but do it with lessened intensity and emotion.

Underachievers begin to change when they understand that other people will not assume their emotional responsibilities. You have not chosen to exhibit the disappointing or disruptive behavior so don't assume the emotions of someone who has. It is your child's choice—a bad choice, but nonetheless a choice. Being dispassionate facilitates the child's becoming aware of his or her own feelings. You do not want to steal the child's emotion. (Yes, this has been stated already, but it is important enough to repeat.) The same is true when the child does well. First, explore how he feels about the success: "I wonder how you feel." Don't press for a response. Then tell your child how you feel in a dispassionate way: "I'm pleased. You did very well." Let the child reflect on his or her feelings.

This sequence is not natural. You'll have to practice it, but the subtleties are important. Don't expect immediate results. These things take time, but keep at it. As an aside, convincing parents that they must adopt a dispassionate approach and helping them to achieve it is a very challenging task for a therapist.

■ **Use withholds.**

Withholds substitute effectively for punishment. The withhold sequence is as follows:

- The child is inappropriate (e.g., disrespectful to a parent, refuses to do a requested task, misses a curfew, etc.).
- The parent dispassionately points out that that behavior or attitude is unacceptable and states "I'll get back to you on that; there will be a consequence."
- Some time over the next few weeks—do not do withholds right away—the child asks for something (permission, access, approval, money and so forth).
- The parent, after giving it some thought, answers with something like, "No, because last Monday you were rude to your mom. That's unacceptable." or "No, because three weeks ago when I said I needed help on that lawn project you disappeared. That's unacceptable." Jog your child's memory of the incident and why you are doing a withhold. "I told you at the time that was unacceptable and that I would get back to you. Now I am."

Deliver the decision in a very businesslike tone. At first, the child will be angry and rail against the injustice of your "withhold." If the child persists in being demanding, calmly reiterate, "That's unacceptable. Please stop. I'll get back to you about this." Eventually, the child will *anticipate* the consequences of his behaviors and attitudes. This could take a few times, but the practice will lead to fewer confrontations, improved behavior and reduced family stress.

Withholds should not necessarily be in direct proportion to the child's indiscretion. They can be a bit smaller or larger, or even once or a few times for that specific incident. ("This is your first consequence for that incident.") It is best that you do not establish a predictable pattern. You want your child to be kept off guard until he graduates to consistently more motivated behavior.

One suggestion is to keep a private card on which you write your child's indiscretions so you don't forget to "withhold." Don't forget to get back to him. You must follow through.

Withholds do work, but why? They work because when underachievers ask for something, they are vulnerable. By their asking, they are undeniably stating they want something. Their guard is down and their defenses momentarily withdrawn. Contrast this with a punishment moment. When you tell your child, he can't use the Internet for the weekend or he can't watch television because he was indiscreet, what does he do? Usually, he adjusts, shows a little irritation, shrugs and says, "So what. I didn't want to anyway." Inside he is thinking that you are mean, that there is injustice and that he will "show you" eventually...somehow. He does not accept blame for his indiscretion and does not change his behavior. Some kids may actually think, "It's worth it." In contrast, withholds build appropriate anticipatory anxiety and lead to behavior and attitudinal change.

- **Unhook the projection**

For months or maybe years, your underachiever has manipulated you by directing the focus away from himself and the real problems. This is *not* necessarily a conscious and deliberate act. This is projection.

Projection is a defense mechanism. It shifts blame or excuses for inappropriate behavior to other individuals or objects. Rather than accepting personal responsibility and exploring what is really going on, underachievers will quickly project their feelings. They will project on to people, on to things, on to situations. Unhooking the projection means focusing attention back to the projecting individual to get him to reflect on his feelings and the underlying reasons for the behavior. You focus the attention back to the child and the real issues by using *processing responses* to your child's projections.

In unhooking the projection, you should not defend or even acknowledge the projected item. The response to projection should be designed to make your child think about his true feelings, rather than reason with him.

Contrast the responses below that you would normally say with the recommended, or processing, responses. Notice the natural inclination to go out of your way to counter your child's comment with a "logical" response.

Child's Comment:	"School is boring."
Projected Item:	School
Typical Response:	"School is wonderful! You learn things you'll need for your job. You have that great library and gym. You do interesting experiments in the lab. You should love it."
Recommended Response:	"You seem to have difficulty getting involved."

Child's Comment:	"Geometry is irrelevant."
Projected Item:	Geometry
Typical Response:	"Knowing geometry really helps if you're planning a big garden. Or some day, you might want to design your own house and you'll need to know angles and distances." (At this point, your bright underachiever is thinking, *Isn't that why people hire landscapers and architects?*)
Recommended Response:	"Concentrating is difficult when you have doubts about yourself."

Child's Comment:	"The teacher can't teach."
Projected Item:	Teacher
Typical Response:	"Your teacher is a wonderful person. She's had a lot of education. Your cousin, Janie, had her last year and she did really well in school."
Recommended Response:	"It's hard to learn if you're feeling anxious or inadequate."

Think about the target of your child's comment and do not defend it. You could go to great lengths to justify your defense. Don't do it. The defense is not the point. Focus on the underlying problem. Also, try not to use any of the words that he is using, such as "boring" or "irrelevant." Responses should try to help your child expand his "feelings vocabulary," as well as gain insight.

When unhooking the projection, you must remain calm and matter-of-fact. Being dispassionate is important to helping your child look inward for answers. If you become emotional, you focus attention on yourself, not on your child's feelings. If you are having a difficult time thinking of a response, repeat one you used earlier or say something like "I just wonder," or "You seem—," and then walk away. Leaving the conversation in mid-stream is acceptable once you have made a processing response. Remember, you are not trying to justify anything. You are trying to trigger a thinking process in your child so he understands exactly *what* he feels.

Appendix E contains scenarios to help you explore ways of unhooking the projections with your child. Notice that no matter what the subject of the scenario is, the parent neither takes the child's comment personally nor tries to indict the child for his comment or behavior. You don't defend the projected item. You don't even discuss it. Instead you make a comment dispassionately about the real issues that are affecting the child.

- **Use processing comments**
  The use of processing comments is a subtle way to get your child

to think. Like the processing responses used when unhooking the projection, processing comments are those that will cause individuals to think about their emotions and their actions. Consistent use of them will help you reign in your emotions and move toward dispassionate responses to your child.

Throughout this book, you have seen several of these formulaic phrases: *"I wonder why—"*

"I wonder how you feel about—."

"You seem—"

"You appear—"

"That's interesting that you choose to—"

Start your comment with these phrases, then add emotion words or description of actions: "I wonder why you choose to take the test unprepared" or "You seem happy." If you say, "You seem happy," you're inviting a response, but not forcing it. It really doesn't matter if your observation is correct or not. Processing comments are catalysts. They prime your child to think about his emotions and actions in a gentle non-interrogating manner.

Make the comment matter-of-factly and **walk away**. Don't expect a reply. If your child wants to talk further, fine, and if not, don't try to elicit a response. The processing comments offer an opportunity for expression, but they don't make it a requirement. Processing comments do not have to be long or require an extended conversation.

Here is how an exchange might play out: You say, "You seem confused today" and walk away. Your child follows after you: "What do you mean I seem confused?" You then point something out. You might say, "Well, you're a junior in high school now. You don't seem to ever want to do any homework, yet you expect to go to college." Then you walk away again.

In another case, you might walk by your child as she watches television and say, "You seem happy." She might question, "What makes you say that?" You answer casually, "Oh, I just got that impression from your look. Did I interpret it wrong?" Then again, maybe she won't respond at all, but she's thinking, *Yes, I am happy* or *No, I'm not happy at all. Why am I giving that impression?* Whatever the response, you want to start a thought process that will help your child *feel*.

Here is another example of a processing comment. Your child does not turn in a class project when everyone else does. You say, "You didn't turn in your project. I wonder why you made that choice." If your usual rule is to give a consequence for certain behaviors, do so—dispassionately—as you make the processing comment. "It seems that you want a consequence for that. I wonder why you made that choice." In a case like this, don't be baited. Don't let him try to justify the inappropriate behavior or tell you he "didn't know." You can repeatedly use the phrase "You knew there would be consequences. It was your choice."

Sometimes there may be no external responses to your processing comments. Your child may say nothing. She may roll her eyes and appear disinterested. Don't give up. Don't give in to her resistance or her fears. The true goal is to activate her thinking process about how she really feels. If you persist, over time she will begin to think about what you are saying and more importantly, what she is thinking and feeling.

Processing comments can be used in all types of situations, positive and negative. Gradually work processing comments into your exchanges. Start with a couple each week to get comfortable and work up to frequent use.

■ Don't interrogate—share

Many parents who come to the Center proudly acknowledge that every day when their children come home from school, they ask, "How was your day?" *Don't do that.* The outcome is so predictable. Especially as they enter their teen years, kids say, "Fine." You say, "What happened?" "Nothing." You respond, "What do you mean 'nothing'?" and suddenly the conversation you intended has been transformed into an interrogation. This type of conversation occurred on a daily basis between Tony, a high school student, and his mother.

Tony's mom admitted that the first thing out of her mouth when her teenaged son came through the door after school was always,

"How was school today?" Tony's standard answer was, "Good." Then the exchange went like this—time after time until she got so frustrated, she knew she had to take a different approach:

"So what did you do?"

"The usual."

"What do you mean?"

"Stuff. You know."

"No, I don't know. What did you do today?"

"Nothing much."

"Have any homework?"

"Nope."

"Tony, I can see you have books in your backpack. Are you sure you don't have any homework?"

"I just told you I didn't. Stop buggin' me."

Occasionally, she would ask how he did on a test or what grade he got on a project. He'd offer a monosyllabic "fine" or "great." Then Mom would probe further: "Are you sure?" Tony's next answer was a trigger for high anxiety: "Sure I'm sure. Geez, Mom, don't worry so much."

Almost invariably, he had done poorly on the test or failed to even turn the project in on the day it was due. Tony wasn't lying to his mother, though. The constant interrogation put him on "automatic" with his denials. He didn't even think about the answers he gave to the questions she asked him day after day.

It's much better to relate anecdotes or make processing comments than to interrogate your kids. Don't ask, "How was your day?" If you mention something that happened during your day, you invite a response. Your anecdote doesn't have to be anything dramatic. Maybe you saw a classic car that reminded you of your grandfather. Maybe an old friend called you or you saw a rainbow. The important thing is that you share something with your child and talk about how you felt about it. Then pause, walk away and continue whatever you had been doing. Don't act like you expect an answer. Kids may actually discount your anecdote and act detached and unimpressed. Don't be deterred. The idea behind your comments and brief sharing is to encourage your child to eventually talk with you because he *wants* to and because he feels that you will be open to discussion.

When you share your thoughts, instead of picking up on the fact that you're anxious about how his day went, your child can focus on what you say. You act nonchalantly to bring him out, to encourage him to talk with you. It's all part of the process of getting an underachiever in touch with his emotions so he starts using his emotions constructively.

When you ask questions in reaction to your anxiety, you cut off any activating tension that your child might experience from wanting to tell you something. If your child is experiencing anxiety—and that should activate her into talking with you about something—you don't want to "steal" that tension from her. Your interrogation takes away from the anxiety that would have activated her to speak. Also, your child will most likely interpret your questions as being "nosy," "bugging" or "nagging."

Kids commonly have little to say the first time they come to the Center. After an initial "Hi," the student may sit in a chair for many minutes without talking. Sometimes the therapist will purposefully not talk either. As the student's anxiety grows, she might break the silence. The youngster might start with "Aren't you going to say something?" or "What do you want me to say?" They're surprised—and eventually responsive—when the therapist says simply, "You seem to want to talk to me. I wonder if you have something to say?"

The key is to make your comments, then step away or silently continue what you were doing without expecting an answer. It is important that the student's internal anxiety is allowed to grow. If your child chooses to follow after you and talk, then it's an opportunity to engage in discussion about various topics. It is important to follow the child's lead with these potential conversations. Stick mainly to those topics that your child provides and remember to skip the interrogation. As an important follow-through, when your child does talk with you, **give him your undivided attention.** Put down whatever else you are doing. Show that you really are interested in him.

- **Don't lecture—react**

As the last chapter indicated, lecturing is analogous to yelling English to a non-English speaker in an effort to get him to understand you. What constitutes a lecture? If you tell your child something more than twice, it's a lecture. Lecturing focuses the attention on you as a nagging person instead of on the topic of the lecture. Anecdotes often do a better job of engaging a child in conversation about an issue.

As another alternative, try reacting. In most instances, your child knows and remembers what you say. So respond appropriately, even if your child insists, "I didn't know!" React with consistency and authority. That may mean giving an unpleasant consequence for actions. So be it. Control your impulses so that you get over any strong desire to intellectually inform your child—again and again—about reality.

- **Use micro-recognition**

Micro-recognition is recognizing small, seemingly unimportant things about people or their behaviors, rather than overlooking these things as insignificant or as something expected.

Sometimes with an underachiever it seems difficult to find anything to comment on positively, because you are so upset and frustrated. Take a step back and remind yourself that your kid is basically a *good* kid. Focus on some of the little things that support that fact. Among the several benefits to your child, she'll get a subtle message that life comprises many small events and accomplishments, not just spectacular ones. Amidst the turmoil of adolescence, she is doing some things right.

Maybe she was helpful to a neighbor last week. Wait for a while— a week or more. (Write it privately in a ledger or on a calendar if you need help remembering.) After some time has passed, tell your child that you noticed her kindness and state how much you liked the action, how much you were impressed, how mature the response was to the neighbor's need. Don't gush, but do make the point.

Some psychologists say that you should reinforce positive behavior immediately, but they don't address the need to revisit the child's accomplishment. Our experience is that recognition at the time has value, but recognition delayed beyond the event has a more powerful effect. This delay allows for everyone's emotionality and intensity to subside. It also means *you* remembered over time; it was important to you. Underachievers don't expect you to remember, because they generally don't. So, if you tell your child that you noticed that he was helpful or creative or whatever, and you do it some time after the actual event happened, that carries more power than only giving the recognition right at the time of the event.

This doesn't mean you should never reinforce at the time. Thank him at the time if the situation calls for it, but in addition, wait a few days and then mention it again. This builds self-esteem, reinforces values and instills pride. It shows your child that his behavior is important to you over time.

Sometimes responsible parents feel that there is very little positive to say to their unmotivated and underachieving child. Look hard. There are many things to reinforce. Most underachievers have pleasant personalities. They usually are not underachievers in *everything* they do or they are intermittent in their underachievement. There is usually something that they do well or they are kind about. Even if you feel it is a struggle, find something to use for periodic micro-recognition. "Thank you for taking those books to the library for me last week. It saved me time and a trip." "I noticed you helped Johnny with his bicycle last week. That was really good of you." Don't go overboard and make a big deal of every good deed and don't say something that isn't true. However, a few times a week, give that micro-recognition.

Sincerity and attention to details are very important in giving micro-recognition. One of my colleagues made the mistake of complimenting a young man on *his choice* of sweater. Unfortunately, it was part of his Catholic school's uniform.

- **Focus on effort**

Help your child develop the attitude that effort is enjoyment. This is a concept that is difficult to live and relay. If you have had a difficult day, week or year, you may not feel positive. You may wish that you did not have to work as hard. Some discontent may have crept into your life. Nevertheless, you need to be a strong role model for your kids in making a consistent effort to do well and letting them see how good you feel about putting in a day's work. Show your effort; show your pride in effort. Focus your attention on *effort*, not necessarily results. If the effort was good, even if the results were less than hoped for, the effort provided a learning experience, which in itself is worthwhile. Eventually, good effort and learning from experiences—and using that new knowledge—will provide positive results. Stress to your child the idea, "nothing ventured, nothing gained."

■ **Avoid cynicism**

Avoid or minimize using cynicism in front of your child. Shelve the negative thinking and expressions. Save your sarcastic comments for when you are with other adults. Try to have your child see you reacting productively to challenges, not observe you finding your job, household chores or volunteer work to be a pain in the butt.

So many outcomes in life are related to attitude. Mature individuals tend to use cynicism periodically to reduce stress, but then they get back to work and do what needs to be done. Unmotivated individuals will observe a person who is being cynical and interpret the cynicism as an acceptable lifestyle. They will use it to further disengage themselves from constructive action.

You don't have to be a Pollyanna, but don't be a Scrooge. Be realistic as the situation calls for it, but try to put a positive spin on situations. When situations are less than desired, look for ways to improve them. Don't focus on inadequacies. See life as challenges to be met and let your child learn from your example. You'll all be better for it.

■ **Prepare for anger**

Be prepared for your child to be angry with you occasionally, because he will be. This is not to suggest that you should allow disrespect, but it is important that you understand that part of the growth process is developing a sense of self, a sense of being different from others. Many times, as your child is frustrated in this process of personal development, he will project his emotions onto others. This is a reflection of his personal inadequacy and uncertainty. He will also question your authority, rules and fairness. Being prepared for and anticipating his challenges will lower the emotionalism of your response and give you more resolve—if you are doing something you need to do, then so what if the boy gets angry? This strategy reinforces consistency in your child's life. It helps neutralize his anger, because he knows what to expect.

An exercise like this one helps some parents put things into perspective. You can do this on your way home from work. Imagine your house has burned to the ground and you've lost everything. Your family is sitting on the curb outside in tattered clothes sadly watching the smoldering embers. Then when you get home and see the house is still there and your family is alive and well, you might be a little less emotional when your kid angrily declares he's getting his head tattooed.

During trying times, you may sorely miss the agreeable little boy (or girl) you knew years ago. Unfortunately, parents of teenagers often feel this way. With underachievers, this stress can be even more intense because underachievers are immersed in their developmental confusions rather than smoothly moving forward to maturity. Their frustration levels are higher than normal. Be prepared for outbursts and develop strategies for handling this stress. It is important to have contingency plans for when things get intense and emotional. Learn how to call for a cooling-off period before things get out of control. Practice personal stress management. (See Chapter 18 for specific suggestions.) It's easier said than done, but try not to overreact to an underachiever's outbursts.

■ Encourage negotiation and compromise

As your child becomes more age appropriate in her maturity and in making decisions, you should begin trying to teach her to negotiate and compromise in areas that have flexibility. This will help her learn useful skills, and your relationship with her will improve. She'll appreciate the fact that you have some flexibility in your thinking and that you don't have to be "right" all the time.

Most adults don't realize how automatically they use the important interpersonal skills of negotiation and compromise. They usually have had years of experience to hone them, with much trial and error. The underachiever tends to avoid the development of these skills, though, because they involve internal control of impulse ("I'm right!"), listening to others and the appreciation that other people may have worthwhile perspectives different from theirs. Underachievers gradually find themselves unable to interact productively, in general because they have not been guided in the development of negotiation and compromise.

For most underachievers, the summer presents a time when some of the pressure for performance is off—both for the children and the parents. Without the tension and frustrations of the school year, there may be a return to a reasonable level of family harmony. Use the summer to begin a family exercise in negotiation and compromise.

During the summer or during the winter holidays, identify at least one issue for negotiation and compromise, such as where to go for vacation or how many hours to devote to a part-time job. Take this issue to resolution by allowing all concerned to become involved in the process. It may take several meetings, but do meet. Write down everyone's perspectives, the pros and cons and ask how each person would like to see the situation resolved. Play "what if" with the responses. Reach a conclusion that is satisfactory to the majority, giving reasons why this is the best alternative. It is very important to make this a somewhat structured (and seemingly artificial) exercise. Doing so lets everyone learn the steps that, over time and practice, will become automatic.

And how might this exercise help with routine events later on? Suppose you tell your fifteen-year-old to wash the dishes and he puts up a fight. You could repeat the order, but he would perceive your unbending will as an excuse to underachieve. Maybe he would wash the dishes, but leave unwashed pots. Instead, when he balks at washing the dishes, ask him if he has a specific reason for not wanting to do it at that moment. He might say he wants to participate in an online chat with some friends. After that, he wants to watch a couple of shows on television. You can then counter with the suggestion that he tape one or both of the shows. As long as the dishes and pots are washed by 9:00 P.M., how he spends the rest of his time is up to him.

Of course, negotiation and compromise do not always work and are not always appropriate, but when they can be used positively the effects are beneficial for everyone. The key to using them wisely is to have familiarity with the concepts and to consider them whenever a potential conflict arises. Learning to use negotiation and compromise is not automatic. Successful use takes training, practice and patience.

Sometimes, as in Tim's case, breakthroughs come quickly.

When Tim was fifteen, all he wanted to do was skate. His early teenage years centered on practicing tricks at the skate park and on the street. Because he wanted to stay in that world, his friends were younger than he was. Other kids in high school had already moved on in their interests. They looked forward to getting a car, not another pair of Rollerblades. Tim's focus on skating to the exclusion of everything else created huge tensions at home. Tim fought with his dad frequently.

The breakthrough that came quickly in the intervention program was that Tim saw the value of negotiation and compromise. He readily understood that making demands and refusing to do anything his parents wanted caused fights, but that honest negotiation and compromise about school work and chores helped him gain privileges and independence.

■ **Remember that kids are not little adults**

Kids are kids. They are not little adults. This concept is sometimes difficult to keep in mind if they have an advanced verbal ability or are precocious in certain areas, but it's important. Your son or daughter is still a child—a child with an unresolved developmental circumstance. He will make mistakes. He has a lot to learn. In general, children don't cope like mature individuals do. They are still developing their values, personalities and viewpoints. Don't overreact to your child when she makes mistakes. Explain reasons. Give examples. State alternatives. You are teaching. Guide with a gentle touch. Don't get rid of expectations, but make sure expectations are appropriate for his or her age.

Every day, nine-year-old Carolyn went in her starched dress to a private international school in Washington, D.C. Her family brought her into contact with sophisticated social circumstances; basically, she hung out with adults. Carolyn could talk about her first class world travel on cruise ships and airplanes and other topics that engaged adults.

When she came to the Center, she always brought Barbie dolls with her. She liked to play with the small dolls and had full-blown childlike fantasies involving them. On the phone, I would not have been able to tell she was nine, but the minute she came into the room, she was every bit a little girl.

General Interventions: Attitude and Communication

1. Be Understanding, but Not Accepting
2. Be Consistent
3. Be Dispassionate
4. Unhook the Projection
5. Use Processing Comments
6. Don't Interrogate—Share
7. Don't Lecture—React
8. Use Micro-Recognition
9. Focus on Effort
10. Avoid Cynicism
11. Prepare for Anger
12. Encourage Negotiation and Compromise
13. Remember that Kids Are Not Little Adults

Change Markers

How will you know when your actions are working? Look for + and – changes in these categories:

Attitude
Willingness to negotiate and compromise
Concern for others
Appropriateness and Balance
Defensiveness
Admission Of Personal Responsibi lity

Behavior
Initiative to do
Initiative to communicate

Mood
Less rigidity/more range
Modulated appropriately
Optimism

CHAPTER ELEVEN

GENERAL INTERVENTIONS: RULES WITH VALUE

Great dancers, doctors, engineers—accomplished people in every field—will readily admit that mastering the fundamentals gave them a foundation for achievement. To a great extent, their mastery reflects an ability to follow rules that support efficiency, consistency, precision and other elements of excellence.

"Rule" has become a dirty, four-letter word to some people, but the ability to follow rules with value is key to mature behavior and high performance throughout life. This chapter, therefore, isn't about nit-picking parental mandates and petty regulations. It addresses the kind of rules within a household that guide an underachiever toward personal responsibility and personal excellence. These rules support the development of an individual who can discriminate between appropriate, responsible behavior and irrational, destructive (including self-destructive) behavior, then act accordingly.

The importance of creating an environment that nurtures personal responsibility cannot be overstated here. Unfortunately, by doing that in your home you are, in a sense, bucking the system. American society appears to be afflicted with a disease that undermines personal responsibility—a side effect is that it nurtures underachievement. It's all too common to hear phrases like these: "I can't do that because they—" "If only they would...then I could—" "They didn't...that's why I'm not—" "What's going on here? Where are the self-determined statements such as "I can," "I'll try, in spite of—" and "I'll find a way to get it done?"

What we often see is an unfortunate focus on the negative, both in regard to the circumstances and to the potential of an individual. By maintaining this negative, blaming view, a person can readily shirk personal responsibility, withdraw from active resolution of situations and assume the role of the victim. By having this view, the negative outcome occurs without the individual assuming personal responsibility for it.

From a historical review of news, it is apparent that a societal shift is occurring. A question does remain whether or not the media accurately reflect society or if they influence it, or both. (We could be influencing society right now!) Nonetheless, this shift in values minimizes the personal contributions to situations and to the resolution of situations. It supports and stresses the existence of the responsibility of institutions such as government and schools. They are supposed to make things right. Conversely, it's their fault if things go wrong. The individual's choices and decisions are minimized as relevant factors.

While we need to work toward eliminating injustice—political, racial, economic, religious—to assume that injustice always disables and makes accomplishments impossible for the "victim" only increases the success of the injustice. Personal responsibility should be a core value. While there are factors like injustice that impinge on our ability to effect change in our situation and in society, personal effectiveness is minimized if personal responsibility is not at the core of our beliefs. Personal effort needs to increase in the face of injustice, real or perceived.

There are two sides to assuming personal responsibility. While on one side we suffer (and hopefully learn from our experience) when we are ineffective, on the other we gain in feelings of personal worth when we have success. The no-excuses lifestyle leads to continuing challenge, excitement and personal growth. The alternative of blaming others leads to mostly negative outcomes, lowered personal effectiveness and distortion of self-esteem.

To help your underachiever or anyone else in your life gain the appropriate sense of responsibility, the first step is to begin to relate personal situations that help the child see that personal responsibility is the preferred choice—no matter how difficult a choice it is. With this mind-set, you do things that are right, even if you don't have to. For example, if your car brushes against another one and scrapes paint off the fender and no one else in the parking lot sees you do it, you still leave a note with your phone number on the damaged car.

Is there a "rule" that says you're supposed to do that? Technically, there probably is, but that isn't what motivates you to leave the note. The "rule" is your internal sense of what's right. It's something you cultivated over time because someone bothered to teach you the difference between acceptable (and commendable) and unacceptable (and condemnable) behavior. Someone bothered to establish rules in your life that were meaningful and durable.

An appreciation of a developmental continuum that leads eventually to assuming personal responsibility must be stressed with your child. A young child is less able in his emotional development to assume as great an amount of personal responsibility as an adult. Authority figures must be cautious that they don't overdo it: Too much pressure to achieve high expectations too soon—including rules that don't make sense for the child at that time—can engender a manipulative perfectionist or a withdrawn and doubting person. Emphasize your can-do attitude with stories that display growth over time and situations. You could talk about your own childhood inadequacies, challenges and successes and move forward from there. Children, as well as adults who are having difficulty accepting responsibility, need to understand that a growth continuum exists in which there is gradual growth replete with mistakes and learning.

Next, model the no-excuses lifestyle. It is important to discuss the assumption of responsibility and how, even as a mature adult, this is not always easy and not always carried out to perfection. Everyone sometimes needs to lessen pressures with rationalizations. A child needs to see how this is not hypocritical, but realistic and human. The aim is to help your child see that while effort is the broad goal, realistically, each one of us must find the level of "no-excuse" that is most productive for us. Temporary rationalizations and relieving pressure is okay, but then appropriate actions to get the job done should follow. A drive toward goals is important.

Finally, give thought to where upon the continuum of personal responsibility your child falls and under which circumstances. This must also be related to other people. You can best do this through discussions about situational "gray areas," the surrounding controversies and the need for individuals to have opinions and options leading to personal standards. Help your child ponder the apparent discrepancies between what some political leaders say and what they do, for example.

The goal of the no-excuse lifestyle isn't perfection, but rather the ability of a mature, responsible person to exercise control in his or her life. A person who attains that goal lives the belief that life is what you make it. That person is an achiever. That person's attitude is saturated with motivation.

With that goal in mind, consider the utility of these interventions focused on rules with value.

- **Facilitate planning ("The Twenty-four Hour Rule")**

Sometimes you just don't have much energy after a long day. Sometimes your children take advantage of that, don't they? Suppose you just got home from work. No sooner do you step through the door when the phone rings. As you answer it, your daughter Julie approaches you to ask if she can go out with her friends, who happen to be waiting outside on the steps. You remember that you talked with your spouse about limits for Julie, but right now you are tired, preoccupied with the phone call and don't remember the details of the conversation. You remember something about Julie staying home after school to do homework, but she keeps pressing to join her friends. You're tired. You don't want the hassle. You say, "Okay," and Julie leaves with her friends. Only later, when things have calmed down, does your spouse remind you that you previously agreed to put more limits on your daughter. What next? The two of you have an unpleasant conversation about not supporting your mutual decisions. You get angry with Julie for pressing you. The message that Julie remembers is that the most effective time and way to influence you is when you are rushed, preoccupied and tired.

On the flip side, has your child ever come to you with a request and you put her off? You might say, "Let me talk it over with your father and

I'll get back to you," then forget to give her an answer. The next thing you know, time has elapsed and she needs an answer immediately or she feels you don't care about her interests.

You can avoid these messes and establish more consistency in your parenting with the Twenty-four Hour Rule. You can use any amount of time that you want—it doesn't have to be twenty-four hours. It can be one hour, twelve hours or whatever is appropriate for your situation. For many people, though, twenty-four hours works well. Whatever time period you choose, stick with it and apply it to all your kids so everyone will know the rule. (Note to managers: It also works well with employees.)

The rule involves letting your children know that all requests must be considered in advance. The "twenty-four hours" is the time you have to decide the answer. If the request has not been presented in advance, then your child should presume the answer is no. Of course, you reserve the parental option to say yes at the time of the request, but it is an option you should use sparingly and only when it's a special circumstance. Otherwise, the automatic answer is no. There is no discussion entertained at the time of the request and no pressure to negotiate unless you feel like it. Everything is done on your schedule. After the period of consideration, the answer may still be no, but at least you've had time to think about it. Your children will soon learn that without the period of consideration the answer will always be no, so to get a yes, sometimes they have to look ahead.

This rule is great for helping your child learn to plan, as well as for minimizing any anxiety and guilt you feel from being pressured. Tell your child not to bother to ask for an exception to this rule (all right, good luck with that!).

Part of the issue around this rule is that many unmotivated individuals are routinely manipulative. They are sophisticated in their abilities to get what they want from parents. If you stick with the rule, it is very helpful in cutting down on manipulation.

Parents, for heaven's sake, don't dismiss this rule as impossible to implement because "today's kids" just don't plan. Forget "today's kids." You are trying to raise one of tomorrow's adults.

A more casual way to facilitate planning than the Twenty-four Hour Rule simply involves exchanging visions for the future with your child. Every so often, as part of a family conversation, talk about what you hope happens in five years or ten years or when you're really old. What does your child see for himself down the road? At first, he might say nothing more than, "I want to graduate from high school and move out of here." Then again, he might offer a vague and dreamlike vision of being rich and famous. As these conversations continue, hopefully he'll absorb the fact that a plan holds inspiration and direction without limiting freedom or possibilities. It's a living document, not a set of dictates written in stone.

- **Establish general rules that reflect values**

One mother expressed the thought that she saw her role of parent as that of a fence-builder. After "building a fence" around her infant, she gradually extended its boundaries over the years to allow him safe limits for movement, growth and exploration. Ultimately, she hoped, she could let go and he would build his own fence of self-motivated rules. This metaphor was colored by her struggle with her teenager and her confusion as to where the fence was. At times, she felt concrete resolution in her limits, at other times, a lack of boundaries. This struggle with rules and roles is a universal phenomenon. This is a particularly crucial issue for underachievers who have yet to internalize the boundaries and discipline needed for independent achievement.

It is especially important to provide consistent boundaries for your child. Remember, you should be friendly to your kids, but not their friend. Be open and available, but for their developmental good, you must be an authority figure for them.

Most kids, especially teenagers, experience confusion about myriad issues, including their senses of limits and values. If they have parents who are similarly confused or are unwilling to take on the appropriate authority roles, this leaves the kids adrift. It makes the transformation from child to adult that much more difficult for them. Even though they might complain at such consistency, young people actually prefer it. It is good for them to have stability, predictability and consistency. This reinforces what is appropriate. They know they can come to you, an authority figure, for straight talk. This helps them to offset some of the other confusions they experience as they struggle to grow up. It helps them resist negative peer pressure and other underachieving influences. When it comes to outside pressures, even if the child knows something is wrong and doesn't want to do it, it is so much easier for her to tell others: "I can't. My parents won't let me." Be reasonable, but be consistent with rules.

Build rules that are appropriate for your family based on your values. As a first step, you need to revisit your values and tell your kids why they are important. Then, examine rules you do have in your house in light of your values and revise them as necessary. Consciously draw the connection between those values and the rules for your kids.

The following is a list of guidelines you may find helpful when examining and establishing rules at your house.

- **Be clear as to which family rules are negotiable and which are non-negotiable.** The range varies with each family. For some, eating dinner together as a family or set study hours are non-negotiable rules. On the other hand, curfews may be negotiable depending on the circumstances. This guideline structures children's needs to test limits and encourages them to problem-solve and negotiate in areas where parents can be flexible. Having some negotiable rules also allows children some input and responsibility because choices are encouraged.

- **Set priority rules.** Emphasis on honesty and staying away from drugs, for example, should be higher priorities than attaining polished table manners. If you set priorities in your own mind, it will help you control your own frustration if your child breaks the rule and it will help you set appropriate consequences.

- **Clearly state and define your expectations for behavior.** Children and parents often have different interpretations of "be good," among other things. Specific expectations of no name calling or completing assigned tasks are less likely to be misunderstood. Some parents find it helpful to emphasize the positive behavior of what they expect rather than the negative behavior of what they won't tolerate. An example would be an expectation that when a child becomes angry, he takes some time to calm down so that he can discuss the circumstances and his feelings more clearly.

- **Be consistent with the rules.** Consistency provides predictable boundaries. To this end, both parents must agree on the family rules.

- **Design enforceable rules and consequences.** If you can't personally enforce a rule or consequence, it is not going to work. Remember, just like "can-I" requests, it's okay to take some time to think and discuss rules and consequences. Be clear with your child as to when you will get back to him, whether several hours or days—and keep the time equivalent to the importance of the situation. Not only does this give you an opportunity to anticipate and plan in a thoughtful manner, it also shows your child how to respond to situations in a non-impulsive way.

- **Make the consequence fit the crime.** In terms of broken rules, modulate consequences to fit the infractions (a bit more, a bit less: remember the discussion on withholds). The purpose of giving consequences is mainly to help kids gain insights and to have a working knowledge of themselves and their responsibilities. If the consequences are too heavy, your child will project his anger outwardly on to you and the consequences rather than toward himself for creating the situation in the first place.

An underachiever can easily drive you to give harsh consequences that instantly become ineffective when you do not or cannot follow-through on them. Suppose as a result of your teenager going to the mall without permission, you order him grounded for a week. Emotions and angry words escalate and the week becomes a month, then a semester. A few more angry words and your child is grounded until the next year. (Laugh if you want, but we've seen it happen.) Levying a one-year restriction for going to the mall without permission is ridiculous and your child knows it. Eventually, when emotions quiet, you won't enforce a consequence so extreme, so you will back down to a more reasonable length of time. At that point, your child feels he has achieved a victory and that makes life even more difficult for you. He plays off your inconsistency. In the midst of such a circumstance, the child will lose sight of his action that sparked the problem in the first place. The focus becomes you and your unreasonable reaction.

In developing consequences for misbehavior, remember that natural consequences related to the act are best. For example, replacing a broken window *versus* restricting television viewing as the consequence of playing ball too close to the house makes sense.

As part of consequences, consider the suggestion made in Chapter 9 under "Punishing": have your child sit for fifteen minutes, then come back and talk to you or bring back something in writing about feelings and responsibilities. If he can't do this, have him go back for another fifteen minutes and think about it some more. If you are not getting good results after a few attempts, tell him that he will have to continue this at some later date when it's convenient for you. Using a notebook helps you remember these incidents and watch for improvement. If, after these attempts, you still don't see any learning, consider a harsher consequence. At this point, you want to discuss with him why the behavior was wrong. Give examples of alternative good responses; explain why you are concerned by his lack of appropriate response and why a bigger consequence seems necessary. Be dispassionate. Don't lecture. Make your points and be done with it. You might want to make a processing comment such as "I wonder why you chose this behavior."

■ **Update rules and consequences as your child grows older and establishes more independence.** As a corollary, the "fence" you design for one child may need adjustments for another child. If you feel like you are the behavior police in your home or like you're living out the Abbott and Costello routine of "Who's on first?" then maybe it's time to re-evaluate your family rules and discuss them with your spouse and children. Rules, like fences, often fall down if they are either too rigid or too permeable and lacking foundation.

These general guidelines on establishing rules and consequences now need to be put into action in a specific way. Exactly what kind of rules should make up that fence around your child? Following are suggestions.

■ **Establish specific rules that encourage responsible thinking and behavior**

You could go crazy figuring out rules for every type of situation and the result would only engender resentment in your underachiever and drive you crazier. Choose categories that correspond to what you feel is important in instilling personal responsibility, then guide your children in seeing the underlying sense of the rules so they can apply them to other situations. The following categories suggest areas where specific rules can truly raise your child's awareness of personal responsibility.

Curfews and other timely limits – The purpose of these rules is to add a measure of safety and responsibility to your child's life, not punish him for something he hasn't done yet. So be sure that you adjust curfews and other limits to fit particular situations: Just do it consistently. For example, a curfew for an average school night may be different from a curfew for vacation times, but school night curfews should be consistent. Special occasions should have different curfews than a school night. You wouldn't expect your teen to be home by 11 P.M. on prom night, even though that may be the normal Friday night curfew.

When setting a curfew, block out the chatter about what other kids are allowed to do and focus on your child's age, level of responsibility, where he'll be and with whom, what he will be doing and what the local laws are regarding curfews.

The rules that apply to curfews can also be applied to other types of time limits. If your child spends an inordinate amount of time on the phone, playing video games or skateboarding, time limits may need to be imposed. Again, the idea is to shape behavior, not punish, so the limits should be reasonable and you should explain the reasons for the limits.

Wake-up calls and other independence issues – You can institute little rules—actually expectations—to promote your child's independence, which is a big issue for underachievers. They want independence, but yet they don't want it. More to the point, they don't want it if it takes effort or planning. You can promote independence and responsibility through expectation and consequence rather than excessive reasoning, nagging or arguing.

To that end, one of the expectations for a teenager might be "Get yourself up for school" or "Do your weekly chores without a reminder." For a younger child you might consider: "Choose your own clothes for school." (That could yield some interesting results, but work with your child, don't preach to her.)

Another expectation for a teen or pre-teen would relate to participation in a sleepover. Have your child commit to some ground rules that mirror what's allowed at home. Both of you are at least slightly better off if she leaves the house with your expectations in the forefront of her mind. At the Center, we commonly have kids admit that they used sleepovers as an occasion to sneak out after dark, drink alcohol, throw an after-dark coed party and, in general, do outrageous and strange things. Discuss the rules before the event. Make your expectations clear and explain why they are important. Get a good sense of the hosting parents, too. Only let your child participate when you have confidence that the other adults involved share your parenting priorities.

Chores – Rules related to jobs at home have to mean more than "If you don't do it, you won't get your allowance." Any child, particularly an underachiever, needs confirmation that she has a place in her environment—that she fits into a family, a neighborhood, a nation and a planet. Awareness that, to some degree, her actions affect other people around her will help her mature. Among those actions are duties; they begin with chores that help her contribute to the quality of life at home. Your child needs to make the connection: Taking out the trash on Tuesday means that she's personally done something so trash won't pile up in the house. She has to understand that she does household chores like that because they are the right things to do, not because a reward will follow.

Having household responsibilities builds maturity, altruism and a sense of pride in accomplishment.

If your child isn't accustomed to doing any chores—if you haven't asked her to put away her toys after playing with them when she was two or three—you may need to help in the beginning. Soon, you'll have to step back from the task though and let your child assume full responsibility. A little reminding might be necessary at first, but reminding can become nagging so set the expectations; enforce them without the continued reminders.

Even if you did have your child pick up toys when she was little and assigned her chores as she grew up, when she got "stuck" developmentally, she also probably got derailed from the pattern of doing chores. Patiently and deliberately, put her back on track.

Start with a list of tasks that relate to your child's ability to complete them—not more than she can handle and not so much that they interfere with the other areas of her life. In assigning chores to your underachiever, you don't want to create either a slave or a princess (or prince). Be specific. Set standards. As your child gets older, allow increasing flexibility as to when and where the tasks are done. You can't change the day when trash bins must be out for pickup, but you can be open-minded about the appearance of her room. You might want to make a standing rule that no food goes into the bedroom, but not require that the room be cleaned every week. You might just say, "If your room isn't neat, keep the door closed," and "If you can't find anything in your room, that's your problem."

Homework – This is every student's chore and your underachiever knows it. What he may need to arouse a greater sense of responsibility about homework though is a rule regarding the time reserved indirectly for homework. At the Center, we don't call those designated hours "study time" or "homework time." The rule we suggest addresses "learning time." This is a certain portion of the after-school hours in which your child pursues learning. He might read a magazine, a book, a newspaper or do homework. It's his choice. The rule is just that he stays away from television, video games or any other electronic entertainment, and studies what he wants and how he wants in relative privacy. What eventually happens is that the underachiever starts to use the time for homework. The other interventions help accelerate this process.

You can promote a desire to be productive by doing your "homework" at the same time and even in the same general area as your underachiever is doing his. Set up your laptop or do your paperwork within sight of your child if his designated learning area is the kitchen or family room. Establish an environment of productivity. Let him know by example that your "rule" is to use that hour or two after dinner to learn and plan for the next day.

Your proximity sets up a natural occasion to help your child see the utility of his homework. You might nudge him into sharing what he's learning by mentioning to him the benefits you're getting from your "homework" or what you learned at the office today. You might also use processing comments to find out what your child is getting out of his homework: "I wonder what your teacher hopes you learn from this." The comment may lead to an exchange about the usefulness of the project or subject.

Conduct – Productively and peacefully interacting usually means following rules of living. It means meeting at least minimum standards of respect, decorum and civility toward others. "You can do whatever you want, just don't hurt anyone" is too vague for most kids and the message actually undermines your interventions with your underachiever. Underachieving kids have a self-centered view and "just don't hurt anyone" gives them carte blanche to play the radio loudly and not pick up after the dog. Set up "rules" that help your child notice other people's sensibilities and act accordingly. Some people call this etiquette.

General Interventions: Rules with Values

1. Facilitate Planning (The Twenty-four Hour Rule)
2. Establish General Rules that Reflect Values
3. Establish Specific Rules that Encourage Responsible Thinking and Behavior

CHAPTER TWELVE

SUMMER AND HOLIDAY INTERVENTIONS

Most people define underachievement as a school issue, but it isn't. It is an issue of emotional development. It may be acted out mostly in school and it may be easier to quantify in terms of bad grades or level of work undone, but underachievement is a pervasive problem. In the summer, the guideposts like homework and tests are usually not there, but the issues remain. **Parents can't take a recess from intervention.**

An important companion to the above thought flows straight from the concept that kids are not little adults. Your year-round attention to intervention does not mean that summer or other vacation periods should be "work time" for your underachiever, as in "let's work on academics" or "let's work on that issue." Some prominent educators and school administrators argue that summer vacation is just wasted time—that a summer break from school is a throwback to agrarian days when parents needed the kids home in the summer to tend the farm. We say: Baloney. Summer vacation is an important time for kids (and parents) to recharge their batteries. Kids need time when they are not heavily scheduled. **Play for play's sake helps them develop emotionally.**

Child psychologists have long recognized that play is the means by which children work through and cope with present and past concerns. Play provides an important education. (Remember your childhood summers.) Through play, a child learns about feelings and can experiment through fantasy with emotions that otherwise may be uncomfortable, overwhelming or anxiety producing. Playtime becomes an onstage experience for the young person who is free to act out many different emotional scenarios from the perspective of multiple characters. If you want to learn to understand your child's inner world in an attempt to guide and enrich, you must learn how to approach play and fantasy without altering, interfering or intruding.

What does a child learn from play? Play allows a kid to work through the expression of and reaction to unfamiliar or uncomfortable emotions in a step-by-step process. It also teaches habits needed for intellectual growth such as goal setting, perseverance and self-evaluation. These skills, once acquired through enjoyable activities, can then be generalized to more stringent requirements and to academically related tasks. For example, when a child builds a tower out of Legos, he learns that it doesn't necessarily stand up the first time. He tries again and eventually builds the tower. This same child later finds the process holds true for addition, subtraction and calculus II. Additionally, play provides an opportunity for fine-tuning of motor development, which is an important confidence builder, among other things.

Game playing with others and the experience of establishing and following game rules contribute to the process of socialization, too. Your child might disagree with another kid about the rules to a game or who scored, but they resolve the issues so they can continue to play. Game playing allows a youngster to experiment with various roles and forms of social interaction—today she's the leader, tomorrow she's the follower—and master interactions involving negotiating, disagreeing and reaching consensus. Play also means occasionally making up a game or changing an established one. In either case, creativity and self-expression grow while self-awareness develops.

A typical parental response to a child's or teenager's need for plenty of space to experiment with ideas at leisure is one of urgent demand to "get busy with the business of life." What these parents fail to realize is that the child *is busy* developing an inner strength that will enable him to tackle life successfully. If you push your child into too many structured activities, you can potentially establish a pattern of dependency upon external events and other's expectations for what constitutes "doing well." An example of doing this would be insisting that your ten-year-old always attend tennis camp on the weekend instead of going skating with her friends. There's nothing inherently wrong with tennis camp, but sometimes you need to let her just *play* so she develops her own measures of accomplishment and satisfaction. The external forces must be counterbalanced by the child's ability to generate positive feelings internally through self-awareness of goals, accomplishments and values.

A second, fairly common response is for parents to impose their own goals and ideas on the child's free activities. For example, if you often impose your organizational and training skills on a child without appreciating her effort and willingness to establish such skills by herself, your well-meaning parental efforts interfere with the learning process and can result in your child losing interest in the activity. (She will refuse to be her mother's daughter...) Many kids dodge "helpful guidance" by sneaking in activities when their parents are occupied elsewhere.

A third, more general parental response is one of not valuing leisure or playtime. The message to the child is that the development of self-directed, inner-motivated leisure activities is frivolous—that, indeed, after childhood and adolescence, there is no more room or time for play. They see no point in play for play's sake. Play is important not only for recreation, but also as a learning experience for developing skills necessary to achieve in life. Parents should see play as a valuable part of a healthy, whole person.

Following are exercises focused specifically on relaxation and play as routes to boosting your child's sense of the interplay between his feelings and someone else's, his actions and someone else's. The exercises can be done at any time throughout the year, but fit well into a program of summer or vacation interventions because they set you and your child up to be more light-hearted than the school year sometimes allows.

Exercise 1:
Indulging in Positive Interaction

Play a game with your child. Emphasize enjoyment of the game and your interaction, not winning. Take time to goof around and high-five.

Having fun like this encourages your child to see a balance in life. It promotes a sense that joy in the process can be at least as important as the end result. You will also encourage your child to get positive feelings from the interaction and understand that being "the winner" isn't always the point of the activity. If he does win in the game you've chosen, make sure it's an honest win, not something you arranged through your own deliberate poor performance.

Exercise 2:
Taking a Break From Chores to
Get to Know Responsibility Better

1. *Agree on a "skip day" with your child—a day on which you put household chores and work aside. Share the "skip day" doing something you both enjoy. (Be sure that you plan the day so that other people don't face inconveniences.)*

2. *During the day, talk about what it's like to "skip out" from responsibilities. Discuss the need to get away occasionally and that it's healthy to take a break from responsibilities sometimes. Also discuss what would happen if you routinely neglected responsibilities. How would that affect others? Affect your self-concept? Change your life? Take the fun out of "skip days?"*

By doing this, you illustrate that perfection and total self-sacrifice are not attainable, nor are they even desirable. This exercise allows your child to understand that doing things for oneself is not necessarily selfish—people need pleasant and relaxing changes from their routines. At the same time, the "skip day" interaction with you fosters responsibility because you make your child more aware of how his own actions can affect others. By affecting others, he affects himself.

Within the context of relaxation and recreation, you can also help your underachiever become less fearful of change. It's especially hard for an underachiever to expect change to be good during the school year because, at least in his mind, it seems like a consequence of his failure. The summer, when the pressure of academics is off, is a perfect time to help your child perceive change as positive and normal, not necessarily a turn for the worse and something to be feared.

The following two exercises related to transitions can reinforce each other. Go ahead and tie the two experiences together for your child by talking about change as normal, often leading to improvements and so on.

Exercise 3:
Promoting Motivation by
Noticing Small, Personal Changes

A natural time for this exercise is just after you've seen your child do something well, such as diving into a pool, sketching a portrait, throwing a baseball or playing chess.

1. *Pick a skill that your child has improved on over time.*
2. *Say something like, "Do you remember when you first learned to (dive, sketch, etc.)?"*
3. *Contrast your child's present skill level with his skill level when he first started. Even if he showed real talent in the beginning, you can remark on how much his practice to improve his skill or strategy has noticeably paid off. State how much your child has improved and in what ways.*

With this exercise, you help your child become aware of personal changes over time and to see them as normal. You emphasize that people continuously evolve by using their knowledge and experiences. On some level, your child will get the message that many small changes affect the total outcome. That awareness feeds his motivation, patience and a sense of perseverance to an end goal.

Exercise 4:
Accepting Transition by
Noticing Changes in the World

Get your child thinking about changes over time as part of normal transitions and development. Exercises like this instill in your child the ability to feel connected to a place (and by extension, people), despite the fact that there have been changes over time.

Take a walk around your neighborhood with your child and spend some time talking about what it's like to live where you do. Point out things that have changed over time and things that probably will change. If you are new to your neighborhood, instead of things that you know have changed, discuss things that probably changed before your arrived (e.g., "I bet twenty years ago you could see the ocean from this street" or "This cornerstone says 1987. I wonder what was here before this building.")

If your vacation travels take you to a historic area such as Colonial Williamsburg, Mystic Seaport or the Ephrata Cloister, talk about changes over time. Follow a progression of events (e.g., from the cauldron in the fireplace to the wood-burning stove to a gas oven to a microwave). Put change in the context of how we have benefited from change.

Your child could also enjoy and get huge benefit from structured "exercise" such as summer volunteer work with a local hospital or some effort with a specific mission like Habitat for Humanity or a clean-up-the-beach project. An underachiever usually doesn't balk at this type of activity because she is not being formally evaluated and doesn't see it as a responsibility. But through such activities, she will learn about responsibility, working within guidelines, how to relate to authority figures who are not her parents, social interaction in a new environment, new skills and facts—so many of the same kinds of things she can learn in school, but without the pressure of school. You don't want a project that will take up her entire summer, though. Something she can move in and out of as time allows will serve your purpose.

In contrast with the structured project, include a vacation exercise such as the following that is deliberately unstructured, full of "what ifs" and requires your child to discover facts and think creatively:

Exercise 5:
Exploring Options, Opportunities,
and Responsibility Through a Family Outing

Your family commits to going someplace unfamiliar to you—a beach you've never visited, a camping or hiking area you've never explored—with no firm agenda. Your child (or your kids together) may even select it.

1. *Have your underachiever investigate the place through magazines, the Internet or brochures and brief everyone on it. This builds his research skills in a painless way.*

2. *When you arrive, keep the trip unstructured. Have your child look for opportunities to explore new territory, develop new interests and coordinate family activities like building a fire, assembling a tent or playing beach volleyball. Talk about what it would be like to follow some of these interests as a career. ("If I were a botanist, I'd probably spend a lot of time wandering in the woods. I wonder how many edible plants we passed today?") Don't make it a lecture, just a few casual sentences here and there.*

3. *Make sure there is quiet time. Don't bring electronic distractions with you like games, radios or portable CD players. You want new experiences. You also want time to reflect and be creative and the freedom to take new opportunities as they arise. Sit around a fire and chat about whatever comes to mind. Be glad if your child gazes at the stars and wonders if there's life on other planets.*

CHAPTER THIRTEEN

HOW TO MOTIVATE A DISTANT UNDERACHIEVER

Of the four types of underachievers, Distants fit the following profile:
- Developmentally, at an earlier stage of emotional development than other underachievers
- Lonely, distrustful and have a deep fear of abandonment
- Focus on solitary pursuits
- Often have an advanced vocabulary and keen ability for philosophical and analytical discussions

Of all underachievers, Distants are the least mature and the most difficult to change. They are afraid that they will be hurt emotionally. On a promising note, though, they won't consciously fight your intervention the way a dependent or defiant underachiever probably will.

Exercise 1:
Helping a Distant Child Become Less Tentative
This will help your child toward dealing with loss and change.
1. *Begin with a plant or consider a low maintenance pet, such as a fish. Have the child take care of it. If necessary, help him take care of it.*
2. *Occasionally, while you have the plant or pet, talk about the inevitable—the fact that someday it won't be around. Put this in the context of how living things such as plants, animals and people come into being, progress, develop, affect others and then move*

on. As part of your conversations, consider how relationships come into being, grow and change because interests change, people change and needs change. Sometimes relationships get put on hold; sometimes they actually end. Draw anecdotally from your own childhood experiences. You'll help the child feel less personally threatened by "endings," because they happen in the midst of continuity.

The lives of distant underachievers are marked by repeated episodes of anxiety followed by their distancing themselves from whatever brought on the anxieties. Therefore, it is especially important to be sensitive to their considerable anxieties and distrust. *Sensitivity*, in this instance, means anticipating their emotional reactions and the concerns they will cause. Distants need to hear and understand your emotional responses to situations. Let them know that certain events make you tense or that being in particular places makes you a little afraid and that these kinds of reactions are normal.

Distant underachievers must be carefully approached in consistent manners. Inconsistencies frustrate them and spontaneity can cause them even more anxieties.

A distant underachiever's ability to trust is fragile. Be careful not to undermine any trust that you may have established. Even small inconsistencies can hurt your relationship, causing your child to distance himself even more.

Exercise 2:
Helping Your Child Deal with Change

While consistency is very important, with this exercise you are trying to stretch the envelope for your child, to help him move toward dealing with change. You will show that within consistency, you can have flexibility. Consistency does not mean rigidity.

1. *Choose one activity that involves your child, such as going shopping or walking the dog together every Saturday.*
2. *Mention in a casual manner how the predictability, while reassuring, isn't necessary for you. ("I enjoy knowing we're going to do*

this together. Some Saturdays each of us will probably want to do something different, though.") How does he feel about that?

3. *After a few months, start doing the event intermittently, substituting something different for the same time slot. Instead of going to the mall, go to a museum. Instead of walking the dog, go rollerblading.*

4. *Each time, discuss in the same casual manner how well everyone handled the change and that the change was good because something else worth doing took its place.*

Interact very gradually with your distant underachiever. Give of yourself without asking or expecting in return. A Distant is easily overwhelmed by forced closeness; don't smother him with attention.

As corny as it may sound, stories of your experiences are a good thing for a Distant to hear. (Be careful that you don't repeat the same stories, as many of our parents still do.) Don't put pressure on him to react in a certain way or to tell his own stories. Your goal is to have him feel at ease learning about someone else and experiencing the closeness that brings. He needs to feel more comfortable with the reasonable risks linked to being familiar with someone, because intimacy is so frightening to him.

Casually telling stories in his presence will allow your distant child to get involved vicariously. Gradually draw him in with short, non-threatening interactions. One of the most effective ways to do this is with planned silence. Pause after your story. Be available. At first, you might even want to leave after telling the story, so it doesn't look as through you're expecting a response. After doing this several times, hang around and pause. Give time for your child to make a response if he wants to, but don't press him for one. If a few moments pause does not bring a response, you might add a few more comments before you go on to something else, such as, "I had not thought about that situation in a long time. I bet that happens to a lot of people." These techniques enable you to make minimal emotional demands on your child while still developing a relationship and giving guidance and support.

Schedule frequent, but short, periods of time with your child, being sure to be consistent, punctual if you have set a time and nonthreatening. For example, take a few minutes in the evening to be with her. If she's watching television, watch with her for a little while. If she's playing a video game, watch. Take an interest, but don't intrude or take over. Be available, not overzealous.

Exercise 3:
Using Predictable Events to Build Trust and Good Feelings
Short-term project:
1. *Early in the day, establish that you're going to be somewhere with your child that day.*
2. *Later in the day, remind him what's going to happen. Talk about the anticipation, the feelings associated with the event.*
3. *Follow through.*

Long-term project:
1. *Make plans about events or situations. Something like: "We're going to a movie of your choice three weeks from today."*
2. *Write it down for yourself—it's important you don't forget it.*
3. *A week later, remind him you haven't forgotten. Ask what movie he thinks he'd like to see. Talk about the positive feelings of anticipation.*
4. *Follow through.*

As this type of project becomes part of your habit pattern, you can do several at once. Select events that you have a high degree of certainty about being able to do. However, if something serious and unavoidable intervenes:
1. *As soon as you are aware of the conflict, tell your child.*
2. *Talk through your feelings about it with him. Anticipate his tensions; stay calm and talk over both his and your disappointment with the change. Discuss how you're going to handle it. Converse about unpredictability and lack of follow-through in various other aspects of life: What can you do about those situations? How can*

you make them better? What can you do to counteract or remedy an
unpleasant situation?

To the best of your ability, *always* follow through on any commitments you make to your distant underachiever. Even saying you will bring her something and then forgetting can be very defeating to a distant underachiever. Such things as you being even a few minutes late when you are supposed to meet her can be extremely anxiety provoking for her. She will immediately begin feeling abandoned, possibly guilty and even more distrustful. She can quickly go from thoughts such as "Mom forgot me" to "She got into an accident and I'll never see her again." Through your reliable, consistent behavior, you will help the distant underachiever toward finding that personal investment is more rewarding than risky.

Exercise 4:
Expressing Feelings About Trust
Discuss trust and how it is created, earned and sometimes lost.
Discuss the emotions around it, such as satisfaction, how calming it
is, the reliance, predictability and relief associated with it. Also talk
about losing that, why that sometimes happens and the anxiety and
hurt that can result. Use anecdotes.

As your child's needs for security are met over time, you will want to stretch his comfort zone—to expose him gradually to situations with the potential for success and failure. Pick something new for your child to try. Make it something that can be done in segments, like baking cookies from scratch. Through this process of letting him handle a "big" project in stages—first, just measuring and mixing the dry ingredients and, finally, doing everything through taking the cookies out of the oven—you'll be able to cultivate some optimism in him about ultimately succeeding. His goofs, like dropping a piece of eggshell in the cookie batter, won't seem so serious when he tastes the outcome of his efforts. He'll start to think: *If I fail, I'll survive. Nothing terrible happened. I'll try again.*

Gradually advance the type of projects you engage your child in, as his skills improve and success occurs. Be supportive along the way and that includes openly talking about emotions such as tension, apprehension, fears, fulfillment and so on that are associated with trying something new. Also discuss the rewarding, positive feelings.

Be especially consistent and explicit when it comes to rules, limits, expectations and consequences. Don't leave the definition or meaning of them to his conjecture. This may mean writing them down for your record and for your consistency of action.

Exercise 5:
Controlling Impulses

Distants often act impulsively without regard for reason or outcome.

1. *Talk about what impulses are and how they feel. Do they happen in response to a rule being enforced? A scary situation? Confusion? Surprise? A strong emotion?*
2. *Share vignettes from your life related to impulses.*
3. *Discuss the impulse and giving in to it versus meeting the impulse and controlling it. When is each reaction appropriate? Talk about impulses versus reason and logic.*
4. *Take a look at the feelings that result from the different responses—a sense of relief in controlling an impulse, a feeling of elation in giving in and getting a great result or perhaps a feeling of rejection or uncertainty after giving in to a misguided impulse.*

Go slowly in expanding your distant underachiever's social circle beyond you and others in your family. Spend time discussing relationships with her in non-personal terms. Try to get your child involved in reading about people, not just things. Especially in crowds, Distants are lost and uncomfortable, so taking her and a group of schoolmates to the circus for a special birthday is probably an unwelcome gift. Be sensitive to your youngster's fears and draw her out slowly.

Exercise 6

Working Toward Intimacy:

Discuss how closeness doesn't mean being engulfed. Be clear with your child that if he feels close to you emotionally, he won't lose his identity and neither will you. Discuss how people can have different likes, viewpoints and interests and still be close friends.

Developing Interpersonal Skills:

Talk about the subtleties of impressions, facial expressions, social cues and others reactions to them. Discuss how the way we act versus what we say influences what people think. Talk about perceptions.

The use of humor with a distant underachiever is especially helpful. That doesn't mean you should tell jokes, do tricks or pull embarrassing stunts. Just lighten up. Much of a Distant's attention is tied to taking responsibility too seriously, setting the stage for anxious anticipation. Humor can help your child tone down the fear he has about taking some control, being the center of attention or making choices in a given situation. Humor coupled with a general lighthearted attitude can take the edge off his anxious feelings and put life's trials into a positive perspective.

Exercise 7:
Helping Your Child Work Through Frustration

Distants often have a low tolerance for frustration, which causes them to quit projects prematurely, retreat from certain situations or act impulsively. Building their tolerance so they can persist to completion is important. This is a "graduated frustration" exercise.

1. *Pick a task that is readily do-able by your child with a little persistence.*
2. *In advance of the project—painting a chair, for example—discuss what you're going to do.*
3. *Stop when his frustration (or yours, if it hits you first) becomes apparent.*
4. *Stay calm. Take a time out if necessary.*
5. *Discuss the situation and emotions. Consider why there is frustra-*

tion and what can be done to overcome it.
6. *Decide on a course of action and work to completion.*

Repeat this with several circumstances. Distants tend to get frustrated doing tasks with multiple outcomes, especially those that involve other people. Follow-up projects might include helping to organize a cookout for his school friends or staging a family party, both of which would involve making calls to several people to invite them, knowing what to say when they ask what to bring and so on. Sporting events and games fit well into this kind of exercise, too, because they invariably involve differences of opinion about rules.

Remember that as your distant underachiever begins to mature, the process will involve several stages. There will be starts and stops, progress and occasional regressions. As he develops, his responses and focus will change. Incorporate the maintenance exercises in Chapter 17 to reinforce his pace of development. Perhaps at some later point, your Distant will seem more like a passive underachiever, for example. Keep moving forward with him and update your interventions as his needs change. It is likely that once your child begins to mature emotionally at a more normal pace, he will go through stages like Dependent and Defiant and you can help make the process of change smoother with those techniques specifically designed for the later developmental needs.

CHAPTER FOURTEEN

HOW TO MOTIVATE A PASSIVE UNDERACHIEVER

Passive underachievers fit the following profile:

- Delayed at a relatively early developmental level or regressed from a higher developmental level
- Focus on the acceptance and approval of others without consideration for their own needs
- Fear of failure dominates them

Overwhelming anxiety underlies a Passive's underachievement, no matter whether she is a compulsive, obsessive, somatic or hysterical Passive, as defined in Chapter 2. You can help a Passive by enhancing her sense of an independent self. A passive underachiever needs to learn that her value as an individual is not singularly based on meeting all the expectations of others. She needs to learn that she herself is important outside the constant approval of others and that it is okay to exist as an individual with individual feelings, needs and expectations. Being your own person carries *reasonable* risks. Help your child to learn to experience her own thoughts and establish her own values, even if those values are the same as yours.

Exercise 1:
Arousing a Passive's Own Ideas

Passives are very hesitant to express their own ideas. By using this game to explore what your passive underachiever thinks about things, you create an atmosphere for him to do that with no (or very little) anxiety.

1. *You and your child each write a wish list with a handful of items. It might include big things—"I wish I had a horse"—and/or little things—"I wish I had a pizza right now." The important thing for him to know is that there is no right or wrong answer.*
2. *Take turns going through your lists in a conversation.*
3. *After that first time, you don't have to write the wishes down. Do oral lists.*
4. *Do the exercise periodically, when it feels natural. A good time might be when you're in the car together.*

The Passive needs to recognize what he feels and what he wants and to assign importance to those emotions and desires. The awakening will help him learn how to appropriately assert himself. Stories and storybooks that focus on a character's feelings and choices, rather than correct or incorrect answers, can entice him to think about his own feelings and choices.

Exercise 2:
Directing Your Child's Reading

Find books for her to read that are not about things, but about people, especially people in situations where they have a lot of choices to make and those choices aren't really "right" or "wrong." The synopses and reviews posted by online bookstores can be helpful guides to selection. Also ask librarians, bookstore staff and teachers.

Exposure to brainstorming sessions involving other people can also pique a Passive's interest in her own thoughts and feelings about issues. For example, at dinner one evening discuss where the family might go for a summer vacation and suggest that your Passive take notes on the ideas put forth. If she wants to contribute thoughts, that is wonderful, but don't force comments out of her. Over time, repeated exposure to such brainstorming situations will help draw her out as long as these sessions involve a variety of answers with no one answer being totally right or wrong. Such situations allow Passives to recognize that it is acceptable to have many and varied ideas.

Exercise 3:
Coexisting With Others

Share anecdotes from your life to illustrate that even people who are very close can have different issues and feelings. Sometimes the two clash. Sometimes they're parallel. Sometimes they're neutral; they just coexist. Talk in terms of it being okay that others are different and you are different from other people.

As with many of these exercises, your child may roll his eyes at first and act like he wishes you would go away. Stick with it in a casual, non-emotional way. The messages will get through.

A passive underachiever has a hard time handling disapproval. He is very likely to think his ideas are "wrong" if you or another significant figure in his life disagrees with him. It is very difficult for a Passive to differentiate among fact, opinion and perspective. The previous exercises set the stage for him to embrace the idea that different people have different points of view without any one opinion necessarily being "right." The following exercise more directly addresses his ability to deal with disapproval.

Exercise 4:
Surviving Disapproval

1. *Pick a topic for conversation that is something trivial, something that in the long run doesn't matter. An example is what to put in the garden this year.*
2. *Agree to disagree. That is, do a point-counterpoint discussion.*
3. *Express incompatible points of view; have a difference of opinion.*
4. *Carry the point-counterpoint through the whole discussion. It would go something like this:*

Parent	Passive Underachiever
"I want to plant tomatoes there."	*"I don't."*
"Why?"	*"Too much work."*
"What do you want to plant instead?"	*"Pumpkins."*
"We don't need a lot pumpkins."	*"We don't need a lot of tomatoes, either."*

"I want to plant some broccoli, too."	*"Yuck. What a waste of space."*
"Broccoli is good for you and	*"I hate broccoli. Let's plant*
I like it."	*carrots."*

5. *Make the discussion time limited.*
6. *End the exercise with a funny comment about what you just did.*
7. *Afterward, chat about how you're both still okay, you're still friendly and everything is still fine in the relationship. Passives have a fear that relationships will collapse after they either express or receive disapproval.*

With the Passive spending so much energy trying to meet other people's expectations she doesn't cultivate a sense of what gives her internal satisfaction. She may pursue activities simply because she thinks that's what you want her to do, not because she enjoys it. By example, show your child that indulging yourself in activities that are relevant only to you can be healthy. Let her know what aspects of your life make you feel good inside—fulfilled. Let her know that people normally do things that hold special meaning or importance just for them; that's an important part of what makes them happy.

Exercise 5:
Developing internal happiness
and personal fulfillment

1. *Pose brief anecdotes about feelings of fulfillment in your life. Those feelings could come from engaging in hobbies, aspects of your work, spending time with the family—wherever you find fulfillment.*
2. *Talk about how that fulfillment leads to happiness and the happiness leads to further fulfillment. Your passive child is worried about external approval and he needs to see that fulfillment is an internal experience, not based on things of which other people like or approve.*

   A hobby can be the best centerpiece for this kind of discussion because the activity is something you like, but one that other people might perceive as irrelevant. Your collection of crystal elephants gives you pleasure regardless of what other people think, say or feel.

By admitting that, you're modeling for your passive underachiever how to appreciate internal fulfillment and respect what's relevant to his own feelings.

Your child needs to know and feel that failure can be positive if used as an opportunity to learn. As part of this discovery process, he'll come to see that perfection is not the goal—it is not a requirement of success and its absence does not make a person a failure. The goal is consistent effort. With consistent efforts, he will still have ups and downs in life, but he will do well and others will appreciate him. With that perspective, your Passive's fear or belief that failing is a final judgment will fade.

Exercise 6:
Experiencing Failure as a Learning Opportunity

1. *Do something together—a household or hobby-related project— and deliberately do it wrong in some minor way. Maybe you're building a model airplane together and paint the top of the wing black instead of white.*
2. *Notice it and show you're okay with it. Figure out some system with your child that would prevent the same kind of mistake next time.*
3. *Anecdotally let him know you did something like this before; point out what you learned and how you were better at doing that activity as a result.*

Books and movies that show others' determination and efforts in the face of continued adversity can be helpful in addition to exercises like the one above. Read the stories or watch the movies together and discuss them afterward. Focus on efforts that ultimately lead to a successful conclusion, regardless of temporary setbacks.

One aspect of these efforts that you'll also want to talk about with your child is how tension is an integral part of the experience. A passive underachiever does not use anxiety as a cue to action. Point out how others who are successful respond positively to tension.

Exercise 7:
Discussing the Value of Anxiety as a Cue to Action

1. *Anecdotally, expose your child to your thoughts on dealing with tension. Talk about how a particular situation made you anxious and how you handled it to create the desired outcome. Express the relief you felt.*

2. *Put yourself in a situation involving you and your child that has some inherent tension. Perhaps you are trying to get someplace at a specific time and hit heavy traffic and red lights. Talk about the tension you both feel, about the fact that cars are in your way and you have no control over that, about how much you'd both like to arrive on time. Take a look at how you are making an effort to be efficient, but these roadblocks keep getting in your way. When you get there in reasonably good time, express relief and how you are glad that you didn't just turn around and go back home. Discuss how, if you had cued into your tension earlier, you might have left earlier or listened to a local traffic report and planned your route better. Talking about it is the important thing in this exercise.*

This intervention program for your passive underachiever not only makes demands on your time, but in some ways it also requires that you make shifts in your demeanor. That will take conscious effort and practice on your part.

Parent Exercise:
Submerging Your Expectations

Do this with your child present, but don't announce your intentions. This exercise is designed to help you submerge your own expectations and instead explore those of your child's.

1. *Offer an opportunity to your Passive to determine the course of an event. You could ask him where he wants to go to lunch if the two of you have plans to eat together, which movie he wants to see or what he wants to buy at the grocery store. Choose a situation in which you are allowing your child to be more expressive and deliberate than he normally would be.*

2. *Let it happen. Do not show disapproval. Submerge your criticisms and feelings about the event.*

   Again, this exercise is for you, so don't tell your child what you are doing. He might be so intrigued that he'll ask you to buy twenty pounds of cookies at the grocery store.

3. *Follow through with what is reasonable!*

As you see your passive underachiever mature, change your interventions as his needs change. When he goes through stages like Dependent and Defiant, you can help make the process of change smoother with the exercises designed for kids at those levels of development. The maintenance exercises in Chapter 17 will also be useful.

CHAPTER FIFTEEN

HOW TO MOTIVATE A DEPENDENT UNDERACHIEVER

Dependent underachievers fit the following profile:

- Commonly fail to set priorities well
- Tend to gravitate toward subjects such as physical education, art or music and away from math, science and English
- Blame others or events for failures
- Express anger through passive-aggressive behavior
- Wait for others to structure and organize them

Most underachievers fall into the Dependent category. Unfortunately, in many ways the Dependent is much more difficult to work with than other types of underachievers. He will be more assertive about maintaining the status quo, consciously manipulating you and going out of his way to sabotage your efforts to disrupt the Dependent life he embraces.

Your challenge is multi-faceted:

- **Persisting through your own frustration.** Day after day, as you attempt the interventions described in this book, you and your child will probably often seem like magnets with like poles adjacent to one another—you will repel her. Your Dependent will make special efforts to engender disappointment and anxiety, in order to make you feel you have to go back to the comfortable way things were before you read this darned book.

- Coordinating the suggested interventions—done on a consistent basis—with a firm grasp of the background information as to the whys and wherefores of failing students in **Part I**. Your child needs insights about why she continually makes choices to be dependent, so your understanding of her situation has to seep into the activities and discussions prescribed in this chapter.
- **Absorbing the fact that the underachievement is *your child's* responsibility and acknowledging that you are at risk of being drawn into the dependency.** You must return responsibility and consequences to the underachiever in a way that reinforces to him that *he* is responsible for the consequences of his choices.

One example of how you can put all this together comes out of a common occurrence for the parents of dependent underachievers: On school days, your child can't seem to get himself out the door on time to take the bus, catch a ride with a neighbor or arrive on time without doing a two-minute mile. When this happens, let him take responsibility for his actions through school detention, extra work, getting himself to school on his own or paying part of his allowance to you for driving him to school. Part of this intervention—or any intervention with a Dependent—should be that he explain the dependent behavior, which led to your initiating a consequence. He should articulate what he did, why he did it and what he could have done alternatively. His initial answers might be "I overslept," "I dunno," "Nothing," respectively, but always work with him to make this a learning experience. If necessary, provide prompts to help him understand the real reasons behind his action and what other options he had. He may not think of any on his own. Don't lecture, though.

Be prepared for your dependent underachiever to dig in her heels and wait you out. Experience has taught her you won't let her fail, but she may be prepared to do that just to keep you involved. You'll have to walk a fine line with a Dependent, between risking failure and providing the interventions that will get her out of this developmental trench. With a Dependent, it is particularly important that all authority figures who interact with her are communicating as a team. The concepts and reinforcements need to come together at once to maximize change. And without question, you will need to let go; it will be a gradual process, but you must do it. For example, if you encounter a situation where you feel you do need to help with a project on which your child has delayed action, help in a way that provides insight. Before lending your assistance, have her either write a paragraph or talk to you about why she procrastinated or was having difficulty. This allows your child to use anxiety as a cue to action and not as a message to withdraw from responsibility by emotionally, intellectually and maybe even physically removing herself from a situation that causes anxiety.

During exchanges like this with your child, point out the irony in how she creates her dependency—the fact that her own behavior results in these situations where she feels restricted. At least several times a week, dispassionately mention the ironic nature of her behavior.

A multitude of situations open the door for this kind of comment; you don't have to contrive anything. A dependent underachiever often says one thing that means *I want independence*, but she's creating the opposite outcome, that is, dependence. For example, your child says, "I'll take care of it. I want to be left alone," in response to your inquiry about her homework. Nevertheless, she doesn't do her homework. You say, "I wonder why you chose not to do it after you said you wanted to be left alone. Your not doing it causes me to want to watch you. Isn't that ironic? You wanted to be left alone, but you chose to do something to get me involved." Bring this point up right when's it happening. Don't nag. Just mention the irony quickly and unemotionally and move on.

Providing assistance to your dependent underachiever should happen only after she's made legitimate and reasonable attempts at resolving her problem. Even then, the assistance should be in the form of guidance as described earlier and not real action to complete her work. This teaches her to accept responsibility, but assures her that others can be helpful resources. For most parents of dependent underachievers, pulling back like this involves internal conflicts. You worry that your children won't be okay without your help, so you get readily drawn into their dependency. Do the following exercise to realign your thinking and feelings.

Parent Exercise 1:
Visualizing Your Child's Independence

Visualization is a powerful technique to train your mind, body and emotions for success. In the context of your intervention, it can help keep you focused on the outcome you want for your child; it can feed your commitment and persistence.

Figure skater Brian Boitano is one of many world-class athletes who used visualization to prepare himself for consistently strong performances. His story of winning a gold medal at the Calgary Olympics suggests how vivid and multi-sensory the visualization of a winner is. Brian had done nightly visualizations of his performance for a year prior to the competition. In his mind, he saw every perfect spin, heard the crowd applaud and felt the tears of joy on his cheeks after giving the performance of a lifetime. The day those events actually occurred, one thing surprised him and woke him up to the fact that this was the moment he had worked so hard for: In his visualization, he "heard" "The Star Spangled Banner" in a slow tempo, but in reality, as he stood on the top platform with his gold medal, the tempo was fast. Just like Brian did, try to engage multiple senses as you visualize your child's independence.

Imagine your child growing up and leaving your home. In your mind, see the details of his success in graduating from school, working in a satisfying job, enjoying friends, decorating a beautiful apartment. Envision your child responding with independence and authority to a challenge at work. See him thriving in an independent life. In this vision, you didn't do a thing.

Use this visualization to develop a mind-set that supports your intervention. You won't be as likely to get drawn into your child's dependent condition if you practice this visualization. When he does-

n't do his homework, for example, you won't feel so sorry for him and so anxious about his success in school that his homework becomes yours. You'll be better equipped to pull away, knowing that will set the stage for his independent success.

The following exercise, which complements the one just described, is focused on your internal struggle over how much control you have to have over your child's life. In this case, because you actually involve the child, your anxiety will probably kick in. Take a deep breath and prepare to let go of your little boy or girl.

Parent Exercise 2:
Letting Go in a Gradual Manner

Work on letting your child assume more responsibility and exercise independent thought, so that both of you feel more at ease with him being out of your influence and control. Do it in a purposeful way. You might feel a slight hesitancy to allow something, but keep that hesitancy to yourself and let him do it. It will help you fight the tendency to be an enabler of your child's dependency.

One sample project is cooking a meal periodically. Establish at least a week in advance which meal will be his responsibility. At first, help him plan the menu, compile the ingredients and get started. Then gradually let him go through the entire process himself by following your guidelines on cost, number of dishes—hot dogs with ketchup are not a complete meal—and when the meal should be ready.

Whatever project you choose is an opportunity for him to stretch and for you to let go, so don't criticize. If his project doesn't turn out well, let him try it again. Work with your child if necessary (to make a meal edible, for example), but do not take over. Guide, but don't assume the job.

Dependents are highly fearful, even though they usually won't admit it. It is helpful for them to explore and discuss their fears and anxieties about specific issues in non-threatening, indirect manners.

Casually bringing up situations in your life or the lives of others you know, that are anxiety and fear provoking to spark productive conversations with your Dependent. Discuss how you would handle these situations. Ask your child to give suggestions and, in a non-threatening manner, discuss the merits of these suggestions. Becoming self-aware and understanding motives and reactions helps a Dependent (and all children) more easily accept responsibility for herself. She learns that by acting on her feelings, she can work through them, be successful and not be overwhelmed. In other words, she doesn't *need* to be dependent, because she can build her own strategies for action. This process aids in raising her self-esteem and maturity. In turn, your child will become more resilient and goal oriented.

Exercises 1 and 2:
Pushing the Independence Envelope and Confronting False Independence Demands

These exercises emphasize the interplay between freedom and personal responsibility. "Pushing the envelope" means giving your child more freedom than he requested. "Confronting false independence demands" means granting a surprise "yes" to your child's request to do something you had not previously allowed. With both exercises, you're setting your Dependent child up for an opportunity to move forward toward greater independence. The degree to which these opportunities are repeated depends on his responsible handling of the new privilege. Do whichever is appropriate depending on the opportunities that arise.

1. *Selectively provide your child with more freedom than he has requested. For example, if he asks to stay out with his friends until ten on a Friday night, give him permission to stay out until eleven.*

2. *At the moment you do it, explore his emotions: "How do you feel about my letting you stay out later than you asked?"*

3. *After he has the experience of more freedom, ask him how he felt about that. Talk about how he handled the added independence. Let him know you're pleased that he had that opportunity and that you hope he made good choices related to it.*

4. *Create a circumstance where you surprise your child with more flex-*

ibility than he expects—a situation that gives him more freedom than he's accustomed to having. For example, he might say, "You act like I can't handle myself. I can't even have some of my friends over to watch movies and hang out." You respond with, "Why don't you have them over on Saturday night? You guys can camp out in the family room and watch movies all night if you want."

5. *If he avoids the freedom you're extending, talk about it. He might come up with excuses not to accept your offer. For example, "the guys" might have other things to do on Saturday or he's sure you're going to change your mind at the last minute. Address the issue of whether or not he wants this freedom.*

6. *If he seizes the opportunity, let him know you're glad.*

With both exercises, make it clear that making the choice to experience additional independence and to handle it well is a sign of maturity. Congratulate him on showing personal responsibility if he does so.

As a coordinated element of the described exercises, you will want to make a list of activities and circumstances that offer your child possibilities for greater independence. Not only keep in mind what is appropriate for her age, but also what other kids her age who appear to be responsible and mature are doing or not doing. Systematically provide your Dependent with the opportunity to have those new experiences, gauging whether or not she's embracing this independence. As you see that your child is making good choices along the way, update the list accordingly.

Playing "what if" scenarios is also helpful to stretch her thinking and get her ready to commit to more independent activities. Explore "what if you did this in that situation? What other possibilities are there?" Through guided conversation, you can create mental decision trees with her. You may even want to do it on paper, illustrating "if this happens, then here are the choices," and so forth. With this kind of help, your Dependent will learn that feelings of inadequacy, doubt or inability can be overcome and that real independence can make her feel good. Your child can start to enjoy the process of maturing and feel successful.

Chapter Sixteen

How To Motivate a Defiant Underachiever

Defiant underachievers fit the following profile:

- Developmentally closest to maturity, with defiant behavior usually surfacing in the mid to late teens
- Insecure in his or her sense of self
- Flaunt their false independence by being contrary
- Given to rage and cynicism, even though they are often energetic and creative

With a defiant underachiever, your goal should be to develop his ability to effectively relate to others, to develop his sense of adequacy and to develop personal control so that he can stop underachieving.

Being dispassionate—staying emotionally calm while still providing guidance and consequences—is crucial in dealing with a defiant underachiever. A consistent, united, dispassionate parental and school approach, which still leaves room for negotiations and compromise, minimizes a Defiant's outbursts and his often belligerent attitude.

Exercise 1:
Staging a Disagreement that Highlights
Negotiation and Compromise

Defiants excel in arranging confrontations, but, in this case, you take the lead. The resolution rests in both you and your child controlling your emotions through a process of negotiation and compromise.

1. Arrange a minor confrontation. It could address, for instance, a haircut or makeup that your child wants to get, but you don't like.

2. *Let him or her know you are open to compromise.*

3. *State your position, indicating that you'll move if and only if he or she is willing to compromise and negotiate with you.*

4. *Discuss options and the pros and cons of each. Remain dispassionate and businesslike. No personal attacks.*

5. *Follow through with a compromise you have both negotiated. For example, you may offer the child this option: Get the haircut or makeup, but not until summer vacation starts. Your child may counter with: "That's four months away! How about spring break?" You might consent as long as he or she agrees to get a more conventional trim or makeup before going back to school.*

A schedule of general rules that allows the child flexibility, but with known and enforced consequences if the rules are not followed, will contribute to a reduction of tension. Keep in mind that Defiants will often experience many consequences before deciding to change their attitude.

Exercise 2:
Shocking Your Child with Independence

1. *Selectively and without notice allow the child to have a previously disallowed freedom, something you have been considering anyway. One example is setting a slightly later curfew. You say, "You know what the rules are, but I'm going to trust you this time to stay out until midnight." It needs to be something you knew she wanted to do and normally would be defiant about: "You never let me do that!"*

   You will shock your child with this concession, but be careful. A Defiant who stays out until midnight one night will probably demand to stay out until midnight all the time. Be very specific in stating that this is an exception to the rules and it's your prerogative to make that exception because you are evaluating her behavior.

2. *Within a few days after the incident, discuss how she liked and dealt with the extra freedom.*

3. *Tell your defiant child why you made the exception. You want to give her a flavor of independence even though she hasn't earned it so that she will work towards it again.*

4. *As she learns to handle these exceptions well, you can choose to grant them more frequently.*

5. *Each time, discuss the result with your child. Let her know you will do this again as long as she acts responsibly.*

As a parent you should be flexible in *how* a Defiant carries out his or her responsibilities. For example, if you want your Defiant to paint a fence, you might let her know that you don't care how it gets done. She can use a roller, a spray can or a toothbrush as long as it is reasonably neat and well done and completed within an appropriate time frame. Maybe the two of you can even negotiate the color and pattern. By giving some leeway, the responsibility and the flexibility to achieve then become hers. You encourage your Defiant's creative freedom and flexibility within appropriate perimeters and that gives her a sense of control. On some level, she feels that she is guiding her own destiny. This is one of the methods you use to plant the belief that "life is what you make it."

Provide casual opportunities for discussions of future hopes, dreams and aspirations. Discuss in a personal way what the realistic paths are to his objectives, but also allow him time for daydreaming. Share some of your experiences; discuss, but don't lecture. Show you value his opinion.

Exercise 3:
Discussing Things on Common Ground

Join with your child in a situation where you can see his logic. It's common for a Defiant to complain about how school or home or life in general isn't all it's cracked up to be. He might, for example, say he doesn't think it's fair that guys on the football team can skip physical education class, but guys who rollerblade after school every day have to go. Even though you're not granting permission to embrace or act on that opinion, you can have a discussion with him that shows you understand and respect his point of view.

That discussion becomes an occasion in which you can anecdotally share your experience of how life isn't always exactly what you want it to be. You deal with it, sometimes you laugh it off, sometimes you try to change it, but you keep your eye on the things that really matter. That's where you invest your intelligence and energy.

Firm outer limits and consistent discipline help shape your Defiant's sense of personal responsibility; they let him know what he has to do to control consequences. Complemented with the kind of flexibility for personal creativity described above, the rules and discipline will lead a Defiant toward more enjoyment about "getting things done." Your teenager should start to see that he can maneuver quite a bit within the confines of what you consider appropriate behavior.

Exercise 4:
Delaying Gratification

Help your child learn to handle delayed gratification, that is, help him understand that he needs to plan and act toward a goal where the positive end result won't come for some time. Introduce your Defiant to the reality that adults regularly have to handle delayed gratification and all the emotions that go with it: anxiety, anticipation and so on.

1. *Let your child do something that he wants to do, but which requires some planning. Part of the requirement is that he agrees to discuss his feelings about the delay before the event. For example, if he wants to go on a weekend camping trip, consent if he agrees to go in three weeks. A week and a half before the trip, have the conversation about his feelings as they relate to the upcoming event.*

2. *In the conversation before the event, explore the things he probably would not have thought about if he had run off immediately. Take a look at the way planning can enhance an experience. Maybe the group had initially decided to take a canoeing trip, but after they talked about it for ten days, they realized they'd rather go for a hike and camp in the back country. Talk about shifts in thinking like this that occur, so the Defiant knows that planning offers*

advantages. You don't want to make any of these conversations very formal, though, because he will resist. Have your conversations in a casual manner, maybe over a meal. The idea you want to put forward is that planning and working toward a goal is part of the reward process and enhances the reward result.

Because Defiants are so prone to contentious behaviors, you should take a close look at how to communicate during conflicts. Although any set of emotions may become so intense that the ability to communicate is impaired, this is most likely to occur when you, your child or your spouse is feeling hurt, frustrated and angry—which can be daily feelings when there's a Defiant in the household. Ironically, during emotional conflict clear communication is what's most needed to resolve issues, but that is usually when it's missing.

Regardless of how well you may be able to communicate during presentations, speeches and sales meetings, at home it's often a different story. There, a strong emotional reaction may lead you to ineffective or inappropriate responses so unlike your abilities at the office. During conflict, communication skills that are usually well honed and refined seem dull. You may find yourself resorting to uncharacteristic behavior and responses during conflicts with your child. That makes sense: Communicating well during conflict is deceptively complex.

Gil, one Defiant who came to the Center, had a standard answer to every one of his father's questions related to responsibilities. His father asked, "Did you feed the pets?" Gil responded, "Are you smoking crack?" Dad inquired, "Is your homework done?" Gil responded, "Are you smoking crack?" The response acted like a trigger for the father's anger and Gil knew it. Over and over again, he simply manipulated his father into conflict. Dad was at his wit's end—what parent wouldn't be?—when he came to the Center, asking, "How do I communicate with him?" In addition to the general tips on staying dispassionate and using processing comments, I took him through the steps in this chapter on communication during conflict.

Following are some strategies for more productive communication with your Defiant during conflict. A few background notes on effective communication may be helpful for you as you restructure your interchanges with your child.

Communication involves several basic components. There must be a "sender," that is, the person who is expressing a specific message. The "receiver" is the listener, the person who is actively trying to comprehend the message being sent. Listening not only involves not talking, but also requires an active attempt to understand the message that is being related. The message itself should be intelligible and clear. Also, both the sender and the receiver must be motivated to cooperate.

These sound like simple requirements, but communication easily fails because myriad blocks can interrupt effective exchange. These include:

1. Language barrier – When conversing or arguing with your underachiever, this refers to the use of slang or jargon. ("You dissed me, man, don't you get it?") The use of slang or jargon can leave one person wondering what was said and becoming ever more convinced that there can be no understanding on any level. This block not only leads to confusion, but it also increases the emotional distance between the two of you. With language barriers, the differences between you, not the commonalities, dominate the exchange.

2. Mixed messages – This refers to a situation in which a sender may be saying one message verbally, while sending a different message non-verbally. For example, you might yell at your teenager, "I want you to feel like you can tell me everything without worrying about how I'll react!" Such mixed messages not only cause great confusion for the listener (or receiver), but also may lead to feelings of distrust on the part of the listener. She asks herself, "Which message is for real?" Do you want the child to feel comfortable talking or will you be very angry and punitive if your child is honest?

3. Inappropriate expectations – People develop expectations about other people's reactions based on previous experiences with that person. In terms of communication, the receiver

often has expectations about the sender based on previous experiences with the sender. These expectations may cause the receiver to expect a particular type of message from the sender. That is, if your son always adopts "an attitude" and barks, "What do you think?" when you ask him whether or not he has homework, you probably won't believe him when he gives a simple, "Not tonight," in response. He may be telling the truth, but the message is distorted by your expectations. He'll probably throw up his hands and yell, "It doesn't matter what I say. You hear what you want to hear," and to some extent, he's right.

4. Change the subject – In this situation, either the sender or the receiver spontaneously brings a new and related topic into the discussion, which results in abandoning the original topic. The consequences of this tactic are that there is no resolution regarding the original topic and additional feelings about the new topic are triggered. For example, you may be setting rules about your teen's use of the family car. In the midst of the discussion, she reminds you of a time when you said she drove better than her older brother. The conversation then shifts to the older brother accusing you of being critical of his driving.

5. Withdrawal – The receiver of the message refuses to listen or withdraws from the sender. The receiver can physically withdraw by going into another room or leaving the house. A more passive way to withdraw is to feign listening, but the receiver is actually daydreaming, reading or engaging in some other activity. The result of this block is that the receiver never takes responsibility for hearing the message and avoids having to give an appropriate response. For example, while your teenager is watching television, you describe an errand that you want him to do. Your teen isn't thinking about that, though. He's focused on an upcoming football game that will be happening at the same time. Later in the day, when he hasn't completed the errand, you blow up. The teenager says quite honestly, "I don't remember you telling me to do that."

6. Deception – This block often involves a situation in which the sender tells half-truths or omits important information about the message. Usually, deception is the result of the sender's expectations based upon previous experiences with the receiver. For example, in response to your question, "How are your classes?" your high school student might respond, "Great. I'm getting an A in Spanish this semester." She's carefully omitted the fact that she's only pulling C's and D's in everything else. When you find out later that the implied message didn't match the facts, your trust in the truth of your child's message drops sharply.

These blocks occur most often during conflict, but they also occur in relationships that have a long history of conflicts. Being aware of them when they occur, however, is an important first step toward changing them. In fact, there are several ways to prevent the blocks or to overcome these blocks when they disrupt your conversations with your child.

1. Make sure that all parties have the same meaning for words. Question the sender, if you are unsure what he means by a particular word. It's also a good idea to request that he avoid slang. Depending on the state of your own vocabulary, your teen may also request that you refrain from arcane terms.

2. If there is any doubt about what is being said, clarify and verify the sender's message. If you think there is a mixed message being sent or you're feeling confused, don't hesitate to verify your understanding of the message. Say, "It sounds to me like you're saying you want—" If you are the sender, you have an obligation to answer honestly and to correct the other person's misconceptions, if any.

3. During conflict, make an effort to stay on one topic until you resolve it. Then you can move on to other issues. In the middle of the discussion, if the original topic slips away from you, just say "changed subject" and refocus on the original topic. Make a note of the other issues for later discussion. It may even be advisable to have separate discussions for separate issues.

4. Give structure to your discussions. Although discussions are often spontaneous, it is very helpful to structure discussions that you anticipate may arouse contentious feelings. Set a time and a place for important discussions that will be free from distractions and interruptions. Also, set a time limit on the discussion. If the issue is not resolved in that amount of time, reschedule for a later time to continue. This strategy helps control the emotional tension during a conflict-ridden interaction.

5. Do not interrupt one another during the discussion. It is often good to set a policy that each speaker has a set number of minutes in which to express his or her views. During that time, no one is allowed to interrupt. This time limit often decreases frustration and facilitates honesty in the discussion. Use it like a debate with a rebuttal period. Successful sports teams and business organizations commonly engage in a practice like this to encourage every member to contribute insights about improving team performance.

6. If the situation gets too tense, take a time out. Recognize that if the discussion becomes too emotionally intense, everyone has the choice to call a "time out." This rule calls for everyone to leave each other's presence for a specific length of time. Then, at a later time, everyone can reconvene. When emotions are intense, conflicts are not likely to be resolved. This rule will help keep the discussion productive and safe for everyone.

Maintaining open communication during conflict is tough. People in conflict have a dramatically reduced interest in cooperating so that messages get through. This is why it's especially important to use rules like these to support your efforts to interact productively.

Exercise 5:
Communicating About Your Child's Unhappiness

1. *Observe and make note of what makes your Defiant unhappy. Your record may include what teachers or neighbors say to you.*
2. *Initiate a conversation about what makes her unhappy. She's defi-*

ant. She'll probably say, "Nothing!" Let her know you've paid attention and help her see how her negative actions make her unhappy. Use processing remarks: "I wonder why you feel this way when you get a bad grade." You want your child to talk about it, but if she doesn't, just make your processing comment and let it go.

Parent Exercise:
Practicing Being Dispassionate

Your ability to communicate dispassionately at particular times is central to a successful intervention program with any underachiever, although a Defiant is most likely to goad you into reacting emotionally. For most people, though, becoming dispassionate takes practice.

Even before you begin the intervention program, make a conscious effort on a daily basis to remain calm on the outside when something bothers you. Even when you are alone in your car and someone cuts you off in traffic, keep your cool. You need to be able to convey nonchalance on cue—and usually your cue will be the emotional outburst of your underachiever.

Being dispassionate does not mean being chilly or negative. Your child should perceive that you are businesslike and in control, not that you are guarded and unloving.

Your practiced dispassion provides the ideal demeanor for using the processing responses and comments described in this chapter. You'll be better able to offer comments such as "I wonder why you chose not to do your homework" without any hint of sarcasm or disappointment.

If you are the parent of a defiant underachiever, take note: Make time for yourself. In the midst of this most challenging developmental stage, it is important that you take time away periodically to recharge your batteries. This is a developmental stage for your child, not a war between the two of you.

Chapter Seventeen

Maintenance and Prevention

Success! Your underachieving student is now motivated and moving forward. You and others who have been concerned breathe easily and feel reassured. But wait: A caution is in order.

If the ineffective and unconstructive coping patterns and defenses used by the underachiever have been present for at least several months, they are not readily displaced by appropriate attitudes and behaviors. Individuals who change from underachiever to achiever have to be aware that, while they have won the initial skirmish, they have not won the battle.

The old, bad habits and defenses become "tendencies." Tendencies keep pressure on the "recovering" underachiever to return to the old ways. For instance, if it has been his pattern to put things off, his tendency will be to procrastinate. If it has been her habit to project, her tendency will be to blame. If it has been her habit to overeat, her tendency will be to eat too much. If he routinely avoided homework, his tendency will be to forget homework. If she was a slacker, her tendency will be to let things go that need to be done.

Fortunately, there are strategies to assist people in beating down their tendencies even though such tendencies may be with them throughout their life. On the positive side, as former underachievers become more established in their new, positive patterns and strategies, the old tendencies emerge less frequently and with less intensity.

Even though they may not totally disappear, a keen awareness of them offsets those tendencies, so they do no harm.

Here are three Maintenance Strategies to adopt:

1. **Boost external awareness.** Forms of *monitoring* work best here. You want to help your child monitor his own progress, quality of outcome, attitude and so forth. You might also include the use of defenses and unconstructive strategies. If he keeps a running record and checks it regularly—daily, at first— he can identify emerging trends so he has the advantage of being able to anticipate and react. It can be as quick as a five-second determination before bed as to whether he met his standards that day. Keep it simple enough so that several months of +'s and -'s fit on a 3"x5" card or a few pages in a notebook. Remember, tendencies are persistent and tend to reemerge, but your child can maintain his motivation and achievement by anticipating and reacting. Such recommitment staves off regression to former ineffective, underachieving patterns.

2. **Cultivate internal self-awareness.** This involves having an honest *internal conversation* that starts with the questions: "Am I clear, every day, about my commitment to positive change? Am I motivated to make that happen?" This weekly self-examination then moves to "How committed am I? How did I react this past week to those old tendencies? How sure am I that I like the results of being motivated? Do I have any second thoughts about this new path?" This internal conversation need only take a few minutes, but it should be sincere and thoughtful in addressing the issues.

3. **Seek reinforcement.** Former underachievers need to find others who are positive and engaged in their lives. While eventually this will naturally occur ("birds of a feather flock together"), they also must actively grow away from former associates and friends who are mired in their own underachievement. Being surrounded by underachieving, negative individuals who are constantly excusing their responsibility, griping, whining and finding fault in others and with life only con-

tributes to regression of underachievement. In contrast, being in a social environment supporting of living the achieving, motivated life greatly assists continuing motivation.

As the parent of an underachiever, besides worrying about your child regressing after intervention, you may also have a concern that one of your other kids will be "stuck." The exercises in this chapter provide you with a convenient, structured method to help you support the continuing emotional development of all your children. By doing them in the systematic way described here, you aren't likely to forget or miss significant developmental interactions that can help your children become independent, resilient, flexible, motivated and, most importantly, happy people. With practice, actions like these will become woven into your parenting habits. You will be spontaneous and comfortable with them.

These actions are *not designed as a substitute* for the interventions covered in earlier chapters. Use the exercises in this chapter with your children before you see a pattern of underachievement or after it's clear that your child is walking vigorously on the path toward emotional maturity.

Please note that this system of actions is primarily designed for children ages five to fourteen, but many actions are appropriate for younger and older children. If you have children outside the age range, consider their maturity level and interests and adjust the exercises accordingly.

As they relate to individual children, the exercises will help stimulate a child's emotional development, build self-esteem, nurture self-confidence, increase self-motivation and responsibility and develop creative potential. As they relate to the family, they can have the effect of encouraging healthy expression of emotions, increasing communication, improving family functioning, creating a supportive environment, encouraging interactive parenting, building compromise and negotiation skills, speeding resolution of conflict, building appreciation of others and increasing the positive feelings that come from being a close family unit.

❋
How to Use the Exercises

1. Plan to do a total of three or four activities from different categories each week. An occasional missed week will happen, but try to be consistent. On weeks when you plan to do the activities, really do them.
2. Pick the day of the week that you want to start your week.
3. At the beginning of the week, choose the action items for that week that you will complete with your child.
   a. Try at least two from the combined categories of Self-esteem, Maturation and Relationships
   b. Try at least one from the combined categories of Self-awareness and Creativity.
   Please note: Only a dozen sample exercises in each category appear in this chapter, so you will want to design others using these as a guide. If you keep repeating the exercises in the chapter, your child might wonder, *Why are we having this conversation about your childhood fears* again? or *Why are we going to a museum* again?
4. Spread the actions out over the week in any order you choose.
5. Don't cram a lot of activities into one week to make up for a week in which you only did one or two.

You may not want to do some of the activities listed in this chapter or maybe it isn't practical for you to do them. After you review all the exercises (and the stated purposes for each one), just eliminate the ones you cannot or do not want to do. Use the ones you like as templates to create additional exercises that fit naturally within your family's lifestyle and environment.

Some of the activities may seem as if they belong in a different category or in more than one category. These activities, like life itself, are not always sharply defined and strictly categorized. The idea is a blending of thoughts, emotions, insights and abilities. You will see overlap because it's intended. When you do an exercise, try to influence your actions by keeping in mind the overall purpose for that activity and category. Read and give thought to each stated purpose before you begin an activity.

If both parents participate, that's great, but for many of the activities the child will still benefit if only one of you does them. If you have more than one child, try to manage doing at least two activities in a one-on-one situation. If that isn't practical, it's better to do the activities with two or more together at the same time than not at all. In fact, some activities work well with a group, especially some of the creativity exercises. You can also have other significant people like grandparents do activities with your child, but have them limit the exercises to one a week in addition to what you do.

❋

BEGINNING THE PROCESS

Some of the activities seem more focused on the parent than the child, but they aren't exactly. The focus is on you teaching your child and to do that well, you may need to reflect on some aspects of your life and beliefs. Children learn best by example and parents are their best teachers. When your child experiences a personal example from you, the message is powerful. Especially when it comes to emotional development and instilling values, you need to know yourself before you can consistently and appropriately transfer your knowledge to your children.

Your child may think this new element of your interaction is great. If you've already successfully performed an intervention with a child, as you engage in these activities, he or she may feel reinforced by your continuing interaction about emotional issues. Then again, you may have a child who acts indifferent or seems to resent your actions.

Feigning indifference or occasionally acting resentful is a defense against feeling uncomfortable with the situation at hand. If you're doing these exercises with kids in your household who have not had exposure to the previous remedial activities and interactions, they may feel embarrassed at the same time that they have a lot of curiosity and interest in the projects. Don't let that response deter you. With continued interaction, this should pass. Analyze your presentation style: Are you making your interactions sound like a lecture? You need to adopt a casual, relaxed, conversational style. Discuss your actions as if you were talking to yourself—and don't force any response, but allow pauses so your child can enter the conversation. Even if it doesn't seem like it at the time, your child wants to learn from you, wants a close relationship with you and wants your love. He may not say much during the activity, but he's probably listening and storing the information. Over time, both consciously and subconsciously, your child will reflect on and integrate much of what you are saying. When similar situations arise for him, your comments will be a reference point.

Sometimes it may feel a little awkward to start a conversation suggested for the exercise. This may happen a lot in the beginning, but with experience, that feeling should dissipate. Often, it's best to set up a situation where you can lead into the topic. For example, if you're driving with your son or daughter and you see a family on the corner, you could say: "See that kid over there with that older man? That reminds me of the time my grandfather and I—." Or maybe while fixing dinner, you make a statement like: "My boss told me today about . . .and that reminded me of—." Sometimes a good introduction is just a simple statement: "I was just thinking—." Your child may think some of what you say is strange at first, but once you get into the action, it won't matter. Eventually, you'll find introductions that work for you and that make your child more enthusiastic. Knowing the subjects you intend to cover during the week will help you take advantage of opportunities for the exercises as they arise naturally. Use your planning skills as well as your imagination in making the process seem less contrived.

❋

THE EXERCISES

The emphasis in this system of activities with your child is in five important categories: Self-esteem, Relationships, Maturation, Self-awareness and Creativity. From these areas spring the motivation, excitement, energy, concern and resilience that lead to productive, happy individuals.

Many similar exercises in each category may come to mind as you review these. As suggested, add to your repertoire with exercises modeled on the ones suggested.

SELF-ESTEEM

The activities in this group are designed to develop positive regard, self-confidence and self-motivation. They focus on the positive aspects of resilience, tenacity, understanding of moods, acceptance of responsibility, conquering challenges, control of one's environment and engagement in life. The activities in this category provide opportunities for you and your kids to show emotional support, nurturing, pride in accomplishment, acceptance of abilities, acceptance of individuality and love.

#1

Action

Choose a subject in which your child has particular interest and/or expertise. Ask for advice or an explanation of some aspect of the subject you want to know more about (avoid questions to which you know the answers). Listen intently. Thank your child for the information.

Purpose

Affirms to your child that his or her opinions are important and that he or she has the ability to contribute in a valuable manner.

#2

Action

Ask your child to help you complete a project. Pick something with which you both can get involved. Be enthusiastic. Praise efforts and accomplishments, even minor ones.

Purpose

Reinforces good feelings of accomplishment, improves self-satisfaction, heightens parental awareness, rewards initiative and motivation.

#3

Action

Call your child from work to say "Hi." If you don't work outside the home or if your child isn't available when you're at work, leave a note that says something like, "I missed you today."

> *Purpose*
> Reinforces that you think about your child even when you are not together. Affirms that you feel the child is important; shows you care.

#4

Action

Choose an area in which your child has applied good effort (school, hobby, volunteering, social). Say you noticed the effort and are pleased.

> *Purpose*
> Fosters accomplishment, promotes persistence to completion, emphasizes the causal link between effort and results. Provides emotional support and affirms acceptance of abilities. Instills motivation.

#5

Action

Discuss your child's favorite hobby, sport or other activity. Show enthusiasm and pride in your child's interest.

> *Purpose*
> Reinforces child's development of interests and improves a sense of self. Helps your child feel good about an activity and the parental interest.

#6

Action

Choose an activity that your child does well. Ask your child to teach you how to do it or take part in some aspect of it—any activity, such as draw a cartoon, do a lay-up shot, lead a cheer, play a video game, spike your hair, skate uphill. Be enthusiastic and have fun; don't criticize or suggest other ways to do the activity unless you feel there will be physical harm.

Purpose

Sharing accomplishments enhances a sense of self. Builds confidence through teaching and concentrating on skills. Builds pride in accomplishments that are noticed and reinforced by parents. Establishes a bond between parent and child. Opens communications and sharing.

#7

Action

Play a game that you can both enjoy. Involve yourself fully and emotionally in the fun of the game and don't worry about winning. Touch your child warmly and often during the play (high-five, handshake, pat on the back, hug).

Purpose

Play is a primary area of self-expression and esteem building. Parental appreciation and involvement in play promote a child's self-worth and feeling of acceptance. Promotes emotional bonding by accepting the child at his or her developmental level. Builds enjoyment and good memories of parental interaction. Physical contact shows love and builds bonds.

#8

Action

Remember a special day you had with your child when something positive happened. Reminisce with your child about the day.

Purpose

Teaches that experiences are valued even after they've passed. Enhances self-esteem by showing your child that he is part of a lasting, positive memory.

#9

Action

Talk with your child about a childhood fear that you had, but overcame. Discuss how you overcame the fear, how long it took, what kind of help you had, how you feel about it now.

Purpose

Imparts the understanding that fears are part of being human, but also allows fears and insecurities to be seen as challenges to conquer rather than obstacles to be avoided. Normalizes fears, allowing them to be overcome and, by doing so, builds confidence.

#10

Action

Send a funny card to your child. Write a short, positive message on it.

Purpose

Helps to develop a sense of humor. Sends a message that humor is an important part of a relationship. Shows your child that parents can have fun; makes you "more human" to your child. Reinforces that you think positively about your child even when you aren't together.

#11

Action

Take your child to a museum. (Note: Many cities have hands-on museums for children.) Let your child decide what to see and how long to stay at each exhibit. Focus on your child's enjoyment. Leave when your child wants to leave. Afterward, stop for a treat like a snack or video game.

Purpose

Reinforces in your child the knowledge that you want to be together. Instills confidence that her interests are important. Promotes an understanding that people can have a good time together while learning.

#12

Action

Say, "I love you" to your child. Add a hug.

Purpose

Creates an atmosphere of acceptance and openness by expressing a feeling that often goes unsaid. Reinforces value of verbalizing positive feelings. Nurtures and gives emotional support. Reassures your child.

RELATIONSHIPS

In the relationships category, the focus for your child is other people. One purpose of the exercises is to build interpersonal values and respect. Another is to nurture appropriate appreciation of other people as they fill certain roles in your child's life: authority figure, teammate, friend and so on. The exercises will help your child spot commonalities of interests and values with others, hone communications skills, develop greater awareness of and sensitivity to other people, practice tolerance and use negotiation and compromise skills.

The exercises are also designed to give insight into the stresses and strains that can develop between people and how to control and overcome these states. You'll support the growth of your child's interpersonal skills so that he finds social interactions fulfilling.

#1

Action

Review this week's television listings with your child. Circle those programs that family members want to watch together. Choose two or three and then watch them together.

Purpose

Teaches cooperation, self-disclosure. Develops awareness and appreciation of others interests, likes, dislikes. Provides practice in setting priorities based on consensus.

#2

Action

Ask your child, "Am I ever unreasonable?" If the answer is yes, don't be defensive. Ask for clarification. Discuss the situation, then, if possible, state that you will try to be more sensitive (and then do so). If the answer is no, talk about an incident when you thought someone was being unreasonable (*not* the child you're talking with). What did that entail? How did you respond and/or how would you change that response now?

Purpose

Showing concern for others' expectations and feelings enhances relationships. Models fair parenting and sensitivity. Gives thought to what reasonable expectations are. Opens communication.

#3

Action

When you are involved in a task, take a break and become interested in what your child is doing.

Purpose

Models being able to interrupt your interests for those of another. Creates "other" focus as well as shows concern and interest in another.

#4

Action

Make an unusual request. Have the request relate to some event that will happen later, but of which your child is unaware. For example, ask your child to pull all his clothes from a set of drawers and put them on a bed. (Your plan, which you don't announce, is to line the drawers with paper.) If your child asks why you made the request, state you will tell him later. Later, ask your child to guess what your motives were for making the request. Involve your child in the task and, as you're doing it, discuss whether he was right or wrong about your motives. Discuss how it is often difficult to know what people are thinking and how important good communication is to a relationship.

Purpose

Enhances your child's ability to appreciate that things that might seem strange or arbitrary may be rational if the intent is communicated properly. Stresses the importance of good communication between individuals.

#5

Action

Include one of your child's friends in a family social event.

Purpose

Promotes concepts of sharing, hosting and being part of a larger community.

#6

Action

Discuss something about which you feel angry (this anger should not be focused on your child). State why you are angry, how long you expect to be angry and what you intend to do to stop the anger.

Purpose

Creates an atmosphere of emotion sharing and conflict resolution. Encourages open expression of "negative emotions" so that anger can be dissipated and constructive interactions can occur. Teaches child that even though conflict can be resolved, anger and hurt may linger. Builds sensitivity to others' emotions.

#7

Action

Do something nice for someone with your child (e.g., bake a cake for a sick neighbor, visit a relative who may be lonely). Let your child know why you feel it's important to do things like this. Talk about your feelings and the response of the person for whom you did the nice deed. If the person's response is negative, discuss reasons why the individual might react that way. Discuss how such situations should be handled.

Purpose

Teaches your child to care about others, builds sensitivity and minimizes self-centeredness. Promotes self-satisfaction through giving to others. Develops a sense of community with others.

#8

Action

Tell your child a brief story about a good friend that you now have and have known for years. Talk about the transition of that friendship to the present. Then contrast that friend to another friend with whom you have lost contact over the years. Discuss why one friendship remained and why one didn't. Talk about changing interests, activities, moves, attitudes, etc.

> *Purpose*
>
> Helps your child understand that friendships are changeable and dynamic and that commonality is the basis of friendship. Opens sensitivity to the factors that can affect friendships.

#9

Action

Choose two or three famous people that you do not know personally, but whom you admire or respect for their accomplishments, talents, personality and so on. Discuss with your child why you feel the way you do about these people. Then discuss the difference between admiring and/or respecting someone and having a true friendship with someone.

> *Purpose*
>
> Develops an understanding of various types and degrees of relationships.

#10

Action

Walk into a room where your child is playing, reading or studying. Give your child a hug and then sit down to read a book or magazine. Spend at least thirty minutes in the same room. It isn't necessary that you do anything special or say anything special. Just be there and be available if your child wants to interact. If your child wants to know why you are there, say something like, "I just want to be around you for a while."

Purpose

Shows that caring and love are not always expressed by "doing" but also by just being together. On one level, responsibility for further interaction is put on the child. This develops an understanding that relationships are based on the action of all involved; that there must be effort from all sides. On another level, your child gains security and comfort from having you just be there. Affirms the complexity of relationships.

#11

Action

Decide as a family project that you are going to make a charitable contribution to someone or some organization. It can be financial (any amount), time, articles of clothing, etc. Ask your child to make several suggestions of what the family should give, to whom and why. Pick one of the suggestions and make the donation together.

Purpose

Promotes a sense of social responsibility and concern for others. Encourages your child to give of self without expecting anything in return. Fosters teamwork and a sense of connection to a larger community.

#12

Action

Discuss situations that make it not "fun" or "nice" to be at home, such as when people are fighting, someone's sick or when there's too much to do.

Purpose

Gives insights into the stresses that others have and feel. Creates empathy; creates a shared responsibility for family unity.

MATURATION

This category is designed to stimulate a child's emotional growth and the intellectual properties associated with emotional growth. It encourages your child to focus on object relationships, that is, how people relate to other people and other things. While imparting useful information, the exercises here also stress values, communication, an appreciation for detail, acceptance of differences, the need for limits and boundaries, control, problem solving, planning and responsibility over time.

#1

Action

Have your child call to check price and availability of a family purchase (television set, computer, etc.) or time and price of an event (hockey game, concert, etc.) and report the information back to you.

> *Purpose*
>
> Develops self-confidence, problem solving with others, accountability, appreciation of finances and planning (in terms of questions to ask and time of day when questions can be answered).

#2

Action

Go to a bank with your child and start a savings account in his name. Have your child help complete the forms and make the initial deposit. Encourage small, systematic savings. (Note: Some banks automatically offer an ATM card with a new account. You'll have to make the call as to whether having this card is an opportunity for growth or a source of confusion for your child.)

> *Purpose*
>
> Develops a sense of financial responsibility, ownership and financial security. Establishes value of savings and investment. Teaches delay of gratification in that the rewards (whatever the savings will be used for) will come over time if properly planned.

#3

Action

With your child do a "time pie." Divide a large circle into twenty-four sections. With your child, fill in your time and how it was spent in the last twenty-four hours. Do the same for the child's day.

Purpose

Develops a sense of time. Promotes the necessity of planning to achieve efficient use of time. Develops appreciation for time required to complete tasks. Makes the time allocated to specific activities a visual experience.

#4

Action

Tell your child about your first job. Discuss your first day of work and how the job evolved. Then tell, quickly and without much detail, how that first job led to others, if it did.

Purpose

Develops a realistic view of starting jobs. Contributes to the mastery of anxieties associated with new experiences. Encourages your child to think in terms of building on previous experiences while planning for the future.

#5

Action

Have a sex education talk with your child (appropriate for his or her age) that encompasses both the physical facts of sex as well as relationships and values.

Purpose

Helps establish awareness that you're in touch with your child's thoughts of sex, intimacy and relationships. Assists development, opens communication about sex, imparts appropriate knowledge and alleviates guilt in your child, who undoubtedly thinks about sex.

#6

Action

Using a watch, time with your child how long one minute is as you both sit quietly. After the minute, discuss how it seems so long when you are not doing anything and just waiting for the time to pass. Then suggest an activity that your child enjoys: "Let's—" (whatever it is). At the end of the twenty or thirty minutes, talk about how time flies when you're having fun. (Go beyond the thirty minutes if you both want to continue.)

Purpose

Develops appreciation of time, a sense of time passing and the beginning of time management skills. Establishes how interest and anticipation affect the perception of time.

#7

Action

Decide to share a movie with your child, either at the theater or at home. One person is in charge of what movie to watch and getting ready for it—selecting it, finding theater times and location, etc. The other is in charge of snacks and other "comfort items." For example, if you're at home, that person could grab the pillows and blankets. After the movie, discuss the activity in a fun way. Did you like the movie? What could have been better or different? Was there enough popcorn?

Purpose

Promotes planning, communication, mutual contribution, cooperation, review and analysis. Sets up an environment for parent/child interaction and shared experiences.

#8

Action

Together, plant a tree, shrub or vine outside or a slow growing plant inside. Give your child the assignment of caring for it. Periodically measure its height and discuss the growth.

Purpose

Promotes awareness of time, growth and development over time. Establishes commonality with you over time. Establishes responsibility and an appreciation of nurturing.

#9

Action

Discuss whether you communicate well about when and where you are going, when you are returning and how you schedule appointments and family events. Is this predictable? Does it take into account the needs of other people? Does your child ever feel "abandoned?" Discuss how you can improve any areas that make your child feel uncomfortable.

Purpose

Models consistency, security, predictability and the importance of sharing life with others. Lessens fears that your child may have regarding "abandonment." Note: It is normal for children to sometimes feel a certain level of apprehension when parents are away from them. It is also good for both the children and the parents, for parents to be away from their children periodically.

#10

Action

With your child do a usually mundane task for someone who may need a little extra help such as mow a lawn or replace a light bulb. Display outward enthusiasm for the chore and the help you are giving.

Purpose

Models excitement and enjoyment where none may have existed before. Gives your child a sense of challenge in seeing the positive in utilitarian situations. Promotes interrelationships and a sense of caring and responsibility toward others.

#11

Action

Ask your child for a loan when you're out together. Say that you want to run into the store and buy something (a soda, bread, a bag of ice, etc.), but you don't want to stop at the bank. Pay your child back the next day. Discuss the important limits of lending money and the responsibility the borrower has to pay it back.

Purpose

Develops trust within relationships. Teaches mutual reliance in relationships and appropriate, healthy limits on interactions.

#12

Action

Ask your child what he or she thinks your job is like. Arrange for a visit or tour of your workplace so your child can better understand what you do everyday. Note: Your job could be paid employment, consulting from a home office, volunteer work or work at home with which your child isn't involved.

Purpose

Helps your child understand responsibility, even when some aspects may be routine. Enables your child to experience limits and controls related to work. Allows your child to better relate to your situation and empathize with you and, by extension, other people who do this work.

SELF-AWARENESS

These exercises allow your child to shape and explore feelings, ideas, reactions, values and desires. You support this process while providing guidance, insights, opportunities and freedom to explore without fear of failure or rejection. The activities will help your child understand that many of the thoughts he has—no matter how emotion-charged—are felt by other people and that having emotions and fears is normal.

Many of the actions in this category involve you, the parent, relating experiences. This is important because there is heavy emphasis here on values and values are best learned by examples from the parent(s). Your child will use your experiences as a guide for future personal reference. Additionally, the exercises in this category emphasize the expression of feelings. To fully express and understand emotions, you need a vocabulary that encompasses a wide range of feelings. This includes terms of moods, intensity and duration. Refer to Appendix C for suggestions of words to incorporate into your conversation.

#1

Action

Recall a funny joke, story or incident that involved your child and share it. Be sure the incident was not embarrassing or hurtful. It should be one that your child enjoyed.

Purpose

Develops a sense of humor and appreciation for small joys. Internalizes in your child pleasure and warm memories.

#2

Action

Tell your child you need a change of pace. Ask to exchange chores, but let your child choose the chores. Do not criticize the quality of work and do not help unless absolutely necessary. Ask why those chores were selected and what he liked and/or disliked about them.

Purpose

Provides an opportunity for your child to explore something out of the ordinary. Gives your child a sense of control of his immediate environment. Provides a situation where your child can reflect on expectations, abilities, wants, likes and dislikes.

#3

Action

Stop with your child at a construction site and observe the work for several minutes. Discuss the work being done and the jobs required to complete the project. Ask how your child feels about various aspects of the job—what looks easy, difficult, complicated, exciting, boring? Why? Talk about the interdependence of the jobs and how these jobs affect the common and end goals.

Purpose

Gives an understanding of the detailed aspects and planning necessary for a major project and how various individuals and skills interrelate. Encourages your child to think of end results in terms of all the individuals that affect the outcome. Gives an appreciation of the need for various tasks, even if thought of as less than desirable by your child. Stimulates your child to think about career options in terms of his or her own feelings toward various aspects of different types of jobs. Develops observation and communication skills.

#4

Action

Tell your child, "People spend a lot of time focusing on negative parts of themselves. Let's make a list of things we like about ourselves." Then do it and talk about it.

Purpose

Encourages your child to look for positives in herself as well as in other people. Stimulates introspection and self-awareness and reinforces what traits are considered positive. While learning about self and others, self-esteem is also heightened.

#5

Action

Ask how your child feels about some situation. Pick something non-personal, such as an item from a news report. It can be happy, sad, good, bad, whatever you wish. After your child expresses a feeling—and if he doesn't automatically express one, encourage him—repeat the feeling back to your child by using the same "emotion word." For instance, if your child says, "It upsets me," you say, "You feel upset about—" then state that other people probably feel the same way (including you, if that's true). If your child has an emotion that seems totally inappropriate for the situation, discuss why it seems so and why your child feels that way. Do it in a calm, relaxed way.

Purpose

Mirroring is an important development of self-expression. Your child learns to concentrate on, recognize and express emotions and from your discussion, learns values that are appropriate for various situations.

#6

Action

Tell your child of an incident where you got into trouble with your parents or some other authority figure. Mention how you felt at the time. Discuss what you learned from the episode and how you feel about it now in terms of your values.

Purpose

As a learning experience from parents, problem incidents have immediate impact on children. Drawing your child's attention to such situations encourages thinking about values in terms of actions and allows your child to analyze different problem-solving scenarios for different types of problems. It also reinforces that conflicts are part of life and that one should learn from such conflicts. Helps develop a bond between you and your child.

#7

Action

Point out to your child someone who is making an extra effort that pleases you (e.g., a friendly and helpful clerk). State what that effort is and why it pleases you. This exercise works best if you can point out the effort while it's happening. To set it up, you might want to go to a place together where you usually get great service and ask for "help."

Purpose

Focuses attention on observations of attitude, skills and appreciation of work. Models what you consider good effort and shows it is a value that you recognize and appreciate. Lets your child understand how to act in terms of what you consider important.

#8

Action

Tell your child about a selfish thing you once did and that you felt bad about doing. Discuss why it was selfish, how it affected others and how you changed, or might have changed, the selfish act.

Purpose

Teaches your child retrospection and reviewing experiences in terms of other people. Conveys that everyone acts selfishly at times, but that occasional lapses don't make a person "bad" nor do they make it impossible to change. Encourages your child to recognize when such situations occur and to take appropriate steps to correct the situation and change the behavior. Helps your child to better understand your personality and values and use them in molding and developing his or her own.

#9

Action

Describe to your child the feelings of satisfaction that you get from doing your work. Ask your child to describe the feeling of being productive.

Purpose

Builds character. Teaches that productive challenges are positive. Promotes self-satisfaction with productivity. Encourages a work ethic that says that the effort itself is an important part of the result and that satisfaction comes not only from the end reward, but also from the effort to achieve.

#10

Action

Choose something that happened to you recently that sparked a strong emotion. It can be something good, bad, routine, exciting— whatever you want. Discuss the incident and talk about the feelings you had at the moment. Talk about how you used, or can use, those feelings as a cue to actions. Ask, "Has anything like that ever happened to you?" Encourage discussion of the incident and related feelings. If your child can't think of a similar situation, have one ready. ("What about the time when—?")

Purpose

Promotes self-disclosure as a means of learning about oneself and others. Feelings of guardedness or defensiveness are overridden allowing more thorough introspection of feelings. Develops a commonality between parent and child in terms of feelings and assures your child that a variety of feelings are normal and, if used as a cue to appropriate action, healthy.

#11

Action

Share an aspect of your work, at home or away, that you enjoy. Ask your child to tell you about a fun aspect of his or her work (i.e., school, chores).

Purpose

Shows that work and play do not have to be mutually exclusive. Enjoyment can be found in work. Focuses tasks on the positive. Allows your child to understand that things that are required can also be positive (fulfilling, entertaining, creative, stimulating). Highlights that sometimes we need to do things we would prefer not to do in order to get positive effects. Shows positive feelings can be found in many ways and settings.

#12

Action

Tell your child about a temptation situation you had and how you handled it. Discuss if the outcome was good or bad and whether you would, in hindsight, have changed your action.

Purpose

Acknowledges that all people are subject to temptation, but how a person deals with it and learns from the incident is an important reflection of character. Encourages your child to think about consequences, values, outcomes and feelings of self and others.

CREATIVITY

Creativity stimulates richness of thought. The purpose of these exercises is to engender flexible thinking, cleverness, openness, problem-solving abilities, a sense of humor and curiosity. You'll find that many of the exercises work well with a group. Creative individuals seek challenges, have a lowered fear of new situations, look for relevancy and develop heightened intuition. Creativity can easily translate into a fun personality and increased productivity.

#1

Action

Pick an everyday object and discuss how everyone's life would be different if that object had not been invented.

Purpose

Stimulates thought and idea generation. Develops appreciation of things we take for granted. Allows your child to assess from a different perspective. What-if thinking gives practice creating alternatives and solving problems.

#2

Action

Go to an ethnic food store that is new to you. Browse together, taking in the sights, sounds and smells. Discuss the things you see. What is interesting about them? Which of your senses are activated the most? Why? Talk about why certain items are popular in an area/culture. Purchase an "unusual" food item that doesn't require preparation and eat it after leaving the store. Comment on the flavor, aroma and texture.

Purpose

Stimulates appreciation of cultural differences and insights into why people are different and how differences can add excitement to life.

#3

Action

Make up a story with your child. Start the story with "Once upon a time" (or if you're Snoopy fans, "It was a dark and stormy night"). Alternate adding sentences with your child, making up the story as you go along.

Purpose

Promotes creativity under continuously changing circumstances. Teaches quick thinking. Promotes acceptance of others' ideas, continuity between individuals and a sense of shared effort toward a common goal.

#4

Action

Select a chore to do with your child that normally requires talking, such as cooking or moving furniture. As you start the chore, announce that just for fun no one will talk for fifteen minutes. Instead, send notes or mime the message.

Purpose

Promotes self-control and self-discipline; controls impulse. Teaches think-before-you-speak skills and nonverbal communication. Encourages your child to invent new ways to reach solutions.

#5

Action

Watch a sunrise or a sunset with your child. Talk about what you are feeling and seeing. Talk about the effect the sunrise/sunset has on how objects look, such as clouds, buildings, hills, the ocean. Talk about how people and animals react to the event, such as going to work, lighting, etc.

Purpose

Enhances observation skills. Allows creativity and self-expression related to an uncontrollable, but predictable, event. Contributes to an appreciation of the interrelationship of objects and activities.

#6

Action

Discuss several career alternatives with your child by imagining aloud what they would be like. Discuss what the jobs entail, educational requirements, the benefits and drawbacks. Include a few positions that are out of the ordinary. Do not be judgmental. Do not say or imply that any are preferred or better than the others.

Purpose

Creates openness to a variety of vocational possibilities within a non-pressuring atmosphere; allows child to safely experiment with different roles without concern for rejection. Stimulates thinking about different aspects of a career. Shows your child that you are open to different career paths.

#7

Action

Visit an airport or a shopping mall. Sit in chairs and observe the people walking by. Each of you make up stories about what you think these strangers' jobs are and where they are going.

Purpose

Helps child expand interest and appreciation for diversity. Focuses on the important role of a first impression, whether it is accurate or not. Allows for creativity in a setting where there are no right and wrong answers.

#8

Action

Ask your child to suggest a place for a family outing and present reasons, pro and con, for the suggested place. Discuss how others might feel about the choice and why. If possible, follow through on the outing. If not, tell your child why, then ask for another suggestion until one can be accomplished.

Purpose

Enhances independent thinking. Elevates your child to being a participant in family decisions (self-esteem booster). Asking your child to suggest how others would feel about the choice develops a sense of consideration of others' needs, interests and abilities, while encouraging your child to think from others' viewpoints.

#9

Action

Go with your child to a library. Agree to meet at a designated place in the library in fifteen minutes. During that time, each of you on your own find something interesting—either something of interest to you or that you think would be of interest to the other person. When you meet, discuss why the "something" is interesting. Don't check anything out.

Purpose

In a time-pressured circumstance, this promotes making choices, looking for the interesting aspects of an idea or object and concern for another. Leads to an ability to differentiate items quickly. Not checking anything out shows that things can be interesting even if they cannot be possessed.

#10

Action

Create a job list with your child. List several people you know and write what they do next to their names. Discuss the characteristics that make each person suited for his or her respective job. Discuss what would be a job better suited to that person.

Purpose

Broadens your child's appreciation of diversity. Creates a sense of uniqueness of individuals. Prepares your child for future career decisions. Encourages thoughts of someone familiar in an unfamiliar setting, thereby eliminating stereotypes.

#11

Action

Ask your child what a good teacher should be like in terms of style and abilities. As your child talks, draw a picture assigning the characteristics. For example, "smart" may translate into a big head; many eyes could represent "sees what kids are doing;" "helps everyone" may be a teacher with a dozen hands. Pick another person and let your child draw as you both talk about the characteristics. Try to come up with different characteristics for each person.

Purpose

Encourages creativity in description and an ability to visualize and document abstract ideas.

#12

Action

With your child and a camera, take pictures of each other with "special" things or in "special" places. Review the photos and talk about why the pictures you each took were special.

Purpose

Encourages your child to differentiate objects and places on a hierarchy. Allows your child to compose feelings visually. Lets your child and you explore together your similarities, differences, interests and insights and to create a lasting memory of them.

Chapter Eighteen

Staying Fit for Intervention

Integrating interventions for underachievers into your daily life can tax you, especially your planning skills. Two strong predictors of success with this intervention are a parent's willingness to do the program without ambivalence and the parent's energy level for doing it.

Other people won't stop making demands on you just because you've embarked on a program with your unmotivated child. As a result, you run the risk of feeling over stressed and overextended with an associated loss of efficiency at work, withdrawal from your other kids or spouse at home and guilt over those shortcomings. How much or how little you feel that way depends a great deal, of course, on your nature and your experience juggling multiple obligations. Nevertheless, it won't take long for any amount of distress to distort your intervention efforts, which you will start to view as a burden rather than an opportunity for growth and change for your child and you.

Take a look at the elements of your life—which now include a commitment to guide your unmotivated child toward personal responsibility—and consciously create balance.

Begin by reevaluating your job demands, satisfactions and attitudes. A frequent trap for people entrenched in their job is the belief that they are so essential that they are the only ones who can do the task. Although a flattering attitude, it fosters isolation and pressure. If you need assistance or clarification, ask for it. Delegate or collaborate before you become overwhelmed. You're likely to get more emotional and professional mileage out of completing a project as part of team than as an overworked solo flyer.

Reevaluate your attitudes to determine if your expectations are unrealistically high. Understanding exactly what your job demands of you will lead you to achieve the kind of balance you need in your personal life. Maybe, for you, the fast pace and intellectual energy demanded of you on the job might best be balanced by more quiet and less stimulating outside activities. For someone else, there may be a need for physical activity or more satisfying pursuits outside of work. Be aware of what's missing in your life, what interests you and what will rejuvenate your energy rather than further deplete it. Be aware of how you may be under-stimulated or over-stimulated in certain areas. You have to make deliberate choices in your life if you want to create balance.

Support your choices with how you manage your time. Treat family activities and individual interests as you would your work schedule. Plan them in advance and schedule them on a routine basis. Don't wait for time to be available—make it available. This is not to say that you take the spontaneity out of life. It means that on a day-to-day basis you respect your own intention to balance time for career, family and self. What you do with the time can reflect a whim.

Take the time to share with your spouse and children how your day went. This encourages them to do the same. When you have to drag work home from the office, do it in a positive manner. Create a quiet time when you and your children do "homework" together or do your work while they read or do a hobby. Take a few minutes out occasionally to chat about "how you're doing." Doing your homework while they do theirs models responsibility and diminishes isolation and resentment for parents as well as children. This creates an excellent opportunity for stress reduction and open communication.

Scheduling career and personal activities may be an easier task than trying to balance family time demands. Negotiating family activities is challenging, partly because your kids also struggle with a balancing act among school, outside interests, friends and family. You are in a position to help them respond constructively to this challenge. All of you need to communicate, clarify desires and compromise.

These techniques for establishing balance in your life will work some of the time, but there will still be moments (or days) when you feel overwhelmed and overextended. Your greatest need at that point is knowing how to deal with stress.

Stress is the body's response to a demand placed upon it. This can be mental, physical or chemical. The effects of stress are cumulative. They tend to build up within us over time unless we do something to manage or release the stress. Both good and bad stimuli cause stress. Just as getting fired from a job can be stressful, so can being promoted to a position with more responsibility.

Keep this in mind when you witness your underachiever acting annoyed or resentful when he does *well* on a test or earns high SAT scores—the pressure of raised expectations from you and his teachers may cause him to "stress out."

The stress response we experience when we react to a stressor is called the "fight or flight" response. It's innate, developed through the course of evolution. When we are under stress or a perceived threat, our body responds automatically by preparing to fight or flee. Our heart beats faster, blood pressure elevates, adrenaline pumps through our veins, our breathing becomes more rapid, our digestive tract shuts down and muscles tense. With reactions like these flaring up, it's easy to see that repeated stress can cause great wear and tear on a body. Chronic arousal of these kinds of body responses can cause high blood pressure, headaches, backaches, stomach problems, difficulty sleeping and general irritability, just to name a few symptoms. Since the response to stress is automatic, it's extremely hard to remove it, but we can mitigate it. We can learn to notice the signs of stress and use techniques to reduce tension and its negative side effects.

The major causes of stress that provoke negative responses are overwork, suppressed emotions, intense feelings and significant life changes. Life changes are not something we should avoid. Changes can be a detriment or they can help us live our lives to the fullest capacity and enjoyment. But too much change in a short period of time can take its toll on the adaptive capabilities of the body, lower resistance and increase the risk of major changes in health.

Personality type is also an important variable in how people react to stress. Some individuals tend to have intense ambition, competitiveness, a need to get things done and meet deadlines, visible restlessness and impatience and they tend to hold in their feelings. Other personalities tend to have a more easygoing and patient manner; they are less competitive and tend to express their feelings more openly. Persons with more of the latter characteristics tend to be more resistant to the effects of stress and manage it better. (Don't be fooled by the superficially carefree demeanor of many underachievers, however. Their laid-back veneer hides a swirl of emotions and stress-related anxieties.)

Other factors that affect a person's ability to deal effectively with stress include nutritional and fitness habits, degree of rest, emotional support systems and the capacity to relax. Here are specific suggestions on incorporating these stress relievers into your life:

1. If you don't understand what a person is saying to you, ask for clarification at the time. How many times have you experienced aggravation with your spouse or your child over a simple misunderstanding about what he or she said?

2. Go ahead and laugh out loud if something amuses you.

3. Avoid self-medication by binging on substances like alcohol, cigarettes and giant pepperoni pizzas. They can reduce the perception of stress, but they do not reduce the stress.

4. Do self-medicate with things like hot herbal tea and a bowl of chicken soup. Be flexible. Accept that you cannot control everything and plan accordingly. Develop contingency plans. Relax your standards when necessary.

5. Plan for stress. Set realistic goals that leave time for breaks and limit work. Find a quiet time each day when you can take a few minutes to rest, maybe listen to music or read just for fun. Take some time to relax your muscles and do deep, slow breathing.

6. Learn to express and accept love, praise and friendship.

7. Keep a sense of humor. That often means giving other people the benefit of the doubt. Think before you say something that would make matters worse.

8. Start thinking about what you really want out of life; plan for it in a realistic way.

9. Take at least one mental health day (i.e., vacation day) every two or three months. Do something different that day. Avoid work and problems.

10. Avoid sulking. Learn how to express irritation constructively. Let people know what you want and how you feel. Change what you can and learn to accept what you cannot change. Do not carry a grudge.

11. Develop a good support base. Find others with whom you can mutually share thoughts and feelings. Talk is a good medicine for stress.

12. Practice time management. Work smarter not harder. Keep a calendar with appointments, errands and so on, so you don't have to rely only on your memory.

13. Organize your home and work space in a way that makes sense to you. Put things you use most in a space that's easily accessible.

14. Practice "preventative maintenance." This includes your health, car, home and stocking supplies before you run out.

15. Allow fifteen minutes extra when getting ready for an appointment or work. Leaving a little extra time will reduce that frazzled feeling. When possible, do things ahead of time, such as put out clothes for work the day before, set the table early and so on.

16. Exercise. Do something regularly, even if it's just walking the dog.

17. Get enough sleep—plan for it.

18. Learn to say no when you don't have the time or energy for a project, chore or engagement. Know the difference between what you think you should do and what you are able to do without making yourself crazy. It's okay to say no.

19. Develop a winning attitude. Be positive about yourself and your choices.

Not only can these techniques work wonders for you, but practicing them can also make you a great role model for your stress-filled underachiever.

CHAPTER NINETEEN

TEACHER/PARENT COOPERATION

Teachers see your child in the environment where his underachievement may be most easily noticed. It's easy for you to assume comfortably that the teacher will therefore be able to offer you special insights and direction. You might also assume that he or she frequently sees this behavior in the classroom and can deal with it effectively. As a result, your expectations as a parent might be that the teacher can solve the problem or at least help you solve the problem. Sometimes that's true and sometimes—with the best intentions of pushing the child forward in the class—teachers will actually feed the underachievement.

As you begin an intervention program with your child, you need to establish a way of working with the teacher to prevent the latter outcome in which everyone loses. The first step is simply having a getting-to-know-you chat with the teacher so you have a foundation for more substantive conversation later.

Teachers have their own ideas on development and their own systems of punishment and reward. They may consciously attempt to build self-esteem according to principles they espouse and they may try to instill their own values. While you may not disagree with the facts they teach or with their values and beliefs, as a result of your exposure to this book your methods of communicating all these things to your child may be quite different from the teacher's methods. They might even be diametrically opposed.

240

For example, as you put the responsibility for homework back on your child where it belongs, teachers may criticize you for not calling their daily homework hotline and not pressing your child every night to get the homework done. When they call you and accuse you of disinterest or of sabotaging *their* efforts to help, they are unwittingly feeding into the dependency of your underachiever. Especially as your child gets older, you need to back off from monitoring his homework; transfer accountability gradually and steadily to your child starting in the pre-teen years. You know that by now, but teachers don't necessarily know it. You may have to educate your child's teacher on the dynamics of underachievement. (Teachers have often admitted to us that they didn't know that underachievement was a real developmental problem that could be treated. Many of them have been schooled to believe that the signs of trouble all point to attention deficit or other disorders or they discount the underachievement believing "they will grow out of it.") As with parents, the natural inclinations of teachers are not necessarily in the best interest of underachieving students. Tell the teachers what you're doing and why. Enlist their help so you can act as a united team with consistency and shared commitment to goals.

The natural urges of school administrators and teachers are to control kids externally and make them conform to standards. They do this through homework hotlines, daily or weekly progress sheets and other devices that shape parents' expectations and monitor student behavior. The schools want parents to hold their kids' noses to the grindstone if the kids don't plunge into the work themselves. Of course, this is antithetical to what you now have learned is effective. Try to get the teachers to understand and cooperate. Ask them to be flexible enough to accommodate your approach. Expect that discussing your new strategy for transforming your underachieving child once will not be enough. You will need to have continuous contact to help your child's teachers understand the process. Teachers operating in information vacuums will interpret what you are doing as being unconcerned. Explain to the teachers that this is not the case and that you have a systematic approach to correcting underachievement.

Mrs. Frank went to her son Kevin's fifth grade teacher to tell her personally that she would support the teacher in her efforts to hold Kevin accountable. She explained that she and Mr. Frank had begun an intervention program with Kevin to develop his sense of personal responsibility. "Treat him like any other kid," she said, "and hold him accountable for his actions. Don't give him special attention or help when he doesn't do the work. He's bright—he can get it."

The teacher said, "That's not my philosophy. That's not how I was taught to handle a child with problems." She refused to accept the Franks' approach. She continued to give him chance after chance, which fed into Kevin's using excuses to manipulate her and the situation.

This teacher didn't completely "undo" what the Franks had done to help Kevin develop, but her rigid thinking and narrow perspective did put the student and his parents at a disadvantage. They had more moments than many other parents when they felt like Sisyphus perpetually rolling the stone uphill.

To avoid a clash of expectations and methods:

1. Establish pleasant contact with your child's teachers and advisers at the beginning of the school year. Call. Follow up with a letter or e-mail. One purpose is to give the teacher your contact information personally. These initial "social" encounters will help you get to know each other in a non-judgmental atmosphere—before anyone feels the stress of unfinished homework and bad test scores. This makes the process of goal setting, and any future adjustments, much more likely to be successful.

2. Find out in written form both the teacher's and the school's standard operating procedures for grading, holidays and school events. Some schools begin the school year by sending an "outreach form" home that contains information like this. It might also list what the school's minimal level of contact with parents will be, such as quarterly parent-teacher conferences. If the school your child attends doesn't have this practice in place, you might suggest it.

3. Get the approximate date when report cards and interim grades appear and know if the school mails them or gives them to students to carry home.

4. Set basic expectations on what type and how much communication *focused on your child* will occur throughout the year. This is in addition to schoolwide parent-teacher conferences, which can involve such a whirl of information for the teacher and parents that everyone forgets what they wanted to say or, at the end of the day, the discussions about your child are hurried or forgotten. Nuances of your child's situation certainly won't make it into a two-minute conversation in that setting. Try to establish that, at least four times a school year, you have some meaningful exchange about how your child is doing. Not only should it be the usual grade reports and interims, but also brief narratives that include comments on attitude, effort, attendance, appropriateness of response to limits, social interaction and so forth. Has his attitude improved at all since beginning the intervention? Is he more prepared for class than he used to be? Does he always show up for class on time? Work out a system that doesn't make the child the bearer of the information. Ask the teacher to mail it or send it to your private e-mail address.

5. Respond with your own report in the form of a written note or e-mail. Let the teacher know what you've seen or not seen throughout the school year—both the positives and the concerns.

6. If you spot an anomaly, such as the teacher reporting that he hasn't even seen your child in several weeks, have a conversation with the teacher in which you articulate the steps you'll take to address the situation. Conversely, ask the teacher how he plans to deal with it. Set a team goal.

7. During the school year, when your child is excited about a class topic, stimulated about an assignment or talks positively about a classroom experience, drop a note to the teacher about that.

Many parents of bright kids, whether or not they're underachievers, face two types of dilemmas regarding teachers and the school system. The first is too much homework and the second is teachers and coaches pulling their talented kids into very time-consuming extracurricular activities.

There needs to be a life balance among homework, extra-curricular activities, play (free time) and home chores. The United States Department of Education 1999 guidelines for teachers suggests two hours of homework for the seventh through ninth grade, but many teachers pummel students with homework. Overworking kids, whether through homework or other structured activities, won't help them learn to establish balance in their lives.

In addition, the schools themselves may not put controls on the participation of bright and talented kids in extra-curricular activities because of the school's agenda. The drama teacher or basketball coach isn't looking at the big picture when he schedules three-hour practice sessions five days a week for three consecutive months during the school year. You have to put reasonable limits on activities so your underachiever's life has balance. Applaud their successes in sports, music, math or in whatever they do well, but *do not* let school staff who want spectacular performances or a winning season undermine your efforts to guide your child toward emotional maturity and lifelong happiness.

In many major metropolitan areas, the challenge is formalized. School systems place gifted and talented kids, some of whom are unquestionably underachievers with great natural abilities, in schools devoted to the fine arts or science and math. Other schools, in communities of all sizes, place so much emphasis on "winning the game" that teachers rationalize why they should give passing grades to strong athletes who are, in fact, failing. And it's not fair to assume that they are failing because they lack intellectual prowess: Their academic progress may be inversely related to the amount of time they spend on the football field.

Consider these stories if the school your talented underachiever attends is pushing him to pursue an activity to the exclusion of others:

Jennifer starred in plays throughout her school years. Occasionally, she directed for the one-act festivals. Jennifer was just sixteen and a dependent underachiever. She was failing every core subject, but the school staff kept asking her parents to let her continue full-throttle with her theater work. After all, she was at a school for gifted and talented students of the arts. Jennifer's parents had already started an intervention program with her for her underachievement, so they said no. From the top level, school officials countermanded the parents' wishes. They actively recruited her for projects that sapped her time and energy. Jennifer's parents had to be aggressive with school officials because they chose not to respond to parental explanations of the intervention program. Eventually, the parents succeeded in convincing the educators that Jennifer had to be held accountable in all classes—but it was a tough battle. Most importantly, Jennifer herself has started to recognize the exclusionary nature of her focus on drama and the fact that she used theater to avoid other issues in her life. (Unfortunately, without parental consent or knowledge, Jennifer's primary teacher met with Jennifer alone and rescinded the accountability demand. Jennifer's parents were livid, but she was pleasantly surprised. The intervention with Jennifer hit a pothole in the road.)

So what's wrong with a talented kid devoting his or her time solely to a passion? In all likelihood, a young person of sixteen does not have the life experiences to allow that kind of narrow focus. Think back to when you were sixteen. Did you have clarity about your future career? A child's long-term success, even in a field he loves, is built on discipline and achievement that he realizes in many areas of his life. Once he builds a well-rounded background, he can afford to put an abundance of energy and attention into just one thing. In the meantime, it's hazardous.

Stereotypically, you see this single-mindedness with sports. Consider the story of this football star:

After graduating from college, Dexter Manley went on to an NFL career that took him to two Super Bowls with the Washington

Redskins. When the defensive lineman's brilliant career faltered, many fans still assumed his NFL laurels should translate into new opportunities and lifelong success. Instead, he sunk into drug use and had to pay the price in a Texas prison. The NFL also banned him for life. His fans were baffled: How could a sports hero and college graduate make a choice to destroy his career and reputation with cocaine?

The fact was, Dexter Manley was nearly illiterate. He had graduated from college without basic reading skills thanks to the "educators" who promoted his athletic talents at the expense of his long-term happiness and success. He had lived a lie throughout his football career and when it was over, it was exceedingly difficult to sustain that lie.

Many people would find Dexter's illiteracy sad and even appalling. Fewer would have that reaction to Jennifer's situation because she is in a school for gifted and talented arts students. A more likely reaction in this society would be to think she's wasting her intellect on plays when she could be excelling at something "practical." So, when an underachiever is a math genius, everyone from teachers to the man on the street may think it's just fine if he flunks English or history because he has no motivation to learn them. They may expect him to be deficient in interpersonal skills because he's so different from other kids. In short, teachers and other key people in the child's life might prefer to say he has a "math brain" rather than an emotional development problem called underachievement. To a great extent, this is what happened to Cal.

Cal: A Math Genius Turned Dependent Underachiever Is Helped Through Interventions

Cal had been an animated child who enjoyed elementary school. But by middle school, it was clear he had a gift that in some ways became a curse: Cal was a math genius, which left him open to bullying from other kids who proclaimed him "a nerd." Some of them called him "cauliflower head" because his head was large and topped with blond curls. This mockery had the effect of making him steadily with-

draw from social interaction at school. His sole extracurricular activity was math competitions.

By the time he reached high school, he had built up a wall to insulate himself emotionally from his family as well as schoolmates. He reinforced his difference by often wearing T-shirts that featured esoteric jokes about math formulas.

His grades dropped. Even his grades in math were merely average. No part of school enticed him to put forth a real effort. Like a typical dependent underachiever, he tried to transfer the burden of schoolwork to his parents. Unlike the experience of many Dependents, however, this strategy didn't work too well for Cal. His parents, who were both researchers, already had enough stress trying to get through a day and raising three other kids. Cal's problem and the special attention it required from them were almost more than they could handle.

The intervention began with Cal's parents making deliberate attempts to show him affection. Cal was unresponsive. He seemed put off by their expression of feelings. At the same time, he showed virtuosity on the piano and scripted funny home movies with his brother and sisters—the whole family knew he had "soul." Cal's father blamed himself partially for the genesis of his son's aloofness. He felt that it was more natural to be affectionate with his two daughters, Cal's younger siblings, than with Cal and his older brother.

(Contrast this part of Cal's story with Bert's, the passive underachiever discussed in Part I. Bert openly and often showed his mother physical affection that was excessive for someone his age. Part of the intervention for Bert was making him pull back. Cal, on the other hand, didn't show the range of emotions or affection that someone his age should have become comfortable with. The intervention for him involved deliberate displays of caring.)

Cal's parents also had to take a number of specific steps to awaken his sense of personal responsibility. One of the steps that annoyed his mother, who foresaw terrible effects on the rest of the kids, was letting his room stay messy. If he couldn't find something, that became his problem.

Because of the intervention, Cal stopped thinking of himself as a freak. As a result, his own talents helped him move forward more. He qualified for the "Math Olympics" and went to an international competition as part of the American team. It woke him up to the value of his abilities and the possibility of going to college. So in his junior year, Cal tried to kick into high gear with all his courses and he succeeded. Duke University welcomed him after graduation.

Cal himself now admits that his lack of motivation to succeed in school caused him a great deal of personal pain. The only friends he had were just like him. They spent day after day reinforcing patterns of underachievement in each other. If his parents had not intervened and had they not insisted that the school not let him slide just because of his math aptitude, Cal might have ended up just like his high school friends, whom he describes as unhappy, cynical, detached dropouts with "math brains" and mediocre lives.

Chapter Twenty

Intervention When You Aren't Around

For many families, a grandparent, a neighbor who provides after-school care or a regular babysitter needs to be brought into the intervention process. You don't want grandma or grandpa pampering your underachiever all the time. Nor do you want anyone else who qualifies as a parent surrogate to give in, get overly emotional about issues or do anything else that will undermine the program you've established to help your child develop. The same concern applies to a non-resident parent who has custody of the child on weekends or for a month in the summer, for example.

It's your challenge to educate them about your child's emotional development, as well as raise their comfort level with the interventions so, at the very least, they won't say or do things that oppose you. Here is one scenario of how to accomplish this that doesn't involve contention:

- Invite the "significant other" to serve as your part-time partner in the intervention process. Ask him or her to be open to the information in this book.

- Explain why you use processing comments such as, "I wonder why—" and so on.

- Once that person has some familiarity with the interventions, discuss them and share some anecdotal information about your attempts to use them.

- Discuss ways that the two of you can work as a team for the common goal of motivating your child.
- Keep the other person informed about changes you've seen in your child since you started the program, even if they're just little things like occasionally "remembering" to do his weekly chores.
- Ask for feedback and keep a dialogue going. Occasionally remind each other of what needs to be done and reinforce your efforts.

Cissy: An Underachieving Child is Turned Around With the Help of a Dedicated Caretaker

Both of Cissy's parents were doctors working sixty to eighty hours a week. They recognized Cissy's underachievement, but didn't spend as much time with her as whatever nanny they had at the time spent with Cissy. When they first brought Cissy to the Center, they had "Nanny #1." Her modus operandi was letting the kids do what they wanted while she watched her daytime dramas. Not only did Nanny #1 expose them to lazy adult behavior, but she also engendered their ability to manipulate her. Fortunately, her stay at the doctors' house was short-lived. Unfortunately, her time with the family was followed by the brief employment of "Nanny #2" who was no better. Luckily, the parents next found Suzie, a native of Northern Europe, who was in her early twenties—theoretically unschooled and inexperienced, but bright and dedicated. They gave Suzie permission to engage in the intervention program prescribed by the Center to help their daughter, who was twelve at the time.

Suzie always brought Cissy to sessions at the Center with Cissy's four-year-old brother in tow. She was key in working with that family and effecting change. One summer, she even took Cissy home to Europe with her to meet her family and neighbors.

The parents did come in for meetings at the Center, but Suzie remained the primary parenting factor in that family throughout the program. She set up and enforced rules. She provided huge amounts of love and consistency. She had a good grasp of the importance of consistent behavior and wisdom about child development—what the kids were capable of doing at what age, for instance.

Because she lived with the family, Suzie seemed like a family member. She literally took over the task of parenting that the parents had essentially abdicated. We insisted that there be communication between her and the parents about strategies and activities; she made that happen, too.

Suzie made it possible for an inherently troubled family to come together. Cissy was the father's child, adopted by his second wife. Her younger brother was the product of that second marriage. Within a few months of hiring Suzie, a stable force in their life, we saw inspiring progress. The daily influence of a caring, consistent adult gave the children a springboard to excellence and happiness in their lives.

Even if a babysitter—whether a family member, neighbor or professional—only stays with your child after school each day, "Suzie" is an excellent model.

What happens if grandparents or a former spouse would rather disregard your program and relate to the child exactly the way they always have? You can't exactly fire them the way you would a babysitter, so special elements need to be worked into your system of interventions.

If they won't be flexible and you see the potential for conflict:

1. Accept it so you don't ruin that relationship. Heightening tensions with a former spouse or grandparent with whom you disagree won't help your child.

2. Stick with the program. Your consistency is especially important since your child will likely have some conflicting experiences with these other people. You face an "in spite of" circumstance, so expect that it may take longer to help your child get past his underachievement.

3. Discuss the situation with your child. Explain that grandpa or mom or dad may have different ideas from you about parenting, but don't try to discredit that person. Let your child know that when he's with that other person, the expectations will be different. Tell him you would appreciate it, however, if he would abide by the rules and practices you've established at

home because you believe they will help him be happy. Emphasize that when he is home with you, regardless of what he's experienced elsewhere, your expectations haven't changed. Your rules are *the* rules.

4. Periodically revisit the issue with the individual(s). Let them know you'd appreciate their giving some consideration to your approach. In addition, acknowledgment of their good intentions sometimes helps them grow more open to your philosophy. It may try your patience, but do whatever you can to avert actions by them that will confuse your child.

If the person is an after-school care giver or other professional, consider switching environments for your child if your expectations are not met.

You also have a challenge if your underachiever is a latchkey kid. You can't control what your child does in the few hours he has to himself. All you can do is set expectations, then try to observe and modify expectations if necessary.

Internet access, for example, could make those after-school hours a very distorting time for your child. The Barnes, one set of parents coming to the Center, said they could not figure out why they had to buy so much ink for their color printer until they discovered that their fourteen-year-old was printing X-rated pictures during his time alone. It's a well-publicized fact that chat rooms can expose kids for hours at a time to distortions, lies and manipulation from other kids as well as adults. Those who demand that we "wire every home" to ensure that all our youth have equal opportunity in a wired world should recognize that our youth aren't born with critical thinking skills, nor do they all acquire them at the same pace. Children learn over time to analyze information and should be guided, enlightened and appropriately protected as they learn that skill.

In terms of the special challenges related to underachievement, the issue of computer use has two sides: time and content. Both excessive use and exposure to material that confuses or overwhelms him can exacerbate your child's problem.

While kids in general can get sucked into computer over-use,

Web surfing and video games hold a special magnetism for many underachievers because they don't involve face-to-face human contact and the emotional complications that go along with it. Time restrictions on computer use is a reasonable rule.

Content restriction—censorship—is not a one-size-fits-all answer to the content problem, however. Your child needs your adult perspective on what he sees and hears; he needs your guidance. He isn't likely to greet you at the door with, "Gee, Dad, I'd like to discuss the porn I found on the Web today!" or "Do you realize that people in my chat room think you're very misinformed about marijuana?" Even with blocking software, things you consider objectionable will get by. So if he has Internet access while he's alone, it's up to you to engage him in conversations that will help him sort truth from lies and gain clarity on his values as well as yours. It is possible to get a history of his site visits with the popular browser software and you may want to do that solely to know where he's wandered and the frequency of his visits, so you can focus those non-threatening conversations. Your child may be getting an overwhelming amount of information about a subject and it's important you know that. Offer your perspective, not your negativity. The importance here is offering your adult perspective, not censorship. Help your child toward discriminating thinking and values certainty.

This same thinking applies to any media activity of your child's—television, music, magazines, films. You can take extraordinary measures to shield your child, but if you don't talk about the "objectionable" things she does see and hear as she goes through a normal day, then you've missed a big opportunity to advance her emotional development and her ability to think critically and access her values. Question statements people make on television shows, on the Web and through other media in a way that helps your child focus on the difference between facts and opinions. Help her tune in to the motives behind the message. Then even during her time alone when she's exploring the vast resources of the Internet or any media, she'll be better able to use her values as a filter for information and an impetus for action.

CONCLUSION

The best intervention you can do with your underachiever is to show your son or daughter that the real kick in life is the process of accomplishing something. The fact that you are merely able to survive or retire after thirty years of work means very little to a child. Rise above that. In contrast, the fact that your life is a string of challenges and opportunities that lead to fulfillment means everything. This is what provides zest and happiness.

By guiding your underachiever toward personal responsibility and accomplishment, you acknowledge that life is full of chances to succeed. You embrace the truth that life is what you make it.

Make the effort to guide your underachiever on the path to emotional maturity. You want him or her to grow, to be full of life, to follow values, to be productive, to grab life rather than just observe it, to thrive rather than just exist.

The emotional foundation for creating this is your sense of wonder. Don't be embarrassed to take time to experience and appreciate the wonderful things in the world. Some people are too cynical, too sophisticated or too intellectual to "indulge" themselves in such childlike enjoyment. They feel foolish, as if somehow, as adults, they should be beyond such things. Wonderment is essential if you are to have a zest for life.

Wonder is excitement, amazement and astonishment. Wonder is curiosity and attention to mysteries and new experiences. Wonder is the spark that lights fires. Wonder is adventure.

One fear you may have seen in your underachiever is that "wonder" appears to have a dark side—doubt and uncertainty. Show your child that this aspect of wonder can lead to possibilities and creative thinking. A quest for solutions often arises from wonder. When used as a cue to action, wonder can make a negative situation positive. There is an inherent sense of optimism in wonder that allows people to surge on, to look for answers and to pursue the unknown instead of avoiding it. Great inventions, solutions and changes happen because someone wonders "what if?" and pursues the thoughts that follow.

It's not that a person should be blindly optimistic. Negative circumstances exist and should be acknowledged. But an optimistic sense of wonder about these circumstances can lead to action that leads to change. Excessive negative thoughts, especially without positive action, are a drain on a person's outlook, attitude, ability to enjoy and eventually on motivation and performance. Negativism also has an undesirable effect on other people. It not only makes the negative person difficult to be around, but also corrodes the attitude of other family members, friends and coworkers.

Many people seem to feel that wonder should be reserved for the heralded events of life. But people who get the most satisfaction from life find wonder in all kinds of things—a sunny day, a child's smile, a great workout and a job accomplished. This appreciation feeds contentment, hope, happiness, excitement and a reason to persevere.

Those who lack the ability to find the wonder in everyday things are unhappy people. That's the real sadness carried by underachievers.

Make the effort to look for wonder in your life so you can help your child do the same. It gives a renewal and an excitement that will make both your lives so much more enjoyable. Remember: Nothing is interesting if you aren't interested.

Just as the emotional foundation for arousing your child's interest in achievement is your sense of wonder, the ethical foundation is your own sense of personal responsibility. Your child needs to see that you live by the belief that life is what you make it. A consistent level of effort reflects that belief and highlights the reality that raw talent is a blessing, but it doesn't take you very far.

Achievers apply their talents and stretch beyond expectations through their hard work, perseverance, flexibility, resilience and positive regard for challenges, small and large. You can support your child's development of such a positive motivated attitude by helping the child understand what he or she feels and why. By giving the child focused assistance in accessing core values and by teaching your child how this can lead to productive action, you help instill motivation. This is a circular process—the Motivational Circle—which ultimately prepares the child to take charge of his or her life. Your child can be an effective, productive, happy person and you can help him or her get there.

CHECKLIST OF UNDERACHIEVING BEHAVIORS

A child with a true motivation problem shows symptoms *over time* that distinguish the problem from "just going through a phase."

The child may exhibit many or all of the following symptoms:

- Detachment and withdrawal from responsibilities—both physical and emotional. Detachment slowly moves even into things the child likes.
- Feigned indifference to many aspects of life ("I don't care").
- Emerging anger, sullenness and agitation.
- Exaggerated sense of being correct. Seldom accepts responsibility for own outcomes. Tends to blame other people or circumstances.
- Diminishing sense of urgency to complete tasks and plan for the future. Misses deadlines.
- Diminishing sense of inquiry. Does not initiate new projects; withdraws from challenges and new ideas.
- Disorganization, especially about schoolwork. "Forgets" to bring homework or turn in assignments.
- Erratic performance. Needs excessive supervision. Is not a self-starter. Appears easily distracted when needing to do work.
- Periodic enthusiasm, particularly at the start of projects, but does not follow through. When confronted may admit a problem "this time," but promises to "do better next time."

- Lack of enjoyment in own successes. Seems sad.

Parents and teachers who are concerned about an unmotivated student also show symptoms such as:
- Feeling ineffective with this particular child.
- Experiencing pervasive worry about the child's actions and future.
- Feeling frustrated that nothing seems to work to motivate the child, but at the same time feeling even greater necessity to help.
- Experiencing increasing concern over time.

As part of this pattern, the family situation is deteriorating. Family symptoms include:
- Tension over academic responsibilities, chores and performance.
- Tension over wasting time that should be used for studying or other productive endeavors.
- Absence of discussions about planning for the future.
- Decreasing communication in general.
- Conflicts over imposed limits and rules.

When these symptoms are present over time, move toward active resolution of the problem.

DEVELOPMENTAL LEVEL INDICATORS – WHAT TYPE OF UNDERACHIEVER IS YOUR CHILD?

Circle the numbers that best describe your child at a particular point in time. See the chart afterward to establish the category of under-achiever.

1. Rarely seems to complete a task in the way expected.

2. Questions your requests and instructions; may comment that they are irrelevant or stupid.

3. Becomes anxious when asked for an opinion.

4. Shows patterns of tardiness/absences from school.

5. Wants to please you, but does not follow through with appropriate actions.

6. Lacks close, long-term, same-age friends.

7. Seems to expect perfection from self.

8. Has a fragile sense of own independence, although is quite independent.

9. Does not accept responsibility for own poor performance.

10. Exhibits low frustration tolerance to the point of "tantrums."

11. Usually smiles, but seems sad inside.

12. Uses physical complaints to avoid circumstances.

13. You are exhausted after trying to work with this child.

14. Respects authority and is appreciative of your efforts to help.

15. Openly questions your authority.

16. Interrupts conversations with you to talk with others.

17. Expresses a much more "liberal" approach to life than you.

18. Interests lie in activities that are isolated from others.

19. Because of narrow "detail" focus, often misses the "big picture."

20. Seems to agree with you just to avoid discussion.

21. Freezes on exams or when called on in class.

22. Seems not to learn from mistakes.

23. Takes openly rebellious attitude toward authority.

24. Gregarious and enjoys social activities.

25. You feel confused when trying to understand this child (as compared to other children).

26. May evoke conflict when forced to engage with same-age peers.

27. You feel on guard with this child.

28. You worry about the types of people with whom he or she associates.

29. Seems influenced inordinately by peers.

30. Seems to agree with you too much of the time.

31. Seems able to profit from mistakes, if criticism is not given in an authoritative manner.

32. Seems to have a selective memory.

33. Seems to do better when rules are constant and concrete rather than flexible.

34. Attaches little or no importance to schoolwork.

35. In spite of the motivation problem, is "a good kid."

36. You would admire this child if he or she were not constantly challenging you.

37. Passively resists your authority or seems ambivalent.

38. Seems to be unable to establish close relationships with authority figures.

39. Disagrees for the sake of disagreeing.

40. Complains of being bored and does not seem to listen.

41. Experienced significant emotional trauma early in life.

42. Much of the time you worry for him or her.

43. Says, "I don't know" much of the time.

44. Attempts to avoid being around responsible adults.

45. Doesn't seem to trust others easily.

❊

TYPE OF UNDERACHIEVER

Circle the numbers in the lines below that correspond to the numbers circled on the previous pages.

Distant Underachiever: 6   10   18   22   25   26   29   33   35
41   45

Passive Underachiever: 3   5   7   11   12   14   19   21   30
35   43

Dependent Underachiever: 1   4   9   13   16   20   24   32   35
37   40   42

Defiant Underachiever: 2 8 15 17 23 27 28 31 34 35
36 38 39 44

The type with the most indications is the predominant level for your child. It is possible for your child to show aspects of various levels, but at any point in time, one level usually dominates.

EMOTION VOCABULARY WORDS

Use a range of words to describe your emotions and encourage your child to do the same.

able	abnormal	abused
abysmal	accepted	accessible
accommodating	accountable	accused
active	adamant	addled
adept	adequate	adjusted
admirable	adorable	adroit
adventurous	affectionate	affirmed
afflicted	affluent	affronted
afire	afraid	aggravated
aggressive	aghast	agonized
alarmed	alienated	aloof
altruistic	amazed	ambiguous
ambitious	ambivalent	amiable
amicable	amorphous	amused
analytic	angelic	angry
anguished	animated	annoyed
antagonistic	anxious	apathetic
apologetic	appeased	appreciated
apprehensive	approved of	apt
arbitrary	ardent	argumentative
aroused	arrogant	articulate

ashamed	assured	astonished
at ease	attentive	attractive
audacious	authentic	averse
aware	awesome	awful
awkward		

backwards	bad	baffled
balanced	banal	barbaric
barren	base	battered
beaten	beautiful	befuddled
belittled	belligerent	benevolent
benign	betrayed	better
bewildered	biased	bitter
bizarre	blameworthy	bland
blank	bleak	blighted
blissful	blocked	blue
bold	bored	bothered
bouncy	bratty	brave
brazen	bright	brooding
bubbly	bugged	buoyant
burdened	burned	

callous	calm	cancerous
candid	capable	capricious
captivated	carefree	caring
casual	caught	caustic
cautious	cavalier	censured
certain	chagrined	challenged
charmed	cheapened	cheated
cheerful	childish	civil
clammy	classy	clean
clever	clobbered	clogged
close	closed	clownish
clueless	clumsy	coarse
cocky	coerced	cogent

coherent

comfortable

compassionate

competitive

complex

compromised

concerned

concocted

confined

confused

connected

conscious

conspicuous

consumed

content

contradictory

contrived

convinced

cool

correct

courageous

cracked up

crass

creepy

cruddy

crushed

curious

daft

daring

dead

deceived

decrepit

defeated

debutante

cold

communicative

compatible

complacent

compliant

compulsive

conciliatory

condemned

conflicted

congenial

conquered

consequential

constrained

contained

contingent

contrary

controlled

convoluted

cooperative

corroded

cowardly

cramped

crazy

cross

cruel

culpable

cut off

dainty

dashing

debased

decent

dedicated

defenseless

defensive

combative

compacted

competent

complete

compressed

conceited

concise

confident

confounded

congruent

conscientious

considerate

constricted

contemptuous

contorted

contrite

controversial

convulsed

cordial

corrupted

cozy

cranky

credible

crowded

crumpled

cunning

cute

damaged

dazed

deceitful

decided

deep

debtor

defiant

defiled	deflated	degenerate
dejected	delighted	delinquent
demanding	dependable	dependent
depersonalized	deplored	depraved
depressed	deprived	deranged
derisive	deserted	deserving
desirous	despairing	desperate
despicable	despondent	destructive
detached	determined	deterred
detestable	devastated	devious
devoted	different	diminished
diplomatic	direct	dirty
disagreeable	disappointed	disapproving
disconcerted	disconnected	discontented
discordant	discouraged	disgraced
disgusted	disheartened	dishonest
disillusioned	disliked	dismal
dismayed	disoriented	dispirited
displeased	disquieted	disregarded
disrespectful	distant	dissatisfied
distinctive	distraught	distressed
divided	divine	docile
dominant	dominated	doubtful
dowdy	down-in-the-mouth	downhearted
drained	dreadful	dreary
dubious	dull	dumb
duty-bound		

eager	earnest	easy
ebullient	ecstatic	effective
egotistic	elated	elegant
elusive	embarrassed	empty
enchanted	encouraged	energetic
engrossed	enraged	entangled
entertained	enthralled	enthusiastic

equal

evil

excuse-maker

exotic

expressionless

estranged

exasperated

exhausted

expectant

extorted

evasive

excluded

exhilarated

exploited

extreme

fabulous

fair

famous

far-gone

fat

favored

feminine

fierce

fit

flamboyant

flighty

flustered

footloose-fancy-free

forgetful

forsaken

foul

frank

friendless

frustrated

funny

faddish

faithful

fancy

far out

fatherly

fearful

festive

filthy

flabbergasted

flattered

flirty

focused

forced

forgiving

forthright

fragmented

frantic

friendly

fulfilled

furious

faint

fake

fantastic

fascinating

fatigued

fearless

fickle

fine

flaky

flexible

floaty

foolish

foreign

forlorn

fortunate

frail

free

frightened

full

futile

gauche

geeky

giddy

gleeful

gloomy

good-hearted

gratified

great

gaudy

generous

giving

glib

glorious

gracious

grave

greedy

gay

gentle

glad

gloating

good

grateful

gray

grievous

grim

growing

grumpy

gun-shy

grotesque

grown-up

guilty

gypped

grouchy

gruesome

gullible

half-hearted

hardened

hasty

haughty

heartbroken

helpless

hesitant

high

homesick

hopeful

horrified

humble

hungry

hyper

happy

hardheaded

hated

hazed

hedonistic

hero

hideous

high-class

honest

hopeless

hostile

humiliated

hurt

harassed

harsh

hateful

healthy

helpful

heroic

hiding

homely

honored

horrible

hot

hung up

hustled

idealistic

ignoble

ill-fated

imbalanced

impassive

impish

impressed

in-touch-with

incapable

incongruent

inconsolable

indecisive

indignant

industrious

infatuated

idiotic

ignorant

ill-tempered

immature

impatient

implacable

impressive

inactive

included

inconsequential

incredible

independent

indistinguishable

ineffective

inferior

idle

ignored

imaginative

immoral

impetuous

important

impulsive

inadequate

incompetent

inconsistent

incredulous

indifferent

indulged

inept

inflamed

inflexible

ingratiating

insane

insignificant

instinctive

integrated

interested

invincible

irate

irresistible

influential

inhibited

insecure

insolent

insulted

intelligent

intimidated

invisible

irrational

irritated

informed

innocent

insensitive

inspired

insulting

intense

intuitive

involved

irrelevant

isolated

jaded

jinxed

jolly

judged

jealous

jittery

jovial

judgmental

jerky

jocund

joyful

jumpy

keen

kindhearted

knowledgeable

kicked-around

klutzy

kind

know-it-all

labeled

ame

late

lecherous

let-down

liberal

lied-to

limited

lively

lonely

lost

loving

lubricous

lustful

laconic

lamentable

lazy

left-out

lethargic

liberated

liked

listless

loathed

lonesome

lousy

low

lucid

lagging-behind

lanky

leashed

less

liable

licentious

lily-livered

little

loathing

longing

loved

loyal

lucky

macabre	mad	magnificent
maladjusted	malevolent	maligned
manipulated	masculine	masked
masochist	mature	maudlin
mean	mechanical	mediocre
melancholy	menaced	merry
messy	miffed	mindless
misbehaving	mischievous	misdiagnosed
miserable	misguided	mistaken
mistreated	misunderstood	mixed-up
mocked	modest	money-hungry
moody	moral	morbid
morose	mortified	motherly
mourning	mousy	multidimensional
mundane	murderous	muscular
musical	mutable	mute
mysterious	mystical	mystified
nagged	naive	nasty
natural	nauseous	neat
needful	negative	neglected
negligent	nervous	neutral
new	nice	noble
nonchalant	noncompetitive	normal
nosy	notable	nothing
notorious	numb	nutty
obedient	objectionable	obligated
oblivious	obnoxious	obscure
observant	obsessed	obsessive-compulsive
obstinate	obstructed	obtrusive
odd	off-beat	offended
open	operating	opportunistic
opposed	oppressed	optimistic
organized	ostracized	out-of-it
out-of-place	out-of-touch	outgoing

outlandish	outraged	overburdened
overwhelmed	overworked	

pacifistic	pained	panicky
paralyzed	paranoid	parasitic
pardonable	participatory	particular
passionate	passive	pathetic
patient	patronizing	peaceful
peeved	pensive	perceptive
perfect	perfectionistic	perplexed
persecuted	persistent	personable
perturbed	pessimistic	petrified
petty	phobic	phony
photographic	physical	picked-on
picky	pious	pissed-off
pitied	pitiful	plagued
plain	pleased	poetic
poised	poky	poor
popular	positive	possessed
possessive	precarious	precocious
predictable	prejudiced	pressured
pretty	prideful	prim
private	problematic	productive
promiscuous	proud	provoked
prudish	punished	pure
pursued	pushed	pushy
put-down	put-upon	puzzled

qualified	qualmish	quarrelsome
queasy	queer	querulous
questioning	quick-witted	quick-tempered
quiescent	quirky	quiet

racist	radical	rage
rambling	rapturous	rash
rational	rattled	ready

reasonable	rebellious	reckless
reclusive	refreshed	regretful
regular	rejected	relaxed
released	relevant	relieved
religious	reluctant	remorseful
remote	renewed	repentant
repressed	repugnant	repulsed
resentful	reserved	resigned
resistant	resolute	resourceful
respectable	respected	respectful
responsible	responsive	restless
revengeful	reverent	revolting
rewarded	rich	ridiculed
ridiculous	righteous	rigid
riled	rosy	rotten
rough	rude	rugged
ruined	rushed	ruthless
sad	safe	sarcastic
sated	satisfied	savage
scared	scheming	scholarly
scorned	screwed-up	scrutinized
secretive	secure	self-conscious
selfish	selfless	sensible
sensitive	serious	servile
settled	severe	sexy
shabby	shackled	shaken
shaky	shallow	shameful
sharp	shielded	shocked
shoddy	shook-up	short-tempered
shy	sick	silly
simpleminded	sincere	sinful
skeptical	sleazy	sleek
slick	slighted	sloppy
slovenly	sluggish	small
smart	smothered	smug

sneaky	snubbed	sociable
soft	solemn	sophisticated
sore	sorrowful	sorry
sour	special	spent
spiritless	spiteful	splendid
split	squelched	startled
steady	stereotyped	stern
stingy	straight	strange
stressed	strung-out	stuck
stuffed	stunned	stupefied
stupid	subjective	submissive
successful	suffering	suffocated
suicidal	sullen	superior
sure	surly	surprised
suspicious	sweet	swell
sympathetic		

tacky	tactful	tainted
taken-advantage-of	talkative	tame
tarnished	tattooed	teased
teasing	tempted	tenacious
tender	tense	tentative
terrible	terrified	terrorized
thick-headed	thorough	thoughtful
thoughtless	thrashed	threatened
thrifty	thrilled	thwarted
tidy	tied-down	timely
timid	tired	tolerant
tormented	torn	torn-apart
touched	tough	tragic
transient	trapped	treacherous
treasured	tremendous	triumphant
troubled	trusted	trusting
truthful	turned-off	turned-on
tweaked		

ugly	unapproachable	unbalanced
unbelievable	unclean	uncommitted
uncool	uncouth	undaunted
undemanding	underachieving	underappreciated
underdeveloped	underrated	uneasy
unfeminine	unfulfilled	unhappy
unhealthy	unimportant	unique
unlovable	unloved	unlucky
unmasculine	unnoticed	unprotected
unready	unreliable	unsettled
unstable	unsupervised	unsurpassed
untouchable	untrustworthy	uplifted
upset	uptight	used
vacant	vacuous	vain
valued	vehement	vengeful
venomous	verbal	versatile
vexed	vicious	victimized
vigilant	vigorous	vile
violated	violent	virtuous
vital	vivacious	vocal
volatile	vulgar	vulnerable
wanted	warm	warped
wasted	watchful	weak
well	well-off	well-spoken
whiny	whipped	whole
wicked	wild	willful
willing	wired	wise
wistful	with-it	witty
wonderful	wondrous	worldly
wormy	worried	wounded
wry		
yielding		
zany	zealous	

APPENDIX D

EMOTION SITUATION GRAM

Use the Emotion Situation Gram to monitor the intensity of your reactions to different situations. After you've experienced a particular event, rate your emotionality and intensity on the scale of one to ten, with one being "not at all" and ten being "the most." Do these ratings every day for a period of time to establish your baseline. Then do them again periodically to increase awareness of your reactions to particular situations. Try to bring tens down to nines, nines down to eights, and so on. The goal is to eventually lower your emotional intensity and become more dispassionate in situations that currently trigger a high response.

Date _____

_____
Situation

0   5   10

\

Situation

| 0 | 5 | 10 |

Situation

| 0 | 5 | 10 |

Situation

| 0 | 5 | 10 |

Situation

| 0 | 5 | 10 |

Situation

| 0 | 5 | 10 |

APPENDIX E

UNHOOK THE
PROJECTION
SCENARIOS

Model scenarios to fit your own circumstances after these suggested exchanges:

Scenario #1

Your child's comment:	"School is boring."
Projected item:	School
Your processing response:	"You seem to have difficulty getting involved."

Possible continuation –

Your child:	"I'd get involved if school weren't so boring."
You:	"Making a commitment can be scary."
Your child:	"What do you mean 'scary?'"
You:	"If people get involved in something and don't do well at it, they have to face their failure. Some people would rather not try than try and maybe fail. Of course, not trying means never succeeding."

Scenario #2

Your child's comment:	"Geometry is irrelevant."
Projected item:	Geometry

Your processing response: "Concentrating is difficult when you have doubts about yourself."

    Possible continuation –

Your child: "I don't have any doubts about myself."

You: "I wonder why a smart kid would
choose to   not do well."

Your child: "Because geometry is irrelevant."

You: "It appears when faced with difficulty some people would rather hide from their true feelings."

Scenario #3

Your child's comment: "The teacher can't teach."

Projected item: Teacher

Your processing response: "It's hard to learn if you feel anxious or inadequate."

    Possible continuation –

Your child: "I could learn just fine if the teacher could teach."

You: "You appear to have some hostility and anger."

Your child: "Of course I'm angry. How can I learn if the teacher can't teach?"

You: "I wonder if another problem is interfering   with your wanting to learn."

Scenario #4

Your child's comment: "I hate school."

Projected item: School

Your processing response: "It's hard to like things when you feel inadequate."

    Possible continuation –

Your child: "I feel perfectly adequate."

You: "People who feel adequate put in good effort."

Your child:	"I'd put in good effort if I wanted to."
You:	"It's hard to want to do something if you feel confused."
Your child:	"I'm not confused."
You:	"People who aren't confused set good goals and follow through."

PARTY GUIDELINES

In support of your attempts to make clear rules as well as engender a sense of planning in your child, it is useful to define what is and is not allowed and what expectations should be met. The following is an example using the situations surrounding parties.

Teenagers and parties—the pairing doesn't have to make you think of loud music, drinking, drugs, sex, gate-crashers, fights and furious neighbors. Try implementing these guidelines:

1. Talk with your teenager at planning time to set the ground rules. Share your feelings and concerns and listen to his.
2. You or another responsible adult should be present throughout the party.
3. Alcohol and other drugs must not be served or allowed.
4. In a subtle way, let it be known that anyone leaving the party will not be allowed to return. This discourages kids from leaving to drink or take drugs.
5. Send out invitations. Do not allow open-invitation parties. Keep a guest list and only admit kids who are invited.
6. Set time limits for ending the party and state them on the invitation. Let a couple of kids stay afterward to help clean up, but have your teen nudge everyone else out the door on schedule.
7. Notify your neighbors in advance and ask them to call if the noise bothers them.

8. Be prepared for kids to consume "mass quantities." Have food that can be eaten while the kids are walking around.
9. Have a variety of activities planned in advance.

Allow your child to attend parties only when you know where and with whom he will be and that similar rules are in place at those parties.

These party guidelines can serve as a template for other kinds of events. The key elements in any similar set of guidelines are planning together so you and your child understand each other's expectations and following through with the plan to avoid being overwhelmed or derailed.

INDEX

ABOUT THE AUTHORS

Peter A. Spevak, who earned a doctorate in clinical psychology from the University of Missouri-Columbia, has appeared on *Good Morning America* and has been featured in the *New York Times, Los Angeles Times, Washington Post, Boston Globe, Wall Street Journal, Newsweek, Ladies Home Journal, Forbes* and *Parenting Magazine*. He established the Center for Applied Motivation in 1984 to research, develop and enhance self-motivation. The Center is located in the metropolitan Washington, D.C. area in the suburbs of Rockville, Maryland and Annandale, Virginia. Dr. Spevak is a resident of Rockville, Maryland.

Maryann Karinch has spent over twenty-five years writing about medicine, technology and fitness and serving as a communications consultant to physicians. She is the author of *Telemedicine: What the Future Holds When You're Ill* (New Horizon Press), *Boot Camp* and *Lessons From the Edge: Extreme Athletes Show You How to Take on High Risk and Succeed.* A resident of Estes Park, Colorado, she holds a bachelor's and a master's degree from The Catholic University of America.

Her web address is www.karinch.com.